Hathor Rising

THE SERPENT POWER OF ANCIENT EGYPT

Alison Roberts

FIRST PUBLISHED IN 1995
REPRINTED IN 2001 BY
Northgate Publishers
3 Court Ord Cottages
Meadow Close
Rottingdean
East Sussex BN2 7FT
www.northgatepublishers.co.uk

COVER ILLUSTRATION

The serpent eye goddess Hathor
holding out her *menit*-necklace
to the king. Relief from the
tomb of Seti I now in the Louvre
Museum, Paris. Photo: Réunion
des Musées Nationaux

ISBN 0-952-4233-08

PRINTED by The Bath Press, Bath

Contents

Dynasties of Ancient Egypt
New Kingdom King List and Chronological Summary

A chronological summary of the main periods of ancient Egyptian history is set out in the next column. As this book concentrates on New Kingdom Egypt, a detailed list of the rulers during that period is set out below:

DYNASTY 18	C 1570–1293 BC
Ahmose	1570–1546
Amenhotep I	1551–1524
Thutmose I	1524–1518
Thutmose II	1518–1504
Thutmose III	1504–1450
Hatshepsut	1498–1483
Amenhotep II	1453–1419
Thutmose IV	1419–1386
Amenhotep III	1386–1349
Akhenaten (Amenhotep IV)	1349–1334
Smenkhkare	1336–1334
Tutankhamun	1334–1325
Ay	1325–1321
Haremhab	1321–1293

DYNASTY 19	C 1293–1185 BC
Ramesses I	1293–1291
Seti I	1291–1278
Ramesses II	1279–1212
Merneptah	1212–1202
Amenmesse	1202–1199
Seti II	1199–1193
Siptah	1193–1187
Tawosret	1187–1185

DYNASTY 20	C 1185–1070 BC
Sethnakhte	1185–1182
Ramesses III	1182–1151
Ramesses IV	1151–1145
Ramesses V	1145–1141
Ramesses VI	1141–1133
Ramesses IX	1126–1108
Ramesses XI	1098–1070

The basic framework of dividing Egyptian history into dynasties originates from the Egyptian chronicler Manetho, who wrote a history of Egypt in the late fourth or early third century BC. Egyptologists also use ancient king lists and other sources, including astronomical dates on papyri for calculating the history. While precise dates for the Late Period are known, a margin of error has to be reckoned with for most other dates apart from those fixed by astronomical information.

The dynasties are grouped into four major periods separated by 'intermediate periods'. These periods are preceded by the two dynasties of the Archaic Period when the cultural identity of a united Egypt emerged under a single literate government.

ARCHAIC PERIOD
Dynasties 1–2 .... c 3150–2686 BC

OLD KINGDOM (PYRAMID AGE)
Dynasties 3–6 .... c 2686–2181 BC

First Intermediate Period   c 2181–2040 BC Dynasties 7–10

MIDDLE KINGDOM
Dynasties 11–12 .... c 2040–1782 BC

Second Intermediate Period c 1782–1570 BC Dynasties 13–17

NEW KINGDOM
Dynasties 18–20 .... c 1570–1070 BC

Third Intermediate Period c 1069–664 BC Dynasties 21–25

LATE PERIOD
Dynasties 26–30 .... c 664–332 BC

GRAECO–ROMAN PERIOD
Ptolemaic Dynasty .... 332–30 BC
Roman Emperors .... 30 BC–323 AD

A NOTE ON THE WRITING OF EGYPTIAN WORDS
Ancient Egyptian writing includes the consonantal structure of a word only, without indicating the vowels, and there is no standard way of rendering Egyptian words for the non-specialist reader. In this book vowels have been supplied in many examples (as in *Ankh, Ka, Menit*), though in some cases the hieroglyphs have been left in transliteration, particularly when Egyptian word play is referred to.

Foreword

My interest in feminine divinity began some twenty years ago whilst visiting the Hathor temple at Abu Simbel during my first journey to Egypt in 1974. Although I was unable to make sense of the beautiful scenes decorating its walls, the temple made so deep an impression on me that I felt impelled to understand its meaning. Later, in 1976, I started research for a doctoral thesis on Hathor.

My initial problem was how to find any coherent pattern in the many representations of the goddess. She was clearly a solar deity, and the goddess of sexual love, beauty, music and intoxication—but such descriptions revealed little about her function within ancient Egypt's complex pantheon. What particularly struck me, however, were the numerous symbols associated with her: in the Dendara temple no less than nine different cult objects of Hathor are listed. This led me to read about the function of symbols in different cultures, especially the anthropological studies of Victor Turner and Mary Douglas, as well as Jung's work on symbols of transformation.

I became convinced that the symbolism held vital clues, and decided to study the use of Hathor's most ubiquitous cult objects, the sistrum and *menit*-necklace, in New Kingdom temple reliefs. Rather than beginning from the written word, my starting-point was temple iconography, although I included texts whenever they helped to interpret the visual imagery. Philippe Derchain had already used a similar approach to trace the meaning of Hathor's 'four faces' in the Graeco-Roman period in his illuminating study of *Hathor Quadrifrons*. In short, the symbols were to be my guide to Hathor, not forgetting that it was the goddess herself I was ultimately concerned with, and the cult objects were, in the end, only a way to tell her story.

This work culminated in a doctoral thesis, *Cult Objects of Hathor: An Iconographic Study* (Oxford 1984 unpublished), in which I differentiated aspects of the goddess as mother-consort-daughter in the solar cycle, and related these to the Pharaoh as the divine incarnation of the sun god on earth. Nevertheless, although I had interpreted the reliefs in the first hall of Hathor's temple at Abu Simbel, I was also aware that the two innermost chambers remained as obscure as ever.

A fresh approach grew out of a meeting with Eileen Campbell, at that time a commissioning editor at Routledge and Kegan Paul. She proposed I adapt my thesis into a book about Egyptian ideas of transformation. Through the challenge of writing such a book, I found myself entering a process of change, having to let all my ideas re-emerge in a different way. I realized that the tools of analysis, so necessary for a doctoral thesis, had somehow obscured Hathor's power and vitality. I also began to see the need to relate the different aspects of the goddess far more closely to the rhythm of the sun's passage from dawn to dusk, to the cycles of sun and moon, and also to religious developments in the reigns of Hatshepsut and Akhenaten insofar as they affected Hathor's cult.

The central theme of the present book is Hathor and the Egyptian 'art of living'. Its sequel, now nearing completion, focusses on Hathor in Osirian religion—on the Egyptian 'art of dying' including royal rituals and cosmography connected with the New Kingdom temples at Abydos and Abu Simbel.

Many people have helped me over the years. I should never have learnt the necessary linguistic skills without the help of the late Kathleen Kenyon, then Principal of St Hugh's College who warmly accepted me to study ancient languages in Oxford in 1973. Nor would my studies have been possible without a discretionary grant from the former Inner London Education Authority.

The guidance of John Harris was invaluable when I was formulating my approach to Hathor at Copenhagen University in 1976-77. He encouraged me to read widely and his belief in the possibilities of my research, however inchoate its early beginnings, was a crucial support. My work also benefited from many stimulating discussions about Sumerian religion with Bendt Alster during that year. I am grateful to the Danish Government for awarding me a scholarship to study in Copenhagen. I should like to thank my friend, Ulla Jeyes, both for her help in bringing me to Copenhagen and for sharing an abiding interest in the ancient world with me. Her untimely death whilst I was bringing this book to completion has been a great sadness.

As a research student during 1977-80 I was fortunate to enjoy the friendly atmosphere of St Cross College, Oxford and I should like to acknowledge the College's award of a scholarship. My work at Oxford was supervised by John Baines, who read through different drafts of my thesis and made many helpful suggestions. For friendship and encouragement, particularly during a difficult phase of research, I should like to thank Alan and Nibby Bullock, the late Albert Hourani, Angela Robinson and the late Jane Scott-Calder OSB.

In 1980 I moved to London and constantly used the Egyptological Library of University College, London, as well as the unique library of the Warburg Institute. To the staff of both these libraries my thanks are due.

I owe special thanks to the Department of Egyptian Antiquities in Cairo for permission to visit and photograph the monuments in 1980-81, and again in 1990. In particular, I should like to thank Aly el-Khouly for his kindness. I am grateful to the museum curators who have provided photographs and also to Vivian Davies, Keeper of Egyptian Antiquities in the British Museum, for permission to photograph objects in the museum. In addition Robert Morkot has been very helpful with photographs.

I am indebted to Khojeste Mistree for helping me discover the ancient world. The late Gerald Eedle's love of Egypt and the many conversations we shared together were another important influence. This book also owes a great deal to the work of Warren Kenton, whose deep understanding and teaching of Kabbalah have helped me in countless ways. I am grateful to Eileen Campbell for her interest at a turning-point in my work, and for encouraging me to transform my research into the present book.

I should like to thank my father for his constant interest in my studies and for other help; also my mother-in-law, Shirley Gladstone, and my brother, John Roberts, who have generously contributed in different ways. Finally, this book would never have come into being without the enduring support of my husband, Francis Gladstone, with whom I have shared so much in Egyptian religion. This support has included the book's design and publication—somehow accomplished amidst all his own work.

Alison Roberts, December 1994

Preface

THIS BOOK is about the power of the serpent goddess in the royal cults of ancient Egypt, more especially in her manifestation as Hathor. Historically, its focus is the period known today as the New Kingdom (c 1570-1070 BC), which was a time of great cultural flowering in Egypt. This is not to deny the importance of the serpent goddess before then; it is simply that evidence about her cult is in short supply at an earlier date. Moreover, the profound religious changes occurring during the New Kingdom, when new forms of rituals, sacred art and architecture developed, make it unlikely that comparisons with the Archaic Period or the 'pyramid age' of Old Kingdom Egypt are possible.

It cannot be coincidental that Hathor's prominence in New Kingdom religion coincided with a time when strong women were inextricably bound up with the Pharaoh's rule; and the functions of the Egyptian Queen as a 'power-holder' in the palace, an incarnation of the serpent goddess in her different manifestations, will be highlighted throughout this book.[1] However, serpent power is not matrilineal power; and it should be said at the outset that there is little to substantiate the often quoted idea that the Pharaoh's right to the throne was always transmitted through the female line, even though brother-sister marriages occurred at the beginning of the Theban 18th Dynasty. On the contrary, Queen Teye for example, wife of the 18th Dynasty Amenhotep III, was the daughter of an overseer of the king's chariotry, a parentage Amenhotep III had not the slightest hesitation in naming on the commemorative scarabs issued to announce their marriage.

During the Second Intermediate Period (c 1782-1570 BC) there was little hint that Thebes would eventually become the most powerful city in Egypt. Until the breakdown of centralized government at the end of the Middle Kingdom, the Pharaohs had usually preferred to rule in a northern capital, either at Memphis or in the neighbouring vicinity. However, after a period of weak government when the unity of the country dissolved, foreign kings, called the 'Hyksos' by later historians, ruled the north from their capital Avaris in the northeastern delta, while a local line of rulers (the 17th Dynasty) was established at Thebes. It was the latter who eventually pushed northwards and took control of the delta region, culminating in the reign of King Ahmose and his sister-wife, Ahmose-Nefertari (pl 3), the first rulers of a reunified Egypt at the beginning of the 18th Dynasty.

Although inheritance through the female was not the norm, there was undoubtedly a strong matrifocal character to the reigns of these early 18th dynasty kings. For example, a stela from Abydos shows King Ahmose offering to his grandmother Tetisheri (pl 2). In the inscription

beneath he discusses with his wife, Ahmose-Nefertari, what benefits he might bestow on their grandmother, saying to her:

'I have remembered the mother of my mother and the mother of my father, the great royal wife and king's mother, Tetisheri. Her tomb and funerary monument are at this moment on the soil of the Theban and Abydene nomes, but I have said this to you because My Majesty wishes to make a pyramid and a chapel for her in the Sacred Land close to the monument of My Majesty'...so his Majesty said, and these things were accomplished immediately.[2]

Apart from revealing obvious reverence for their grandmother, the text shows that the parents of Ahmose and Ahmose-Nefertari were also brother and sister. Elsewhere, a hymn from Karnak praises their mother Queen Ahhotep as the sovereign Mother of Egypt, rallying the army and putting a stop to rebellions. Clearly, the royal women were no bystanders in the emergence of a powerful new dynasty at Thebes.

Nevertheless, the queen who featured most prominently in the eyes of later Egyptians was Ahmose-Nefertari herself, whose status is unparalleled in Egyptian history. Already in her lifetime she was the first queen to occupy the position of 'God's Wife' in the cult of Amun at Thebes, so inaugurating a long line of temple high priestesses, not all subsequently of royal descent, who played an important role in the temple.[3] After her death, cults devoted to her worship sprang up both at Karnak and on the west bank at Thebes, especially in the Ramessid period. Together with her son, Amenhotep I, she functioned as a powerful mediatress, interceding on behalf of humans in the divine sphere.

If Ahmose-Nefertari was revered by later Egyptians, the same cannot be said of Hatshepsut (pls 4,5) judging, at least, by the evidence from official

sources. Despite the fact that she ruled Egypt as pharaoh for a period from fifteen to twenty years, and her reign saw the emergence of new religious and artistic forms which were to influence Egypt for centuries to come, she was omitted from the 19th Dynasty Ramessid king lists and her name was erased on monuments.[4] Nevertheless, it was her reign that most profoundly shaped and changed the religious landscape of Thebes; and in our search for the serpent goddess, again and again it will be necessary to return to Hatshepsut.

Her familial relationship with the early 18th Dynasty rulers is unclear. After the death of Ahmose-Nefertari's son, Amenhotep I, there seems to have been no obvious successor, with the result that the throne went to Hatshepsut's father, an army general who ruled as Thutmose I. It has been

4 *Hathor and Amun-Re crown Hatshepsut (Relief on a block from Hatshepsut's dismantled quartzite shrine at Karnak)*

suggested that Hatshepsut's mother, Ahmose, was a sister of Amenhotep I but this link is unproven. Nevertheless, by serving as the embodiment of divine power on earth, Thutmose I upheld Egypt's tradition of an unbroken genealogy of rulers who had all maintained cosmic order throughout the Two Lands. Under Thutmose I Egypt's horizons began to expand again. The king re-established connections abroad, taking his army as far as the Euphrates and beyond, laying secure foundations on which his successors could build.

Thutmose I was succeeded by his son Thutmose II, Hatshepsut's half-brother and husband, with whom she now shared rulership as queen of Egypt. But his reign was brief and after his early death events took a dramatic turn. His heir, a son by another wife, Isis, was only a child, too young to rule alone. Hatshepsut took command.

At first she seems to have been content to act as regent for the young Thutmose III, directing the affairs of the country on behalf of her step-son. But around year 7 of his reign she took the unusual step of having herself crowned ruler of Egypt, even going so far as to have an inscription carved at Deir el-Bahri in which she declares that her father, Thutmose I, had appointed her to rule, crowning her as his successor before the assembled court whilst he was still alive:

His Majesty *[Thutmose I]* said to her: 'Come, O Glorious One, whom I have placed in my embrace, so that you may see the arrangements for you in the palace . . . glorious in your magic, mighty in your strength . . . You shall appear in the palace, your brow adorned with the diadem resting on the heiress of Horus whom I begat' . . . His Majesty had brought to him the royal nobles, the dignitaries, the companions, the courtiers of the residence . . . into the audience chamber of the great west . . . Then his Majesty said to them: 'This daughter of mine, Khnumetamun Hatshepsut, may she live, I appoint to be my successor upon my throne. Obey her words, unite yourselves under her command' . . . Then the royal nobles and dignitaries . . . kissed the earth at his feet when the words of the king fell upon them.[5]

All this, of course, blatantly ignores the historical reality of Thutmose II's rule, but Hatshepsut, for whatever reason, was determined to rule as the true heir of her father, to whom she was strongly attached.

Her reign was by no means just a stop-gap. Superb building enterprises were undertaken at Thebes and elsewhere. There was also the famous expedition to Punt which returned to Egypt with exotic trees, animals, minerals and spices, shown in reliefs adorning the southern colonnade of her temple at Deir el-Bahri. Nor does she seem to have been inclined to deny her feminine identity. In many of her royal texts the female grammatical gender was used in place of the standard male form, although she appears as ruler dressed in male attire. And the limestone statue from her temple at Deir el-Bahri (pl 5), showing her wearing the royal kilt and headdress characteristic of Egypt's male rulers, has delicately sculpted breasts and fine facial features, giving a distinctly feminine impression.

Writers on ancient Egypt have frequently dramatized Hatshepsut's actions as a ruthless usurping of the crown from Thutmose III. But this is only speculation; it does not explain why the co-rulers should be shown together on monuments such as Hatshepsut's quartzite shrine from Karnak, a monument which Thutmose himself completed. Or why he seems to have honoured her memory, at least until late in his 54 year reign. Just as plausible is the view that Hatshepsut moved to preserve a dynasty that was scarcely a century old, in an Egypt which had recently escaped a long period of foreign intervention.

Although there is no evidence that Thutmose III perpetrated 'a nephew's revenge' on Hatshepsut immediately after her death, he did exclude her from the genealogy of Egypt's illustrious rulers, as did the Ramessid rulers in their king lists.[6] The succession from father to eldest son, the archetypal pattern of Horus succeeding Osiris which had prevailed in Egypt since early dynastic times, was too powerful a vessel of transmission to be easily changed.

Her name may not feature in the king lists but Hatshepsut's achievements were not rejected. During her reign there were profound religious developments, including as Jan Assmann has shown,[7] a concerted move to define the threefold nature of the Theban deity, Amun-Re. It seems that Hatshepsut sought a deep renewal of Egyptian traditions, including ways to express the shifts in religious consciousness which had been developing since the Middle Kingdom.

Hatshepsut's successors evidently valued what her reign had accomplished. Her innovative monuments were carefully preserved even if her cartouches were often replaced by those of Thutmose I and Thutmose II. Her figure may be obliterated from certain scenes in her temple at Deir el-Bahri but Ramesses II went to great lengths to restore the temple itself, which had suffered brutal damage during Akhenaten's reign.

There can be no doubt that women of strong character—especially Tetisheri, Ahmose–Nefertari and Hatshepsut—played a vital role in the development of 18th Dynasty Egypt; but for the Egyptians themselves, the rulership on which ancient Egypt was founded ultimately had its roots in the mythical and divine spheres. It is impossible to separate state and religion in Egypt, they form an 'indivisible theopolitical unity' ruled by a king who has been installed on earth by the sun god himself.[8] And this divine rulership was symbolized above all by the presence of the cobra on the royal brow.

5 Restored limestone statue of Hatshepsut from her temple at Deir el-Bahri, Thebes (Metropolitan Museum, New York)

1 Introduction: The Wild Goddess

WHAT TRAVELLER IN EGYPT could fail to notice the cobra rearing up on every Pharaoh's brow? Indeed, so familiar is the image of the uraeus (as the Greeks called the cobra) that it is usually dismissed as a detail or passed by in silence. Reluctance to explore the meaning of the serpent goddess may be prudent, for understanding her nature means venturing into elemental fiery regions:

Exalted is your power,
O Burning One, O Sated One,
O Mighty One, Powerful, Skilful of Flames,
Lady of the Sky, Mistress of the Two Lands
O Eye of Horus, and his guide . . .
Lady of Eternity, Fiery One,
O Red One, whose Flame burns
Serpent Uraeus, who guides the people
O Lady of Fire, O Searing One
O Devourer, O Scorching One
Sovereign of Thousands . . .
May your awakening be peaceful![1]

This incantation comes from a sequence of ten hymns praising the uraeus as the crown goddess and protectress of the Pharaoh, recorded on a papyrus from around 1600 BC. But the origins of the serpent goddess lie

6 (previous page) Cobra from the tomb of Tutankhamun (Egyptian Museum, Cairo)
7 (left) Detail of a statue of Amenhotep III (Luxor Museum)

very much earlier. Already in the Old Kingdom, a *Pyramid Text* proclaims that 'sky speaks and earth trembles' when the 'living uraeus of Re' feeds the risen king. Still earlier, her rearing cobra head adorns the brow of two women figures, each standing beside the Horus name of the king on a Second Dynasty seal.[2]

Although images of the female cobra occur in many different contexts, identified by a bewildering variety of names, this book focuses on one in particular—Hathor.[3] For the power of Hathor is so ubiquitous, and so identified with serpent energy, that it is impossible to understand the core of Egyptian religion without going more deeply into her nature.

Hers is no ordinary power, as the early Christians were well aware. So much so, that they were driven to knowledgeable acts of desecration, chiselling out the features of the Hathor faces surmounting the columns of her temple at Dendara and badly damaging the huge face on the temple's exterior wall (pls 19, 20). Though they might not be able to veil her, they did their best to erase her.

Did they succeed in obliterating her? Almost, it seems, for the acceptable

face of Egyptian feminine divinity has long been Isis, whose cult eventually spread to be practised in every region of the Roman empire. Even today we still hear little about Hathor, her qualities being frequently regarded, even by distinguished scholars, as no more than peripheral to the main thrust of Egyptian religion.[4] This book seeks to challenge that perspective, reasserting the central place of the serpent goddess in the religion of ancient Egypt.

SERPENT POWER: SOLAR EYE

Like her companion, the sun god Re, Hathor is a fiery solar deity. As goddess of 'many colours' she constantly shifts her shape, becoming now 'Female Hawk', now 'Cow of Gold', now 'Lady of the Sycamore Tree'; again, as 'Great Lady of Punt', she is the patroness of the fabulous land where the Egyptians went in quest of sweet-smelling incense, myrrh, gold, spices and exotic animals.

Again and again, however, the texts return to the face of the sun god—and that of the Egyptian king—in order to describe her. She is the venomous cobra coiled around his head, rearing up on his brow as an irritable, dangerous presence in the realm, breathing flames against his enemies (pl 9). Only the sun god is able to tolerate her fearsome heat. According to the *Book of the Dead* a huge swelling develops on the head of Osiris, after he places the cobra on his brow in order to appear like Re. He is unable to endure such a sudden infusion of power and has to be healed by Re, who lances the boil, causing a great lake of blood and pus to run out in the city of Heracleopolis.[5]

Hathor is also known as 'Eye of Re'. She can be the *Wedjat*-eye—the 'whole eye'—meaning the eye as a bodily

8 Hieroglyphic name of Hathor written as a hawk within a temple enclosure (Tomb of Queen Nefertari, Thebes)

organ. But as the *Iret*-eye, she also acts as the agent of the god's activity, since *iret* in Egyptian means 'doer'. The solar gaze becomes an activity as the eye—the instrument of divine energy and power—is projected out into the world:

> The Eye of Re
>   appears against you,
> His force
>   is power against you,
> His Eye
>   is powerful against you.
> She devours you,
>   She punishes you
> In this her name
>   'Devouring Flame'.[6]

She is also capable of turning in rage against the sun god himself, causing severe disturbance of his faculty of sight. Chapter 17 of the *Book of the Dead* tells how the initiate 'raised the hair from the *Wedjat*-eye when she was raging', and goes on to explain this irritation as

> The right Eye of Re when she became enraged against him, after he had sent her forth. It was Thoth, indeed, who raised the hair from her, bringing her back alive, whole and healthy.

Yet, although this serpent eye frequently manifests as a wild and potentially destructive force, she also emanates radiant beauty and attraction in the world. It is her magical power which compels the sun to rise each day for Re 'illumines the sun disk when he sees her, beautiful of face in the boat of millions'. Others are said to be intoxicated, overwhelmed by her glittering appearance.

10 The Serpent Eye (Tomb of Neferabet, Deir el-Medina)

One male devotee declares, in a hymn to Hathor inscribed in his tomb at Thebes:

> The beauty of your face
> Glitters when you rise,
>   O come in peace.
>
> One is drunk
> At your beautiful face,
>   O Gold, Hathor.[7]

And a love charm found at the workmen's village at Deir el-Medina invokes the magnetism of Hathor which draws male to female, a woman to her children, a herdsman to his cattle.[8]

Her warmth is indeed life itself. Chapter 162 of the *Book of the Dead* reveals that if a certain spell is recited over a cow of gold, the person will become 'a lord of the phallus . . . shining with rays . . . a lord of transformations' and heat will be throughout the person's body just 'as the cow did for her son Re'. When Naville excavated Hathor's shrine at Deir el-Bahri, he found many wooden phalli deposited there as votive offerings offered by supplicants seeking her blessings. To Hathor belong the gifts of sexual attraction, radiance, fertility and love. Of all the pantheon, it is she who sparks the desire for relationship and life.[9]

Her warmth and colour penetrate even into the deepest depths of mountains, into the interior and heart of the earth. In the inhospitable desert regions of Sinai she was venerated by the miners who came in search of the turquoise which was hers to give.

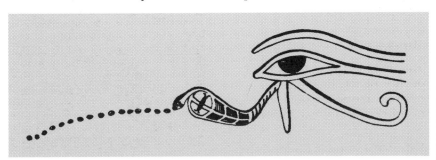

11 Statue of Hathor from the cache found buried in Luxor Temple (Luxor Museum)

Shrines were built there in honour of the 'Lady of Turquoise', whose loveliness is seen when 'the rock is split' and 'the caverns of Hathor are broken open': a goddess rising 'in turquoise from the eastern horizon', says Spell 486 of the *Coffin Texts*.[10] Similarly, New Kingdom copper miners dedicated a small temple to Hathor beneath the legendary 'King Solomon's Pillars' at Timna in the copper mining region of the Arabah, south of the Dead Sea.[11]

No stranger to the mineral realms of earth, Hathor also initiates ascent to the sky:

Flame of Gold, beloved of Horus,
O you, whose head is black,
Who is around the neck of Re,
If you are bound for the sky,
I am bound for the sky.[12]

Both heaven and earth are within the scope of this volatile goddess, she who holds the power both to burn and to bless.

HATHOR-SEKHMET: DREADFUL DESIRE

The need to transform violent, uncontrolled female rage into a radiant, beneficent force—or as Graeco-Roman texts express it, 'to put turquoise in place of carnelian'—lies at the core of myths about the serpent Sun Eye. This beneficent-destructive polarity is reflected in the pairing of Hathor with Sekhmet.

As a savage lioness stalking the land, Sekhmet—whose name means 'the powerful one'—is a terrifying manifestation of the fiery, double-sided goddess. Cobra with the head of a lioness, or lioness crowned with a cobra, she too is 'the Eye of Re', incarnating the burning dangers of the sun (pl 12).

The *Myth of the Destruction of Humanity*, as inscribed near the celestial cow

12 *Sekhmet crowned with a solar disk (Statue from Tutankhamun's tomb. Egyptian Museum, Cairo)*

in the tomb of Seti I, tells how the subjects of Re are in rebellion on earth.[13] Re himself is ageing and withdrawing to the sky as his body crystallizes into silver, gold and lapis lazuli, no longer able to rule his people, nor in control of his bodily activities.

Having sent out his Eye to strike down the rebels, he becomes horrified by the havoc which the blood-thirsty Sekhmet wreaks among his erstwhile subjects. She is 'the confused one in the night', totally out of control, 'wading in their blood as far as Heracleopolis'. All this, says the goddess, 'is balm for my heart'.

To prevent her from completely destroying his people, Re has to resort to a trick. He orders that beer, dyed red to resemble blood, should be poured out over the earth during the night. When day dawns the goddess sees this mass of red liquid and greedily drinks it, becoming so drunk that she forgets about destroying humanity. Pacified by the beer, she returns once more to Re, a transformed goddess whom he welcomes back as Hathor, 'the Beautiful One'.

Re depends on her prodigious powers—he delights in her—but also recognizes that her ferocity must be controlled. And to this end he decrees that bacchanalic festivals should be celebrated for her throughout the year.

The myth also relates to the end of the Egyptian year, at the height of summer when the sun was at its most implacable, the land burned up and no respite could be found as the dry *khamsin* winds blew. It is not surprising that the subjects of the sun god were tempted to rebel against such tyrannical heat. It was, however, also the time when the Nile was beginning to rise, in harmony with the heliacal

13 Hapy, the inundation god, pours water within a rocky cavern, surrounded by a serpent (Detail of a relief on Hadrian's gateway at Philae)

rising of the star the Egyptians knew as Sothis.

The reappearance of this star—the Dog Star, Sirius—just before dawn, after an absence of 70 days, heralded the start of the Egyptian New Year, a time much feared by the Egyptians because of the diseases, pollution and fevers brought by the heat and the returning waters. The epidemics of Sekhmet were rife as her merciless demons plagued the earth, 'bringing about slaughter, creating uproar, hurrying through the land, shooting their arrows from their mouths'.[14] The inundation flooded into Egypt

like a river of blood. Longed for but feared, this annual flooding of the Nile continued until the construction of the Aswan Dam, and the vivid account of the turbulent inundation waters by the 19th century Egyptologist, Maspero, illustrates why the Egyptians might have associated them with the raging Eye:

The first contact is disastrous to the banks; their steep sides disintegrated and cracked by the heat, no longer offer any resistance to the current and fall with a crash, in lengths of a hundred yards and more. As the successive floods grow stronger and are more heavily charged with mud, the whole mass of water becomes turbid and changes colour. In eight or ten days it has turned from grayish blue to dark red, occasionally of so intense a colour as to look like newly shed blood.[15]

Yet accompanying these perils of heat and water was also the promise of renewal, greenness and prosperity, once the Nile had inundated the parched arid land. Moreover, there was the prospect that the solar heat

would soon diminish, the sun having passed its peak. But before this happened, the returning Nile, coupled with the hot sun, meant a difficult passage from the Old Year to the New, a time when destruction and life seemed inextricably interwoven in a natural seasonal cycle, displaying all the characteristics of the destructive-beneficent sun goddess.

Another myth, painstakingly pieced together by Junker from inscriptions in Graeco-Roman temples, tells of *The Goddess in the Distance*.[16] This time the Sun Eye is a wild lioness roaming the desert and wadis of Nubia beyond the boundaries of Egypt, spending her time in rage, eating the blood and flesh of her enemies. Fire flames from her blood-shot eyes, fire issues from her breath, and her heart burns with anger.

But Re desires her return, for without her he has no protection from his enemies. So he sends the moon god, Thoth, and the air god, Shu, disguised as monkeys, to entice her back to Egypt with songs and dances, promising her sacrificial animals, festivities and drunkenness if she returns with them (pl 14). Scarcely had they arrived back in Egypt, when Thoth plunges her into the water of the Abaton, on the island of Biga near Philae, in order to cool her heat. Here, in the Late Period, the source of the Nile was believed to lie in a dark inaccessible cavern, deep under the island (pl 13). Once again the fiery eye and the natural rhythm of the annual waters are reconnected, when the lioness returns to Egypt as the joyful, beautiful goddess Hathor.

The Egyptians were well aware of the dangers lurking in potentially lawless female rage and attraction. A cautious contributor to the *Wisdom*

14 The air god Shu as a monkey, enticing the raging lionness back from the South (Relief from the Graeco-Roman period in the temple of Dakka)

Literature goes so far as to warn about the dangerous power of women with the words 'One is seduced by a body of green faience, (only for it) to become like red carnelian'[17].

Yet the sun god Re is wedded to just such a goddess. Loving and desiring her, he must also appease her wrath in order that they may be reunited for the benefit of Egypt.

For without her—like Shiva without Shakti in Tantric religion—he would be reduced to nothing but a lifeless form, unable to rule, devoid of power and life. The angry, destructive aspect of the serpent goddess must be recognized and accepted if her helpful, beneficent character is to be available.

SOUNDING SYMBOLS: INTOXICATING RITUALS

Crucial at the turn of the year, Hathor-Sekhmet also manifests throughout the annual cycle, feared and desired, particularly in those unpredictable times which periodically recur in nature. Festivals for her were celebrated in each of the four-month seasons

which made up the Egyptian year: *Akhet* (Inundation), *Peret* (Coming Forth) and *Shemou* (Summer). Some were simply local festivals restricted to her temples, such as those at Dendara; but others had a wider significance.

As the year drew to its close, the Pharaoh, as the Son of Re, performed propitiatory rituals for the angry goddess. Litanies were chanted for the goddess, aimed at calming her and preventing her from unleashing her awesome might against the king. Some are preserved on the walls of Graeco-Roman temples such as Edfu:

O Sekhmet, Eye of Re, great of flame,
  Lady of protection who envelops her creator,
Come towards the king, Lord of the Two Lands...
  Protect him and preserve him from all arrows,
And every evil of this year . . .

O Sekhmet, who fills the ways with blood,
  Who slaughters to the limits of all she sees,
Come towards the living image, living Hawk,
  Protect him, and preserve him from all evil,
And every arrow of this year.[18]

On and on the litany continues until the king has been protected from all the baleful influences of the 'Mistress of the Year', all diseases and demons expelled, so that the renewal of time can be repeated once again. The anger of the goddess is always smouldering, always threatening to break out. She is a permanent danger and requires a permanent response in the cult.

It is thought that the black granite statues of Sekhmet, now scattered in museums throughout the world, once formed a huge monumental litany in stone. Jean Yoyotte has estimated that over seven hundred of them must once have stood in the now ruined funerary temple of Amenhotep III, on the west bank at Thebes, each one

16 Dancing Bes, with harp (Temple of Hathor, Philae)

15 Lute-playing monkey (Temple of Hathor, Philae)

dedicated to a particular day of the year.[19] Alternately seated and standing, each lioness figure is crowned with a solar disk and fiery cobra snake, and holds either an *Ankh*-sign of life, or a papyrus sceptre, to symbolize the life-giving greenness of her propitiated state.

Once the passage to the New Year had been safely accomplished, the 20th day of the first month was marked by the joyous 'Festival of Drunkenness'. *Menou*-jugs were filled with wine and beer and offered in thankfulness to Hathor, 'Lady of Drunkenness in the Place of Drunkenness'.

As the yearly cycle moved into the springtime season of *Peret*, the time of sprouting grain and growth, the return of the angry goddess from Nubia was celebrated in southern Egyptian temples in the festival of 'She is Led'.

The Ptolemaic Hathor temple at Philae still bears witness to the festivities which once resounded through an alcoholic haze of intoxication, music and dance. Scenes on the columns show the dwarf god, Bes, playing the harp and dancing in wild jubilation at the return of the 'Lady of favours, mistress of the dance, great of attraction . . . Lady of drunkenness with many festivals' (pl 16). Carved on other columns are tambourine

players and monkeys strumming lutes. All are part of the triumphant band celebrating the return of the goddess.

Through the Philae temple, priests and priestesses would have come, some carrying sacrificial offerings, others doubtless part of that retinue of dancers and musicians who performed acrobatic dances and rhythmically shook their sistra—musical instruments which 'drive away the rage' of the goddess.

Together with the turquoise-beaded *menit*-necklace, worn by Hathor and her priestesses, the sistrum is the representative cult object of the goddess; and both necklace and musical instrument, with its full-face of Hathor between the handle and frame, appear again and again as symbols of her power (pl 17).

The year continued, passing into the searing heat of summer when all of nature lay exhausted, incapable of further growth. In the third month of *Shemou*, came one of the most splendid and ancient festivals of Hathor. Amid a convoy of boats, the holy cult statue of Dendara made the voyage southwards to Edfu for the festival of 'The Beautiful Reunion' with the hawk god, Horus (pl 18).

Halts were made along the way for the goddess to visit other sacred shrines of the land, including the temple of the goddess Mut at Karnak, with its great lake in the form of a lunar crescent; and the ancient city of Hierakonpolis, across the river from the cult centre of the archaic vulture

goddess Nekhbet. Finally, on the day of the new moon, 'Gold of the gods' sailed into Edfu, accompanied by her retinue of soldiers and youths, all waving tree branches along the river-banks.

For thirteen days she resided in the Edfu temple together with Horus, while celebrations took place in the temple and surrounding villages. Then, on the fourteenth day, the fleet set off downstream for the return to Dendara. The festival is portrayed in great detail in the temple of Edfu, and the inscriptions make it clear that one purpose of Hathor's visit was to ensure the return of the Nile inundation waters. She is the one who

Opens the sand
  Causing vegetation to grow . . .
The inundation
Comes at her word,
And the winds arrive
  According to her command.[20]

Even the cycles of nature depend on this goddess of desire and love, whose influence pervades the whole of life.

Right 20 Huge face of Hathor, now damaged, which was originally protected by an overhanging canopy on the exterior south wall of the Dendara temple. It is perfectly aligned with the temple's central axis, so that the power of the goddess is particularly channelled at this southern-most point. In the temple's inner sanctuary there is a niche for a cult statue, which is located behind the damaged Hathor face on the other side of the wall. In the crypt directly beneath this sanctuary, a sistrum carved on the south wall is the focal point of the decoration

She is 'the mistress of the stream who makes the river rise'.[21] When the Nile first began to rise it even displayed her sacred colour: the first phase of the inundation was marked by a greenish tint to its waters—the so-called 'Green Nile', which only lasted a few days but was the herald of the

real flood when the red, mud-laden waters flooded back.[22]

New Kingdom love poetry also takes up this theme of the attractive-aggressive goddess in her yearly rhythm. In one evocative sequence of seven stanzas, a lover and his beloved sing of their love for one another. It opens with the youth praising his beloved's glorious epiphany on New Year's Day. In her loveliness, she is the divine incarnation of the goddess:

The One, the sister without equal,
* The most beautiful of all,*
She resembles the rising morning star,
* At the beginning of a happy year.*
Shining bright, fair of skin,
* Lovely the look of her eyes,*
Sweet the speech of her lips. . .
* True lapis-lazuli her hair,*
Her arms surpassing gold. . . [23]

In the next stanza the girl takes up the refrain, and so they continue, until in the closing seventh stanza, we find the cycle coming to a close.

Now the youth lies sick, at the end of the year, when the sickness and epidemics caused by the demons of Sekhmet were rife in Egypt. His beloved is absent, his body is in a tormented state of disequilibrium, stricken by a malady which no ordinary physician can heal. He languishes under the sickness of love; and his beloved is both the sickness and its remedy:

Her coming to me is my amulet,
* The sight of her makes me well.*
When she opens her eyes my body is young,
* Her speaking makes me strong,*
Embracing her expels my malady.
* Ah, seven days since she went from me.*[24]

So this perfectly composed sequence of seven verses is brought to a close, only to begin once more with the coming of the Beloved on New Year's Day. Just as there were seven demons associated with Sekhmet—and also seven verses recited at the end of the main litany for the propitiation of Sekhmet at Edfu, aimed at protecting the living Horus from the seven arrows of the year—so also these seven stanzas are magically arranged to attract the raging-beneficent goddess and her blessings for the lovers throughout the year.[25]

Yet although we can follow Hathor-Sekhmet through the Egyptian year and see how she was invoked and propitiated, feared and desired, we glean little about her transformative power, except as an oscillating, volatile goddess, now wild and terrifying, now appearing in shining beauty.

To understand her transformational role we must turn to another rhythm of time, the movement of the sun from dawn to dusk, rising in the eastern horizon each morning, crossing the sky at noon, and then sinking each evening into the west. As a solar goddess, the beneficent-destructive Hathor-Sekmet participates in this daily rhythm, a rhythm which also links her qualities with the biological life-cycle of birth, maturity and death.

21 (below) Female guest at a banquet, typifying the refined beauty and elegance of New Kingdom Egypt (Relief in the tomb of Ramose at Thebes)

22 (facing page) Face of Hathor on a statue of Ameneminet (Luxor Museum)

Part 1
Rhythms
of Change

23 (previous page) The winged scarab, Khepri, in the solar boat, is an image of 'Becoming'. Standing at the prow are the solar goddesses, Hathor and Maat. (From the papyrus of Nesikhonsu Egyptian Museum, Cairo)

23 (previous page) The winged scarab, Khepri, in the solar boat, is an image of 'Becoming'. Standing at the prow are the solar goddesses, Hathor and Maat. (From the papyrus of Nesikhonsu Egyptian Museum, Cairo)

24 (left) Lady Ankhesenenmut sails with the hawk-headed Re in the solar boat (Vignette on the papyrus of Ankhesenenmut, Egyptian Museum, Cairo)

LIKE THE EGYPTIAN year's division into three seasons, the day was also divided into three phases—dawn, noon and evening. Each day the sun god journeys through these, hour by hour, changing his name and form in each one. Of these three phases he declares in a magical text:

I am Khepri in the morning, Re at noon,
And Atum in the evening.[1]

As Khepri he is the scarab beetle of the East (pl 23), his name being derived from the word *kheper* which means 'become'. This is also the name of the scarab, an insect renowned for its habit of laying its eggs in a ball of dung which it then pushes around with its legs—a habit symbolizing for the Egyptians the sun's eternal 'becoming' as the solar disk rolled, like a great ball, across the great heavenly circuit.

At noon the sun god is Re, triumphantly sailing across the sky in his boat (pl 24).

Then, as Atum, whose name means both 'The Complete One' and 'The Not [yet] Existent One', he is the Old Man of the Evening appearing as a ram-headed figure within the solar disk (pl 26).

Though night is not strictly part of the day-time cycle, sun-hymns sometimes mention it as a fourth phase, the time when the sun god enters the Netherworld, the realm of Osiris, in order to bring light to those dwelling in darkness.

These phases of the solar journey are also related to growth and change in the human life-cycle. Sun-hymns describe Re as a child, secretly nourished and protected by his mother before appearing as 'the beautiful youth of attraction' in the eastern horizon. When he reaches the meridian at noon he triumphs as a mature ruler, crowned and adorned with the two cobras on his brow, ready to do battle with Apophis, the demonic power, which threatens his life at the zenith. Then, at the approach of evening, old age and decline set in and he sinks down once more, either into the arms of the mother in the West or into the primordial waters of Nun, to be renewed and reborn again next day.

The blossoming of solar religion in the New Kingdom, brought an abundance of hymns praising the sun god in these different phases. Inscribed in the tomb chapels of state officials and clergy, these hymns aimed to help the

26 Ramesses X offering a sacred eye to the scarab beetle of the East, Khepri, and to the ram-headed god of the West, Atum, within a solar disk. Behind the king are the sisters, Isis (left) and Nephthys (right), raising their hands in praise. Sometimes called 'the two kites', these goddesses wait in the horizon realms of East and West, assisting the rebirth process (Scene over the entrance to the tomb of Ramesses X at Thebes)

tomb owners join Re in his nocturnal descent and become absorbed into his great daily rhythm—his death, his rebirth and his eternal return.

The serpent uraeus is very much part of this daily cycle, as a text on a 21st Dynasty funerary papyrus makes clear:

Re has initiated him in his boat,
He has seen the sacredness
of the one who is in his serpent,
He has seen Re
in the three forms which he takes . . .
He has adored him in the morning
In this his name of 'Khepri';
He has praised him at midday,
In this his name of 'Re';
He has propitiated him in the evening,
In this his name of 'Atum' for ever.[2]

The cryptic reference to seeing the 'sacredness of the one who is in his serpent' suggests that the serpent goddess plays a part in the mysteries of the sun-boat. But neither sun-hymns nor vignettes on papyri are very informative about what such initiation may involve. Rather they provide a kaleidoscope of different images, with each image characterizing a particular phase of the continuing solar journey, as Jan Assmann has shown in his study of New Kingdom sun-hymns.[3]

Plate 26, showing the king offering two sacred eyes in the disk, provides a striking illustration of how the serpent eye goddess may be incorporated into the cycle. However, the meaning of this eye offering is not explained, and it could easily be passed over as an unimportant feature.

But in fact the serpent goddess always accompanies Re (pl 27). When the sun god 'shines in his beautiful boat' at midday

It is your uraeus snake
*   who has enchanted your enemies[4]*

When he sank down in the evening they would sing

Hail Re-Atum
*   at your beautiful crossing . . .*
You set in life
*   in the holiness of the western horizon*
Your uraeus snake surrounds you.[5]

And she is also present at the wondrous dawn birth when the sun god rises to new life, as encapsulated in images showing the young sun-child

25 *Maternal arms protectively holding the young sun child within a womb-like sun-disk. The disk rests upon the two lion guardians of the eastern and western horizons, and is encircled by a snake feeding on its own tail, symbolizing the eternal cyclic nature of rebirth (From the papyrus of Heruben, Egyptian Museum, Cairo)*

secure within a womb-like solar disk, held by maternal arms (pl 25).

Henri Frankfort found the presentation of the solar journey in Egyptian sun hymns deeply unsatisfying. To him the hymns lacked any sense of either achievement or real conflict, and he compared them unfavourably with

the Mesopotamian *Epic of Creation* which deals with the struggle between chaos and creative order. In Egypt the solar order is always re-affirmed, the passage of the sun god always accomplished, the threats of Apophis, the evil snake constantly seeking to retard the progress of Re, forever surmounted. For Frankfort, 'The thought that risks were entailed, that an issue was at stake, is never allowed to arise. From the first the tone is set; there is nowhere epic grandeur; there is throughout a static splendour'.[6]

This verdict may be true of the sun-hymns' presentation, praising as they do the apparently effortless movement of Re through the different stages. But the hymns are by no means the whole story. A very different picture of the solar circuit begins to emerge, once it is traced from the perspective of the female and her transformative power. Certainly, such expressions as 'static splendour' are hardly applicable to her unpredictable fiery nature. In order to understand her involvement, however, we must look to other sources than hymns—to royal rituals, iconography and descriptions of rulership—and how these are also harmonized with the diurnal course of the sun.

In Egypt, the Pharaoh's rule replicated the rule of Re. His accession to the throne was timed for dawn, and when he 'appeared in glory' the word ⌂ [*ḫ'j*] was used which also denotes

Below 27 Propitiating the sacred uraeus. The arms of a tree goddess pour cool water over Neferabet as he touches both the fiery uraeus coiled around the sun-disk and the crowned uraeus beneath. The snakes guard the Horus hawk of the horizon (Relief in the tomb of Neferabet at Deir el–Medina)

Facing page 28 Sed Festival dancer (Relief in the tomb of Kheruef in Asasif)

sun-rise. The hieroglyph itself represents the first rays of the rising sun shining over the primeval hill. So too, the king's face resembles the divine face of the sun—with the venomous cobra rearing up on his brow, coiling round him like a circlet of flame, just as she coils around the head of Re and the disk of the sun.

The next few chapters follow the angry-attractive goddess and her consort, the sun king, as they move in a dynamic rhythm of change from dawn to dusk.

Their journey is not at all passive and anything but static. How could it be otherwise? For in the sphere of Hathor nothing is certain, nothing fixed, nothing assured.

The king must do everything within his means to harness and channel her irascible power, if he is to be reborn, thrive again, and reach the zenith of the sky.

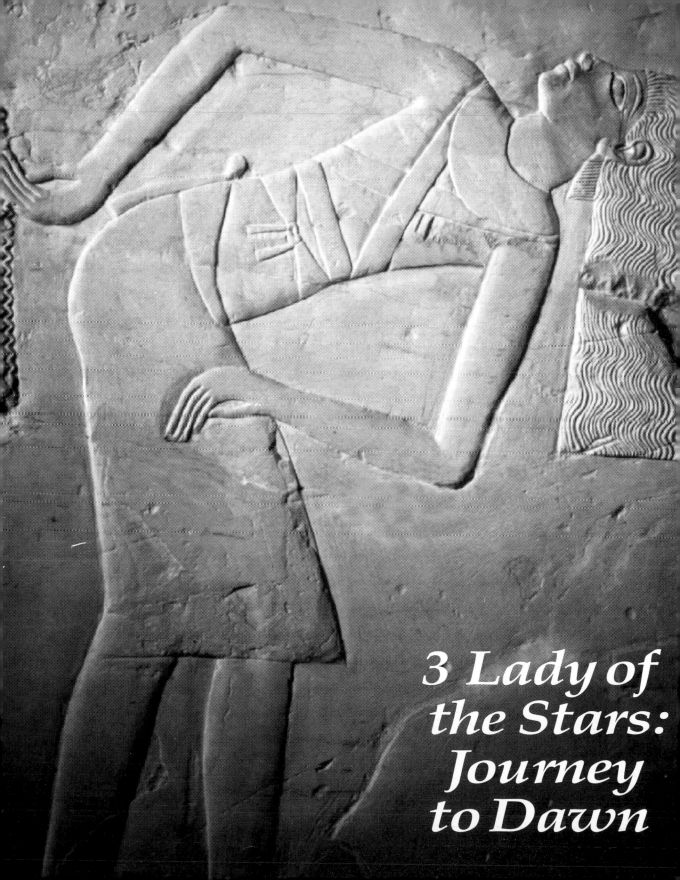

*3 Lady of
the Stars:
Journey
to Dawn*

TO MARK HIS THIRTIETH year on the throne King Amenhotep III, accompanied by his wife, Queen Teye, celebrated a splendid Sed Festival of renewal at Thebes. Often described as 'Amenhotep the Magnificent', his long and peaceful reign had reaped the benefits of the exploits of his 18th Dynasty predecessors, both at home and abroad. Presiding over a court renowned for its opulent luxury and elegance, Amenhotep had entered fully into the spirit of cordial detente which now prevailed between Egypt and her eastern neighbours—especially the kingdoms of Babylon and Mitanni.

Judging by the diplomatic correspondence recorded on thousands of clay tablets discovered at el-Amarna, these foreign rulers were keen to attend the festivals celebrated by Amenhotep.

In one letter, the king of Babylon complains bitterly that he had neither been invited, nor received a present marking the occasion.

How is it you have organized a great festival and you did not send your messenger saying 'Come, eat, drink'? And you have not sent a festival gift.[1]

The gift most desired by the Babylonian king would have been Egyptian gold. Evidently the foreign rulers could never have too much of this precious metal, frequently sending for more in their letters to the Egyptian king. But the Babylonian king was also disappointed that he had not been invited to the celebrations, a reaction particularly understandable if the festival in question was one of the three Sed Festivals celebrated towards the end of Amenhotep III's reign. That foreigners were invited to such occasions is clear from plate 30 (facing page) which shows the daughters of foreign

29 Statue of King Amenhotep III from the cache found buried in Luxor Temple (Luxor Museum)

chieftains pouring libations before the throne of Amenhotep III.

Moreover, the Egyptian Sed Festival was no ordinary occasion. Often referred to as the 'Jubilee Festival', it was an ancient festival, usually celebrated in the 30th year after a king's accession to the throne and, if a king was fortunate enough to enjoy such a long reign, it could be repeated again in later years. This happened with Amenhotep III, who celebrated three such occasions towards the end of his life.

Intended as a renewal of royal vigour, the Sed Festival lasted for several days and—at least in the form practised during the reign of Amenhotep III—culminated in nocturnal rites in honour of the serpent goddess. Perhaps the details of these rites were recorded as explicitly as the pleasantries exchanged between the Egyptian king and his foreign contemporaries in the Amarna letters but no such account has been found. Instead, the little we know depends on a sequence of exquisite reliefs carved in the tomb of Kheruef, Queen Teye's chief steward at Thebes.[2]

In his heyday Kheruef must have wielded considerable influence since scenes in his unfinished tomb, one of the largest private tombs at Thebes, show him being rewarded with gold necklaces for his part in the Sed Festival. Kheruef had been given the task of organizing the festivities in the Malkata Palace on the west bank at Thebes. Known as 'the Palace of the House of Rejoicing', this huge royal dwelling had a lavish audience hall and rooms adorned with painted walls and ceilings. There were also parade grounds, shrines, villas for officials, workshops, offices, kitchens and, not least, a huge harbour, all of which have long since disappeared apart from the barest outline of their foundations.

As Queen Teye's chief steward, administering her estates and wealth, Kheruef enjoyed a position of great

trust and responsibility at court. However, his ultimate fate is unknown. His figure is badly disfigured in some of the scenes in his unfinished tomb, suggesting that he fell from grace; or he may have been a victim of the upheavals in the Amarna Revolution during Akhenaten's reign.

Rarely visited, the tomb lies hidden away in the maze of tombs cut into the limestone rock at Asasif, south of the great desert bay enclosing Hatshepsut's temple at Deir el-Bahri. Towering above the temple is the 'Great Peak', some 200 metres high, overshadowing an area renowned from days of old as a sacred centre for Hathor, goddess of love, drunkenness, music and dance.

Hathor's beneficent presence is evidently important at the close of the

30 Daughters of foreign chieftains pouring libations before the throne of Amenhotep III (Tomb of Kheruef at Thebes)

31 Detail of relief showing dancers (Tomb of Kheruef at Thebes)

Malkata festival nearby, since in beautifully carved reliefs in Kheruef's tomb portico we see king and goddess enthroned together, Hathor being crowned with her horned headdress and uraeus snake on her brow (pl 33). Behind them stands Queen Teye in all her solar splendour; two cobras, wearing the crowns of Upper and Lower Egypt, ornament her brow, a circlet of uraei surrounds her head and to cap it all, perched on a platform crown, the horned headdress with plumes. All this elaborate regalia leaves not the slightest shadow of doubt that the Egyptian queen incarnates serpent power. A serpent queen indeed!

This triad of king, queen and goddess surveys nocturnal rites, performed by women musicians and dancers at the close of the first Sed Festival—dancing which marks the climax of rituals for replenishing the king's powers (pls 32, 34-6). Above the dancers, in the uppermost register on the wall, a group of officials are shown towing Queen Teye and Amenhotep (who is clothed in his special Sed-festival garment and insignia) in 'the evening boat of the sun god'. Like the ageing sun god in the West, life has taken its toll of

Amenhotep. His zest and vitality have gone, and he too must sink into the West, following the way of the sun. Now he must enter the darkness and perils of the Netherworld in order that he—and with him the whole of Egypt—may regain his energy and youthful vigour.

DANCING IN THE DARK: INVOKING GOLD

The two lower registers on the wall are pervaded by a very different atmosphere. Young braided girls, dressed in short skirts with bands crossed over their breasts, are shown performing sacred songs and dances for Hathor, Amenhotep and Queen Teye. They are continuing a long tradition of sacred dance and music in Egypt, for similar dances are known from fragments of Old Kingdom reliefs in the temple of King Sahure at Abusir in the north of Egypt (c 2490 BC), and also in Middle Kingdom tombs.

It could be argued that the Kheruef reliefs are not a true reflection of New Kingdom dances on the grounds that Kheruef had simply imported artists from Memphis, the city in the North where arts and crafts had long

flourished; and that these artists had simply chosen scenes from their ancient 'pattern books' to illustrate the New Kingdom Sed Festival celebrations. Certainly the style of the reliefs suggests that Memphite artists, well used to carving high quality reliefs in limestone, might have come southwards to work on Kheruef's tomb.

But it has to be remembered also that Egypt was a culture in which continuity was highly prized. Plato particularly singled out the Egyptian musical tradition, not only because it imparted traditional values to the young but also because it was firmly rooted in ancient practices.[3] His remarks are supported by these dance reliefs in Kheruef's tomb with their long history—reliefs which were also much admired by later Egyptian visitors to the tomb during the Ramessid period, who, in the manner of modern graffiti writers, had no hesitation in scribbling their names amongst the young dancing girls.

The ritual meaning of the dances, however, is very much in the spirit of New Kingdom Egypt, as can be gleaned from the songs inscribed above the young performers, who are accompanied by women musicians, playing flutes or clapping their hands in rhythm. Over the dancers and musicians in the lower register is a powerful invocation to the starry snake goddess of the night, Hathor 'Gold', whom they call on to rise and be propitiated through the dances they perform in her honour.

But they dance not only for this beneficent queen of the night, shining in her fiery brilliance, but also for Amenhotep who has great need of her power. In their chant to the goddess they implore her to take him to the east of the sky, to the place where at

32 Dancers performing at the Sed Festival of Amenhotep III (Tomb of Kheruef at Thebes)

dawn 'the doors of the sky open and a god goes forth pure'. And this is what they sing:

Make jubilation for Gold
  and sweet pleasure for
The Lady of the Two Lands,
  that she may cause
Nebmaatre [Amenhotep], given life,
  to be enduring.

Come, rise. Come
  that I may make
Jubilation at twilight for you
  and music in the evening.
O Hathor, you are exalted
  in the hair of Re, in the hair of Re,
For to you has been given
  the sky, deep night and the stars.

Great is her Majesty
  when she is propitiated.
Adoration of Gold
  when she shines forth in the sky.
To you belongs everything
  in the sky whilst Re is in it.
To you belongs everything
  in the earth whilst Geb is in it.
There is no god who does what you dislike
  when you appear in glory . . .

O my Lady, come and protect
  King Nebmaatre, given life.
Make him healthy
  on the east side of the sky,
So that he is happy, prosperous
  and healthy in the horizon.
All people propitiate her
  while there is Gold.
If you desire he should live,
  cause him to live
For millions of years
  without ceasing.

O pray that this may be protection[4]

The Hathorian spirit of excitation is awake in their music, bringing the king into a night-time realm of rhythm and movement in which all divisions between sky and earth are annihilated by the fiery goddess. Not sleep and death are longed for here, but the coming of Gold, who reinfuses him with

life and vitality, initiating him to a new shining existence at dawn.

The song above the dancers in the upper register is difficult to understand. Translated by Edward Wente in the publication of Kheruef's tomb,

33 The focus of the Sed Festival celebrations: the throne of Amenhotep who is seated with Hathor. Behind them stands Queen Teye (Tomb of Kheruef at Thebes)

34 Dancers at the Sed Festival of Amenhotep III (Tomb of Kheruef at Thebes)

35 Detail from the Sed Festival dance scenes showing monkey, pintail duck and a leaping bull-calf (Tomb of Kheruef at Thebes)

it compares the night-time sojourn of 'the high one' with the roasting and grinding of seeds, which the granary-keeper has provided. And this roasting is, in turn, linked to the coming forth of a new, exalted body:

He has given to me a pod of seeds,
  Has the garner-man.
As for the pod of seeds,
  I have roasted it a roasting,
I have ground it a grounding,
  O garner-man,
What I have protected has been removed,
  What I have protected has been removed,
So that what should be high is exalted.

You spend all night,
  exalted one, being exalted.
And my eyes are bloodshot
  Through staring whilst they are inverted.
O you . . . whose tongue and throat . . .
  are high, you are high.
O you with sharp nails . . .
  Come forth from . . . the field.[5]

Juxtaposed with the nocturnal song to the serpent goddess beneath, it strongly suggests that we are dealing here with rites for the fiery Egyptian matrix, the

sacred vessel of transformation which renews the Egyptian king. A new royal body has to be roasted and created by the female if the king is to be reborn again at the close of his Sed Festival.[6]

The king of the dancers is being made new again within the fiery female furnace; and these dancing girls, with their swinging braids and ritualized arm gestures, have been trained to perform bending, spiralling, acrobatic movements, which render visible his transformations with the night-time goddess who brings him to dawn.

Renewal through Hathor only comes about by surrendering, letting go and moving to her rhythms. And, indeed, it is clear that Amenhotep himself, though apparently seated so impassively beside the goddess (pl 33), is also to be understood as her musician.

36 Girls clapping for the Sed Festival celebrations (Tomb of Kheruef at Thebes)

37 Hathor, 'Lady of Dendara', embracing Amenhotep III at his first Sed Festival. Wearing her characteristic horned head-dress, menit-necklace and uraeus on her brow, the goddess also has signs of renewal, symbolizing millions of years, slung over her arm (Tomb of Kheruef at Thebes)

For as an inscription over a group of kneeling dancers in the lowest register says:

Behold him,
  as he makes for you pure Ihy-music,
The King of Upper and Lower Egypt,
  Nebmaatre,
The Son of Re,
  Amenhotep, Ruler of Thebes
So that he may celebrate
  his Sed-Festival.[7]

To show the king actually dancing before the goddess in a private tomb would have been unthinkable. Indeed to show such scenes of a royal ritual at all in a private tomb is highly unusual, and can only be explained by the high position Kheruef must have held at court, and his considerable involvement in organizing the festival.

But as musician, seated though he is, King Amenhotep is continuing a long tradition of royal music-making at Thebes. In inscriptions on a stela which Herbert Winlock found among the rubble at Deir el-Bahri, the Middle Kingdom ruler, King Antef, describes how he too, some 700 years before Amenhotep, was a night-time music-maker for Hathor, accompanying Re on his journey through the Netherworld:

My body speaks, my lips repeat
  pure Ihy-music for Hathor.
Music, millions
  and hundreds and thousands of it,
Because you love music,
  a million of music for your ka,
In all your places.[8]

Through such music-making, both Antef and Amenhotep become open to renewal through the shining, beautiful goddess. As a hymn at Dendara says about the king dancing before Hathor:

His heart is straight, his inmost open,
  No darkness is in his breast,
O Lady, see the dancing,
  Companion of Horus, see the skipping.[9]

But as important, by making music they also become incarnations of Hathor's musical and mercurial child, Ihy, whose presence at the Sed Festival of Amenhotep III is symbolized by the leaping frisky bull-calf at the head of the dancers (pl 35).

FLEEING WITH IHY: THE MERCURIAL CHILD

Ihy is one of the most unusual figures in the Egyptian pantheon. Though rarely shown in reliefs before the Graeco-Roman period, this child of Hathor was known already in Old Kingdom times. By far the most

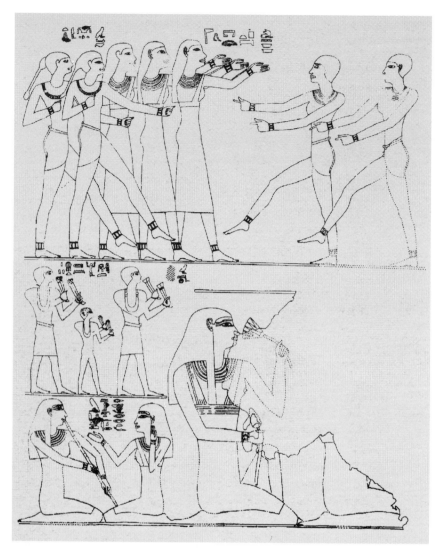

38 An erotic dance celebrating the coming forth of Re with Hathor 'Gold' at dawn. A group of women clap their hands as two young dancers on the left make movements to draw the dancers on the right towards them. Beneath are three male Ihy-musicians, wearing menit-necklaces, who add to the rhythm by playing clappers (Middle Kingdom relief in the tomb of Senet, a priestess of Hathor, at Thebes)

striking images of him are a pair of New Kingdom wooden statues, coated with a black resinous substance, discovered by Howard Carter amongst the treasures of Tutankhamun (pl 39). Naked as usual, and wearing the sidelock of youth on his head, the god's body is black, apart from the gold inlay surrounding his eyelids and eyebrows, which gives a hint of the sun. In one hand he boldly holds aloft a naos sistrum, showing that his mother's musical rhythms belong to him too. Similarly, male musicians sometimes appear as incarnations of Ihy in reliefs, wearing a green-beaded *menit*-necklace around their necks and holding sistra or clappers as they accompany dances for the sun god and Hathor (pl 38).

By no stretch of the imagination can Ihy be described as a tranquil child, and something of his turbulent nature may be gleaned from *Coffin Texts* aimed at capturing his prodigious power. He is invoked as a 'Bull of Confusion'; or as a new-born child who breaks out of the primeval egg. To 'become Ihy', a person must be prepared to experience the raw materiality of existence—blood, faeces, and bodily fluids—all the messy substances and liquids which are there when life is pushed forth from the female womb. Such a birth is graphically described in Spell 334, inscribed on a coffin from Gebelein:

My awesomeness precedes me
As Ihy, the Son of Hathor,
I am he who begets a begetting,
I flowed out from between her thighs,
In this my name Jackal of the Light,
I broke forth from the egg . . .
I escaped in her blood,
I am the Lord of blood. I am a turbulent bull . . .
I came into being, I crept, I travelled around.
I grew, I became tall like my father[10]

This child then, 'the Jackal of Light', is like the animal whose tracks are followed by travellers in difficult desert terrain—indeed a guide for those in the difficult passage to new birth.

In another spell, bodily excrements are confronted by Ihy. 'Turn around faeces. But faeces is not your name. Your name is Re, your name is Ihy'.[11] A person invoking this spell rejects the fate of the damned, who are condemned to eat faeces in the Netherworld, and seeks instead to join the solar circuit together with Re and Ihy. Clearly Ihy enjoys no remote ethereal existence; but rather one which demands complete involvement with the heart and guts of nascent life. This 'Lord of Hearts', as he is called, is not for the faint of heart.

It is to be expected then, that this remarkable child of Gold, 'the splendid lotus flower beside his mother' is much sought after by those in quest of new life at dawn. 'He has fled with Ihy. He has reached the horizon as a great hawk', it is said about one seeker

in a *Coffin Text*.[12] For Ihy is deeply connected with renewal in the solar cycle, involved with the processes of rebirth. According to Spell 334 he has lain motionless in the state of death, has been 'an inert one in Nun', (the watery abyss into which the sun god sinks each night for regeneration). There he has 'rotted' and 'smelt' as 'the brotherly one' of gods and people, his body blackening and decaying. But eventually in this place of dissolution and decay, when all seems lost, something stirs within its depths, as the sound of Ihy is heard. Out of the stench and foulness rises up this miraculous shining child, fragrant like the goddess, apparelled with all her adornments, her power residing deep within his bowels. And he describes this wondrous new body given to him by Hathor:

My perfume is the incense
  which my mother Hathor uses for her censing,
My efflux is the sacred oil
  which my mother Hathor uses for her flesh . . .
My intestines are the beads of her menit
  which my mother Hathor places at her throat,
And my hands are her sistrum
  which my mother Hathor
Uses for her contentment.[13]

No wonder then that this child of Gold should be so close to the hearts of those music-makers desiring rebirth for Amenhotep III at the end of his Sed Festival. Yet to tread this path to new life a person must also be prepared to seize and take possession of Ihy, for he eludes those who wait passively, afraid to summon up his zestful powers: 'I show the paths of Khepri, the Netherworld dwellers follow me, this Osiris N takes possession of Ihy, this Osiris N captures Ihy for eternity',[14] declares another of Ihy's followers.

Seizure, possession, ardour, turbulence and rhythm—all characterize

40 *A herdsman entices his anxious cattle across water by carrying a young bull-calf on his shoulder. A similar scene in another Old Kingdom tomb names the calf as 'the Ihy of cattle' (Fifth Dynasty relief in the tomb of Ti at Saqqara)*

Hathor's musical offspring, who rises 'from his secret mansion like Re shining in his horizon' to bring renewal and life.

How his zest for life drives out all fear, is touchingly encapsulated in an Old Kingdom tomb relief showing a herdsman fording a stream with his cattle. The herdsman must somehow overcome his cattle's antipathy to the water where unknown perils and dangers lurk, and for this purpose, he carries on his shoulders a young bull-calf (pl 40). Knowing Ihy's ability to entice others into making difficult journeys, the herdsman has armed himself

with an incarnation of Hathor's fearless child.[15] Through this ruse, which must have have been much used by Egyptian herdsmen, his cattle's affections are stirred, their fears forgotten, as they boldly plunge into the water, lured to their new pasture-land by the frisky young bull. A vignette from chapter 109 of the *Book of the Dead* also shows a young bull-calf before Re-Harakhti, patently included here as a helper for those seeking rebirth in the East.

One wonders, too, how far these Egyptian themes lie behind the celebrated episode of the Calf of Gold, fashioned by the Israelites during their Exodus from Egypt.

According to Hebrew tradition, the Israelites saw a vision of a bull before them as they made their perilous crossing over the Red Sea. Once they had

arrived safely on the far side, they proceeded to make a golden image of the calf in joyful celebrations. For this was the Calf of Gold who had led them to safety out of Egypt, and so must be worshipped, thanked and propitiated. Old habits die hard. And not even the fear of Jahwe's wrath or the displeasure of Moses could prevent such backsliding into familiar customs.[16]

MAAT: GUIDING ECSTASY

But we have not yet done with the Egyptian king's rebirth in the East. Behind Hathor and Amenhotep stands another figure, richly adorned with serpents on her head and brow—'the beloved great royal wife', Queen Teye, who brings another crucial solar goddess into play; for we are told in the

text inscribed behind Hathor's throne that Teye is 'in the following of the king, like Maat in the following of Re'. As an incarnation of the goddess Maat, Teye also plays an important part in the solar rebirth of her husband, an exalted role indeed for a queen who began life as the daughter of Tuya and a royal official named Yuya, who was overseer of Amenhotep III's chariotry and priest in the temple of Min at Akhmim in Upper Egypt.

Teye was by no means the king's only wife. Also at the Egyptian court, to mention but one, was the king of Mitanni's daughter, Gilukhepa, for whom Amenhotep had to send five or six times in a great flurry of negotiations and diplomatic exchanges. Eventually the princess arrived in Egypt with a retinue of 317 ladies, so cementing the ties between these two countries.

Yet all were to live in the shadow of Teye, eclipsed by a queen who was so renowned abroad that foreign rulers wrote to her on the death of her husband. Her influence was to continue well into the reign of her son, Akhenaten, but in the Jubilee scenes in Kheruef's tomb Amenhotep still rules, with a queen alongside him who, according to the text inscribed behind the throne, appears in the retinue of her husband 'like Maat in the following of Re'.

Significant words indeed, betokening the presence of another important solar goddess. For it is Maat who emphasizes the rightness and order which has reigned since the very beginning of creation (pl 43). She embraces all creatures, humans, rulers, deities alike, all the periodic movements of the seasons, everything lives 'by Maat, in Maat and through Maat'. She is the way of the world which the Egyptian king seeks to uphold as the Son of Re, and Amenhotep III himself is said to be the one 'making Egypt flourish like the first time through the precepts of Maat'.[17]

There is no single English word, however, that can adequately translate her name—truth, justice, morality, and order all fall short of the mark—and probably the best translation is the one offered by Wolfhart Westendorf, 'she who guides'.[18]

Individuals, too, could realize Maat in their lives by following that path of truth, honesty, goodness and moderation, urged upon them by scribes in the *Wisdom Literature* with an insistence which remained undiminished throughout Egyptian history. For a breach of Maat causes quarrels, offends neighbours, disturbs the natural order,

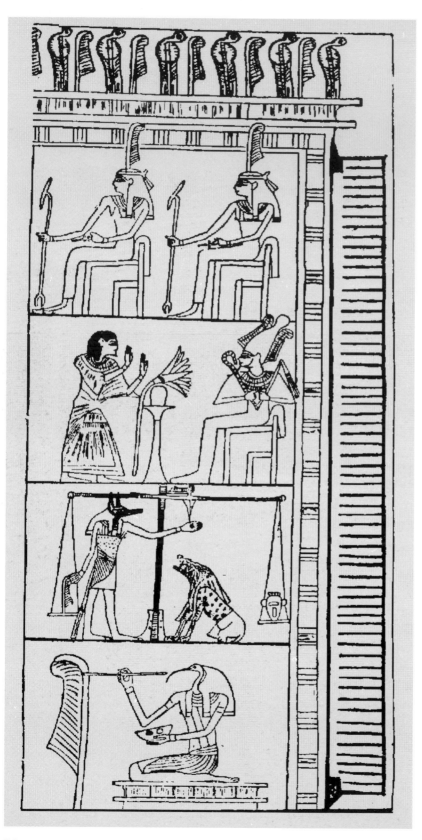

Left 42 Four vignettes at one end of the Hall of the Double Truth where the deceased recited the negative confession before a tribunal. At the top are two enthroned Maat goddesses holding emblems of life and power. Beneath is the scribe, Ani, adoring Osiris. Next Anubis steadies the plumb bob of the scales before weighing Ani's heart, which is placed in one pan against the feather of Maat in the other. At the bottom is Thoth, the ibisheaded god of writing and wisdom, who paints a large feather of Maat. The hall is surmounted by a frieze of uraei serpents and feathers symbolizing the fiery serpent goddess of truth and justice (Detail from the Book of the Dead papyrus of Ani, British Museum, London)

Right 43 The goddess Maat (Painted relief from the tomb of Seti I at Thebes, Florence Museum)

producing that disequilibrium in nature and the cosmos known as *Isfet*—the strife, the robbery and enmity which is the opposite of Maat. In the famous judgment scene in the *Book of the Dead*—the Weighing of the Heart—it is the feather of Maat (the hieroglyphic symbol worn by the goddess on her head) against which the heart is weighed (pl 42). So, the passions and actions of a lifetime are placed in the balance and judged according to her order.

Maat is no empty abstraction. She is vitally real and alive, the very bread of life, sustaining those in the circuit of the sun. As the 18th Dynasty ruler Hatshepsut says:

I have magnified Maat, whom he (Re) loves.
I know that he lives from her. She is my bread,
I feed off her dew and I am of one body with him.[19]

Yet, strange though it may seem, it is also abundantly clear that Maat can only truly guide if united with the volatile Hathor. Both goddesses are 'daughters of Re'; and both are shown standing erect at the prow of the sunboat during the solar journey—one goddess crowned with her characteristic feather, the other with her horned

headdress. The son of a wise old priest of Amun at Karnak succinctly sums up this paradox of 'sober drunkenness' as he prays to the retinue of Re, asking for their blessings on his father:

Let his hands receive your offerings,
For see he has pure hands.
Let his mouth be filled with provisions,
For see he spoke truth (Maat) in his sobriety.
Let him drink from your libations,
For see he loves drunkenness.[20]

His prayer displays a profound awareness that Maat and Hathor, order and drunkenness, are both needed in the solar circuit.

Right action by itself was never the goal of the Egyptian solar cult; nor were excess, delight, wine and fire ever suppressed for the sake of duty-bound moral worth alone. And if it can be said that Maat directs and guides, equally it must never be forgotten that Hathor is the power who moves the desire for life and existence. Both belong to fiery serpent power, as is illustrated, for example, in rebuses of New Kingdom pharaonic names (pls 45-6).

Nowhere is the interdependence of the two goddesses more clearly

44 King Seti I offering Maat to Osiris
(Temple of Seti I, Abydos)

revealed than in Queen Nefertari's temple at Abu Simbel, where a relief on the southwest wall of the Hall shows her husband, Ramesses II, offering a small figure of Maat on the palm of his hand to the Theban god, Amun-Re. Directly opposite this, next to a scene of Nefertari shaking sistra before Hathor, the king offers wine to the sun god, Re-Harakhti.

Allied with Hathor, the guidance of Maat becomes something living and beautiful, not a mechanical activity. Without Hathor, however, the duties, judgments and responsibilities of the solar king would be in danger of turning into arid works, cut off from the radiance and joy of solar life. In short, 'ought' was never severed from 'desire' in ancient Egypt.

Which brings us once more to the Sed Festival of Amenhotep III, who seeks rejuvenation in the nocturnal, inebriate realm of 'Gold'. For all this helps to explain why Queen Teye, as Maat, should be included with the king and Hathor. Like a conductor with an

orchestra, she reminds us that music-making for Hathor needs to be regulated and guided. Music and intoxication, long recognized as powerful instruments in many religious cults, have their dangerous side. Hence the presence of the snake-crowned Teye, watching over the king's new birth. She can provide the necessary guidance to ensure that Hathor's excitable power is not dissipated in a euphoric mood of collective emotion.

If the king is indeed to rise up to new life in the East, he will need both these female powers who ceaselessly keep in motion the circuit of the sun. For one is a dangerous goddess, whose nature, once roused, always threatens to run amok, her helpfulness gone in a flash, as already seen in the *Myth of the Destruction of Humanity*. All too quickly her beneficence may change into savage destruction. Consequently, some measure of control needs to be brought to bear in this festival of renewal, if the glittering serpent goddess is indeed to renew the king, and take him safely through the perils of the night to new life at dawn.

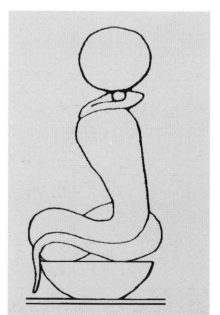

Left 45 Rebus of Amenhotep III's name, Neb-Maat-Re ('the Lord of Maat is Re') with the uraeus representing the Maat element. The rebus is composed of a basket (reading 'lord'), a serpent (Maat) crowned with a solar disk (Re) (Frieze in the 18th Dynasty temple of Luxor)

Facing page, 46 Granite statue of the royal official, Senenmut, holding an image of the serpent Renenutet, goddess of the harvest grain. The serpent and her accompanying symbols can also be 'read' as a rebus of Hatshepsut's throne name Maat-Ka-Re ('Maat is the Ka of Re'), which is normally enclosed within a cartouche. The rebus is composed of Ka arms enclosing a uraeus serpent (Maat) crowned with a solar disk (Re). In this way both Maat and the Pharaoh are proclaimed as nourishers who support and feed Egypt. Elsewhere, the highly creative Senenmut states that he devised the rebus (Brooklyn Museum, New York)

4 Rage and Radiance: The Dawn Gates

Dawn comes. Green and rosy hues bathe the Two Banks in soft colours, a streak of vermilion shows where the sun is rising over Egypt. Slowly, the gates of the sky open to reveal, in a flash of sudden brilliance, a purified fragrant god. It is he, the youthful Re-Harakhti, whom his people acclaim as

Lord of pleasure,
Sweet of attraction,
Shining of rays,
The Lord of Light.¹

The perils of the night are over, a new day breaks. Invigorated and renewed, the handsome dawn hero returns, radiating warmth, joy and attraction into the hearts of his wonder-struck followers, darting his rays to earth, rousing Egypt to new life once more. This is the epiphany of the dawn youth in the eastern horizon—'the beloved', as he is sometimes called—who is so much praised in Egyptian sun-hymns. But it also characterizes the Pharaoh's appearance before his adoring subjects, for right from the beginning of his reign he rules in harmony with the course of the sun. So, for example, King Ahmose, founder of the 18th Dynasty, is seen by his people as a vision of the rising sun. An inscription says of him:

All hearts are filled with his attraction,
Eyes are dazzled by this king,
Hearts leap because of him,
When he is seen like Re at his rising.²

His people are 'captured' by their leader's radiant attraction, raised into a state of ecstatic celebration whenever he appears before them, shining like the dawn god in all his beneficence.

Yet the very words used to describe Ahmose's effect upon them—especially 'hearts are filled with his attraction', 'hearts leap', or 'eyes are dazzled'—arouse suspicion that more lies behind this youthful masculine rising than the prolific eulogies in sun-hymns and royal inscriptions are prepared to reveal. Such expressions hint at the leaping, attractive qualities of Hathor, suggesting that it may well pay to investigate other 'solar appearances' of the Egyptian king.

CORONATION GODDESSES: VITALIZING REGALIA

An initial clue can be gleaned from the coronation inscription carved on the back of a double statue, now in the Turin Museum, which shows King Haremhab together with his wife, Queen Mutnodjme (pl 48). This records how the former military general of the boy-king Tutankhamun travelled to Thebes for his coronation, having taken control of Egypt at the end of the 18th Dynasty.

The auspicious date that he chose for his crowning was the annual Opet Festival, celebrated at Thebes during the second month of the inundation season. Then the city rang with the songs of the temple musicians, as boats carrying the sacred cult images of the Theban triad—Amun-Re, his consort Mut, and their child, the moon god, Khons—sailed from the vast temple of Karnak, to Luxor, lying about three kilometres to the south, where they resided in the Luxor temple for the duration of the festival.

Almost certainly Haremhab was also crowned in the northern capital of Memphis, but he needed to cement his ties with this important southern city. So, bringing with him a statue of Re-Harakhti, he journeyed southwards to Thebes for his coronation, where on arrival he was led by the Theban god, Amun-Re, to the palace for the coronation ceremony.

It should be said at the outset that the purpose of the inscription is not at all to describe the ceremonial details of the ritual, as might be needed by priestly officiants taking part in the coronation. Such descriptions of royal rituals do exist but unfortunately nothing about the coronation ritual itself has survived. Nor, for that matter, will Haremhab's inscription probably satisfy those in quest of prosaic historical facts and data.

On the contrary, the inscription gives a highly symbolic picture of a king in the process of deification, of being transformed and taken up into the exalted realm of the deities who guarantee his rule over Egypt. And one deity, above all, is crucial for the king during the opening phase—the serpent goddess, called here by yet another of her names: Weret-Hekau, 'the-Great-of-Magic'. She is often shown in reliefs as a leonine-headed goddess, crowned with a sun-disk and uraeus; but plate 49 (facing page) shows her in all her serpent splendour as a human-headed cobra nursing the young Tutankhamun. Hers is the

49 *The snake goddess Weret-Hekau*
—'The-Great-of-Magic'—suckling the
Pharaoh (Gold pendant from the small
golden shrine of Tutankhamun, Egyptian
Museum, Cairo)

'magic' which inheres in the gleaming crowns given to a king during his robing and adornment at the beginning of the ceremonies. For, to the Egyptians, crowns were not simply physical objects but potent regalia, charged with magical power and endless fascination.

An ancient invocation to the royal crowns, in the *Pyramid Texts*, makes this abundantly clear:

O Red Crown, O Inu Crown, O Great One,
O Great of Magic, O Fiery Snake.

Grant that the terror of me
  Be like the terror of you,
Grant that the fear of me
  Be like the fear of you,
Grant that the awe of me
  Be like the awe of you,
Grant that the love of me
  Be like the love of you.

Let me rule,
A leader of the living . . . (PT §196-197e)

And it is the connection with this magical power which concerns Haremhab in his coronation inscription. We are told that Amun-Re leads the king to the *Per-Wer* or 'Great House', the ancient shrine of Upper Egypt originally associated with the vulture goddess, Nekhbet. Here 'the-Great-of-Magic' waits to greet him, making the ritual *nini*-gesture of welcome by holding the palms of her hands outwards to the approaching king. Then she embraces him, before settling herself upon his brow, marking him with the indubitable sign of solar rulership:

Then he (Amun-Re) proceeded to the palace, when he had placed him (Haremhab) in front of him, to the *Per-Wer* of his august daughter, Weret-Hekau, her arms making the *nini*-gesture. She embraced his beauty, and placed herself on his brow. The Divine Ennead, the lords of the *Per-Neser*, were in exultation at his glorious rising . . .[3]

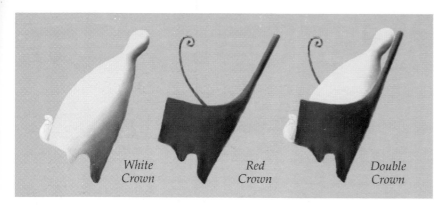

White Crown   Red Crown   Double Crown

50 The White Crown of Upper Egypt, the Red Crown of Lower Egypt, and the Double Crown, symbolizing the union of Upper and Lower Egypt

Only after the palace snake has coiled herself around Haremhab's brow does he make his 'glorious rising', acclaimed by the lords of the *Per-Neser*—the 'House of Flame', which is the Lower Egyptian counterpart to the *Per-Wer* shrine. Only then is he empowered to go forth for the zenithal proclamation of his 'great name' and royal titulary, enacted in an embrace with Amun-Re, who bestows on him 'everything which the sun encircles'. Once more god and king go forth together at the climax of the ceremony, as a great paean of praise fills sky and earth:

The entire people cry aloud to the sky,
  Great and small are seized by gladness,
The whole earth rejoices.

Here then is evidence enough about the crucial importance of the serpent goddess when a king 'rises' before his people. It is also significant that this coronation inscription is located on a statue of Haremhab seated with Queen Mutnodjme, whose role seems unlikely to be simply that of a passive female ornament.

But there is another important clue that needs to be followed up—the reference to 'the-Great-of-Magic' in the *Per-Wer* shrine.

This shrine was known from archaic times as the sanctuary of the vulture goddess, Nekhbet, 'the White One of Hierakonpolis (Nekhen)', who, as the ancient crown goddess of Upper Egypt, was paired with the cobra goddess, Wadjet, 'the Green One' of Lower Egypt. Stylized representations of Nekhbet's shrine appear as early as 3100 BC, showing it to be an edifice with a wooden, or possibly a reed, framework, covered with the skin of an animal, the tail of which is visible at the shrine's back.

But huge religious changes had occurred in Egypt since these early beginnings (see chapter 7) and by the time of second millennium Thebes, influenced by solar religion, Nekhbet's shrine had become almost exclusively the domain of the serpent goddess in all her different manifestations. And usurpers though they may be, these fiery goddesses of the *Per-Wer* shrine, hold the key to royal theophany. Moreover, once coronation themes are seen from this feminine perspective, a much more complete picture of the rising sun king begins to emerge, one which takes us a little further on the track of Hathor.

NURTURING BEAUTY: THE CAVES OF HATHOR

We return to the west bank at Thebes, to an area close to Kheruef's tomb where Amenhotep III's Jubilee Festival reliefs are preserved, an area where the cliffs are honeycombed with ancient tombs. Our destination is Hatshepsut's gleaming white limestone temple, which is built in the semi-circular rocky bay at Deir el-Bahri known to the ancient Egyptians

51 Hatshepsut's terraced temple at Deir el-Bahri. The shrine of Hathor lies on the far left of the middle terrace. The Middle Kingdom temple lies beyond in the south side of the cliff bay

as 'the Holy Place'. Contained within its limestone walls, especially in the shrine dedicated to Hathor, is an abundance of coronation imagery featuring the serpent goddess in her *Per-Wer* shrine. Here cow-eared faces of Hathor, the 'Lady of Punt', patroness of the fabulous riches which were brought to Egypt, stare out from the top of the columns at her shrine's entrance. And scenes, carved in delicate low relief on the entrance facade, show Hathor, as cow, tenderly licking the hand Hatshepsut holds out to her.

On entering the court of the Hathor shrine (which is now open to the sky), the mood shifts noticeably from the rest of the temple, for its pillars are in the shape of huge monumental naos sistra, displaying all the distinctive features of Hathor's sacred musical instrument (pl 52). Yet there is also a strange predominance of cattle imagery everywhere on the walls of the court. In one scene, Hathor, as cow, suckles a tiny figure of Hatshepsut crouching at her udder; in another the cow steps out of the coronation *Per-Wer* shrine. Over on the west wall too, there was once an anthropomorphic figure depicting the Apis Bull of Memphis (though his figure has, at some stage, been intentionally erased, probably in Akhenaten's reign). The Apis, according to his inscription here, is the virile bull 'who impregnates the vital cows', and he informs Hatshepsut that he has established for her 'the limits of your herds'.

However, such cow images should not impede an understanding of Egypt's serpent cult. The ancient Egyptians seem to have perceived an

53 Gold pectoral showing paired figures of Hathor as cow suckling the 12th Dynasty ruler Amenemhet III. A royal figure stands in front of each cow lovingly stroking her neck. The central uniting motif is a prominent sun-disk, from which Ankh-signs of life extend as well as two serpents, coiling downwards to touch the head of the standing king. Above each cartouche on the cow's back is yet another serpent, snaking across the royal name, whilst above on either side, beams a great eye (The pectoral probably came from Byblos on the Lebanese coast where Hathor was worshipped as 'Lady of Byblos' and is now in the Beirut Museum)

esoteric homology between the cow and deadly cobra, probably because they saw their life energy as the same in essence.

Interestingly, two separate statues of the Hathor cow and the cobra (plates 62 and 73) show the goddess in a similar pose, protecting King Amenhotep II as he emerges from a papyrus swamp, a location represented by papyrus stalks surrounding the head of the cow and serpent. The papyrus swamps at the desert's edge have long since vanished but in ancient times, according to Louis Keimer, they would have been a natural habitat for both cow and cobra.[4]

That cow and cobra are indeed bound up with each other is shown in the clearest possible way by the uraeus snakes, eyes and suckling cow motifs of a gold pectoral dating from the reign of the Middle Kingdom ruler, Amenemhet III (pl 53). From this pectoral alone it is evident that the uraeus snake, serpent eye and Hathor cow are all manifestations of the same solar life energy with the cow form emphasizing the nurturing, vitalizing aspect.[5] Moreover, these motifs indicate that this fiery life energy is inseparable from the Pharaoh's rule.

Similar themes pervade the imagery in Hathor's shrine at Deir el-Bahri. Within the darkness of the mountain, three small chambers have been hewn, each one receding further back into the interior of the rock (pl 54). First comes the offering room, then the outer

54 The interior of the Hathor shrine in Hatshepsut's temple at Deir el-Bahri: view from the offering room.

sanctuary and finally the inner sanctuary, with its scene on the back wall of Hathor and Amun-Re blessing Hatshepsut, who is standing between them wearing the White Crown of Upper Egypt.

The first revealing clue is the name of the doorway leading into the small outer sanctuary:

The doorway of Maatkare (Hatshepsut), who is imbued with the vitality of Hathor, the supreme one of Thebes.

It is a significant name indeed, charging the room with all the nurturing power of the solar goddess, who is shown on each side-wall. There is only space, however, for a single scene, and it is the same identical image on each side, portraying the majestic cow, her reddish-brown colour still preserved, standing in a boat within the coronation *Per-Wer* shrine (pl 55). At her udder crouches Hatshepsut, drinking in the sacred milk, exactly like the much earlier Middle Kingdom ruler, Amenemhet III, represented in the pectoral in plate 53; whilst between the cow's forelegs stands yet another figure of Hatshepsut (erased), encircled by the colourful necklace of the cow goddess.

Amidst this abundance of cattle imagery, Hathor's serpent aspect has not been forgotten, for above the *Per-Wer*

shrine is a frieze of cobras, each one crowned with the solar horned headdress and supported by upraised *Ka*-arms (pl 55). Each forms a rebus of Hatshepsut's name 'Maat is the *Ka* of Re' (Maatkare), which is normally enclosed within a cartouche as part of the title 'King of Upper and Lower Egypt'. At the same time, this frieze of serpents reinforces the central theme: that Hatshepsut is drinking in the life-giving magical power of the fiery goddess within the coronation shrine.

Hatshepsut's nephew, Thutmose III, must have shared her enthusiasm for this conception of Hathor because he dedicated his own rock-cut dwelling to the goddess high on the hill immediately to the south of Hatshepsut's temple. Discovered in 1906, undisturbed by robbers, this shrine contained not only wall-paintings but also a marvellous life-size statue of the Hathor cow suckling the king (pl 62).

But what kind of power is Hatshepsut imbibing here? 'Power' by itself is too vague an expression, and it is important to attempt a more precise definition of terms. An answer is provided by the name inscribed on the

55 Hathor as cow suckling Hatshepsut and encircling her with a menit-necklace as a symbol of royal attraction. The figures of Hatshepsut were subsequently erased, and she was never included in the pharaonic king lists. To emphasize Hathor's connection with sexuality and erotic vitality an erect monkey named 'Flesh' stands behind a mirror to the left of the Per-Wer shrine. Above the monkey are two seated baboons. These animals often occur in Egyptian scenes with erotic meaning. Above the scene is a frieze of solar cobras, with each cobra forming a rebus of Hatshepsut's royal name as in plate 46 (Relief on the side wall of the outer sanctuary in the Hathor shrine at Deir el-Bahri)

56 *View of the Speos Artemidos temple hewn out of the rock at the entrance to the wadi. Though dedicated to the local leonine goddess, Pakhet, the entrance pillars have unfinished Hathor capitals. The long inscription over the entrance describes the chaos under the Hyksos foreign rulers, and praises Hatshepsut's prosperous reign. Inside the temple is a small vestibule and beyond this a corridor leads to the sanctuary which has a niche in the back wall for a cult statue*

jambs of the doorway, giving access to the innermost sanctuary:

The doorway of Maatkare, enduring of attraction in the temple of Hathor.

In a flash we are once again brought to that shining quality of the rising sun god in the eastern horizon—'attraction'. By drinking in Hathor's milk, Hatshepsut has become 'enduring of attraction', a quality vividly symbolized by the *menit*-necklace which, like a noose, binds together the goddess and youthful ruler within the *Per-Wer* shrine. So, for example, a 19th Dynasty scene at Karnak shows Hathor, on this occasion in human form, holding out her necklace to King Ramesses II, beckoning him to her with the words:

Come, come, O Lord of the Two Lands,
O ruler, possessor of attraction,
Sweet-lipped, whose eyes are the sun and moon.[6]

The goddess has shifted her shape here to appear more in the guise of a lover with the radiant king, holding out her necklace to him as if to take him in her arms and enfold him in an embrace of love. But whether as Mother or as Beloved, the qualities of this oscillating female clearly belong to the dawn phase of the solar cycle. For if the Pharaoh is to appear in the eastern horizon like Re-Harakhti, 'the beautiful youth belonging to attraction', he needs to be nurtured by the goddess of attraction and grow strong.

However, the opposite pole cannot be ignored—the aggressive face of death and destruction. This is particularly evident if we leave Deir el-Bahri and journey northwards to Middle Egypt where Hatshepsut constructed another rock-cut temple which she dedicated to the goddesses (pl 56).

Located at the entrance to a ravine, not far south of the famous tombs at

57 A menit-necklace combined with a scarab beetle symbolizing Hathor's erotic power connected with the rising sun god (Monochrome relief in the tomb of Inherkau at Deir el-Medina)

Beni Hasan, and called by the Greeks *Speos Artemidos* (Cave of Artemis), the temple is yet another instance of Egyptian female cave dwellings situated in the transitional realm between the desert and cultivated green land. It is dedicated to the wild lioness of the locality, the goddess with 'sharp eyes' and 'pointed claws' named Pakhet, 'she who scratches', who haunts the nearby desert area and lonely wadis, hunting for food in the night. Scenes on each wall, flanking the entrance to the corridor and sanctuary, show leonine goddesses investing the Pharaoh with emblems of their power—fitting decoration for a shrine dedicated to such a fierce goddess.

On the left side aggressive themes predominate. The Pharaoh is shown kneeling before the enthroned Amun for his blessing, whilst the crown goddess, named here as Weret-Hekau-Pakhet (or 'Great-of-Magic-She-who-Scratches'), tells that she, the fiery serpent, is responsible for spreading fear of the Egyptian ruler throughout the lands:

I place your terror in all lands,
I rear up between your eyebrows,
My flames are fire against your enemies.[7]

In the scenes on the right, however, a very different atmosphere prevails. Immediately next to a relief showing the Pharaoh offering incense and making a libation before the leonine Pakhet comes another depiction of the same goddess, who now, quite clearly, is a

46

58 Seti I touches the sacred beads of Hathor's menit. The tenderly clasped hands of goddess and king, as well as Hathor's empowering gesture with her necklace, eloquently convey the Pharaoh as the beloved of the serpent goddess (Relief on a door pillar from the tomb of Seti I at Thebes, Louvre Museum, Paris)

channel for Hathor's beneficence. All is greenness and propitiation as she holds both a *menit* and sceptres with cobras entwined around them. And, placing great emphasis now on her appeased, protective nature, she tells the Pharaoh:

I have placed the two cobras on your head, so that they appear between your eye-brows. My *menit* belongs to you, providing protection for you whilst you appear on the throne of Horus.[8]

All this makes it crystal-clear that Hatshepsut, and all those other Phar-aohs associated with the *Per-Wer* shrine, are not merely putting on the physical signs of rulership at their investiture—their crowns and other insignia—but also taking to them-selves the dread and attraction of the feminine powers. Patently, if a dawn king is to 'appear', he has need of the crown goddesses.

SPELLBINDING LEADER: THE RISING SUN

But why does a ruler need dread and attraction? Of what earthly use is such power in the rulership of Egypt? A great deal, if modern statements about the kind of qualities needed by young leaders are to be believed. For, as one writer succinctly puts it, the talent to 'command affection and communicate energy' is crucial for effective leader-ship.[9] Admittedly, this statement was made in the context of a contempo-rary society very different from that of the ancient Egyptians. Nevertheless, the aptitude for leadership seems to be of abiding interest. Certainly, it was of deep concern to the Egyptians, who, perhaps of all ancient Near

virtues of Senwosret I to a local ruler, telling him that the king of Egypt is

A possessor of charm, great in sweetness,
Who has taken possession through attraction.[10]

But Sinuhe also warns that this same king terrorizes anyone opposed to his will, boasting that he 'smashes foreheads—no one can stand in his presence'. Likewise, he tells how Senwosret I's predecessor, Amen-emhet I, emanated the same qualities: 'Fear of him was throughout the land like Sekhmet in a year of plague'.[11]

Apart from its enjoyment as pure narrative, the purpose of the *Story of Sinuhe* is also quite clearly didactic. Much copied by pupils learning the art of writing in scribal schools, it encapsulates, most strikingly, both the prevailing mood of the age and perceptions of the Egyptian king at a time of great religious and social change. As such, it contains important clues about the essence of Pharaonic rule.

Sinuhe's observant characterization of the king's double-sided nature deserves close attention. For he states quite categorically that royal dread and attraction are inseparable qualities in the art of rulership, qualities which make it impossible for subjects or enemies to remain as passive bystanders whenever the king appears.

Attraction draws loyal followers close to him; the fear he inspires repels those opposed to his will. All this is, of course, the very same ambivalent power which emanates from the serpent eye goddess. So it is now more obvious why a king needs relationship with her: it is she who empowers him to rule.

At the core of such qualities is heated, sexual power. So, for instance, an inscription on a stela from the Middle Kingdom tomb of Akhtoy describes

Eastern cultures, bequeathed the most complete testimony of the qualities they esteemed in a ruler. And a crucial element in all this is the ability to 'command affection'. To rule effectively a Pharaoh must be able to 'capture the hearts' of those in his following.

The popular Middle Kingdom *Story of Sinuhe* gives a vivid picture of the captivating qualities emanating from Senwosret I (1971-1928 BC). The first

part of the story tells how Sinuhe, an Egyptian courtier, takes flight from Egypt at a time of instability. He flees to an area somewhere in Syria-Palestine where he successfully adapts to nomadic life and becomes the chief of a local tribe.

Why he had to flee is not revealed in the story, but his underlying loyalty to the Egyptian king is never really in doubt. At one point he extols the

60 Statue of a Hathorian queen, probably Meritamun, who was both daughter and great royal wife of Ramesses II. She holds a menit-necklace with a human-headed counterpoise, and is crowned with a coronet of solar cobras. On her brow are the paired cobras of Upper and Lower Egypt (Egyptian Museum, Cairo)

how highly this royal official was regarded by foreigners because he was a subject of the Egyptian king. Akhtoy was responsible for bringing back precious minerals (including turquoise) from abroad, and he tells how awe of the king

Instilled respect for me.
His influence spread terror of me,
Those lands in which I came
Cried 'Hail', 'Hail', to his Bas.
His attraction coupled (snwḥ) the Two Lands.[12]

The use of the verb 'couple' *(snwḥ)* to describe royal attraction as the force binding together the Two Lands [Egypt] is an apt choice of words. It underscores the sexual basis of the king's rule, since the verb also means 'to make love', showing that the fire of sexual passion indeed burns at the heart of the Egyptian kingdom.

At issue is leadership exercised by a physically well-endowed, warm, strong, youthful ruler, qualities which are shown to be his, for example, when the Hathor cow surrounds him with her *menit*-necklace of attraction and suckles him at her udder.

Such scenes are not confined to Egypt. The motif of the suckling cow and calf can be seen on a wide variety of objects throughout the ancient Near East—in Crete, Syria, Mesopotamia and Greece, as well as on Phoenician objects.

Othmar Keel suggests that this motif expresses the joyous tenderness, warmth and contentment that sustains the flow of life and he draws attention to the verb 'to be joyful' in Egyptian, which is determined by the hieroglyph of a cow turning round to a young calf

61 The Hathor cow in her rock shrine at Deir el-Bahri before removal to the Cairo Museum. In one of those chance moments of excavation every archaeologist dreams of, a workman employed in Naville's excavation in 1906, loosened a large stone in the rubble of the mountain-side with his pick, to reveal a gaping hole behind. And there, peering forth in all her glory, stood the marvellous Hathor cow within her mountainous cavern, an awesome epiphany of the Lady of the Western Mountain

nestling at her side from the New Kingdom onwards.[13]

Milk-giving, feeding and affectionate warmth are all contained in this image, as well as a sense of the zest for life mediated by the animal world. And whatever its significance in other cultures, this nurturing motif became meaningful in a royal context in Egypt, especially from the Middle Kingdom onwards, when there was a marked shift towards emphasizing the 'heart' and 'feeling' qualities of the Egyptian king in connection with his followers.

In short, the king as a youthful 'dawn hero' appeals to the collective experience of his subjects, 'his herd', as the Egyptian people are sometimes called. Moreover, to lead them he relies strongly on the animal world of feeling and emotions.

He is their guardian and preserver and they, in turn, are bound to him as loyal followers. It would be a mistake, however, to dismiss this group relationship as merely animal, or to minimize the appeal of attraction to group feelings. For experience of such power brings an awakening into the richness, the wonder and beauty of life, a profound sense of relatedness and belonging in the world.

Yet the dawn king cannot remain forever with the Mother-Beloved in the eastern horizon, nor can Egypt rely solely on these charismatic qualities of verve and enthusiasm to focus group aspirations. The sun must continue its course towards the zenith, towards a realm containing different qualities that also need to be brought to bear upon the rulership of Egypt. To discover these it is necessary to turn to a different manifestation of the serpent goddess—the daughter of Re.

62 The life-size statue of the Hathor cow with King Amenhotep II (son of Thutmose III) from the shrine of Thutmose III at Deir el-Bahri (Egyptian Museum, Cairo)

5 Mediatrix:
The Noonday Sun

H E HAS OUTLIVED that rage of early youth. He is no longer impulsive, but implacable. A godlike serenity, an almost superhuman pride, an immutable will, breathe from the sculptured stone. He has learned to believe his prowess irresistible, and himself almost divine. If he now raised his arm to slay, it would be with the stern placidity of a destroying angel. (Amelia Edwards, *A Thousand Miles Up the Nile*[1])

So wrote that intrepid Victorian traveller, Amelia Edwards, about the face of the 19th Dynasty King, Ramesses II she saw on one of the seated colossi before the large temple at Abu Simbel. Whether or not her heartfelt assessment of the king holds true for all who see this massive figure of Ramesses, or whether indeed, it was the intention of the ancient sculptors who chiselled away at the features to convey such qualities, is not the point here. For what Amelia Edwards admirably summed up are certain characteristics of the zenithal sun god in the fullness of power—his 'superhuman pride', his

'immutable will', manifesting with 'the stern placidity of a destroying angel'.

However, our own starting-point is not this colossus of Ramesses II but a relief, equally impressive, on the west wall of the hypostyle hall in the temple of Karnak. It shows Isis rattling her sistrum, as she leads King Seti I, father of Ramesses, into the presence of Amun-Re (pls 63, 65). Like the Abu Simbel colossus, the very size of this relief is striking; unlike other reliefs which normally occupy a single register, this one extends across three registers of the west wall, a sure sign of its importance.

Scenes of this type, showing the king led by a sistrum-shaking goddess, date from the 19th and 20th Dynasties when Egypt was ruled by the Ramessid kings (c 1300–1070 BC). To King Seti and his father, Ramesses I, an erstwhile military general, had fallen the unenviable task of restoring Egypt in the aftermath of Akhenaten's radical departure from traditional solar rulership. His revolution had meant,

to mention but one of the consequences, the exile of the serpent goddess, at least in her different manifestations within the transformational solar cycle. Akhenaten's unswerving dedication to the trinitarian solar father god had shattered the pantheon, and now these Ramessid kings, fuelled by a spirit of earnest piety and devotion, were intent upon making amends. So we see here Seti I, reverently stooping as the goddess brings him into the presence of Amun-Re, reaffirming his dependence on her mediation before the zenithal Theban father. She has returned with a vengeance under these pious rulers, who placated her in no uncertain terms after the traumatic events during Akhenaten's reign.

But what is initially puzzling in this scene at Karnak is the identity of the goddess. Neither Hathor nor, for that matter, any of the other goddesses we have seen linked with serpent power is shown here. Rather, leading the king in all her fiery snake glory is none other than Isis, more familiarly known as the sister-wife of Osiris and madonna-like mother of Horus. Yet here we see her with a uraeus snake rearing up on her

brow, a sistrum in her hand and, to crown it all, a horned headdress resting on a circlet of serpents adorning her solar head. Nothing in her iconography would lead us to believe that here before our eyes is the sorrowful widow or solicitous mother of the Osirian family. Nor is she evidently to be understood as such, since, in the speech inscribed above her, she surprisingly declares herself to be 'the august daughter' of Amun-Re, child of the majestic sun god worshipped at Thebes.

Does all this mean then that we are plunged into that 'disarray' of the Egyptian pantheon, at which Adolf Erman threw up his hands in horror whilst writing about Egyptian religion,[2] in a world where there seems to be neither rhyme nor reason? Was Erman perhaps justified, for have we not seen first this goddess, then that one, taking on each other's shapes and functions with remarkable alacrity? Surely not. Even though the Egyptians never conformed to the rules of Western logic quite in the way some might wish, their pantheon was certainly not confused.

Nor is this weaving in and out of each other's realms by the goddesses simply an incoherent muddle. On the contrary, Isis must be understood here in the light of the reaction to Akhenaten, of the pressing need to reconnect members of the pantheon with each other, and of the wish to show explicitly the interrelationship of their different spheres.

Lying behind such an uncharacteristic portrayal of the goddess is the notion that she too is needed in the solar circuit. The Ramessid temple designers were leaving nothing to chance, leaving not the slightest possibility of misunderstanding that Isis too served an important function in the solar realm. And to make this connection absolutely obvious, she is represented here as a manifestation of the serpent goddess.

Clearly, however, the music she plays with her sistrum does not belong to any nocturnal rite of renewal involving the glittering night-time goddess, 'Gold', who brings the king to dawn. Nor, for that matter, does Isis here resemble the goddess of the *Per-Wer* shrine, nurturing the youth of attraction in the eastern horizon. There is yet another feminine transformation shown here. This time, with her protective power completely wound around the king, her attention shifts towards encounter with Amun-Re, towards his 'wonder-working' countenance, as texts sometimes describe the gleaming brilliance of the Theban god. In the inscription above her head, Isis refers to the seeing of the father god, reminding Amun-Re, in no uncertain terms, that he has 'seen' his son, Horus, acknowledging him to be the ruling hawk king of Thebes:

You have seen your son, Horus,
Appearing in Thebes.
May you imbue him
With life and stability
As a son, glorious and complete.

Here then we have another transformation of the serpent goddess, this time involving the solar father and the king, his son, brought face-to-face at

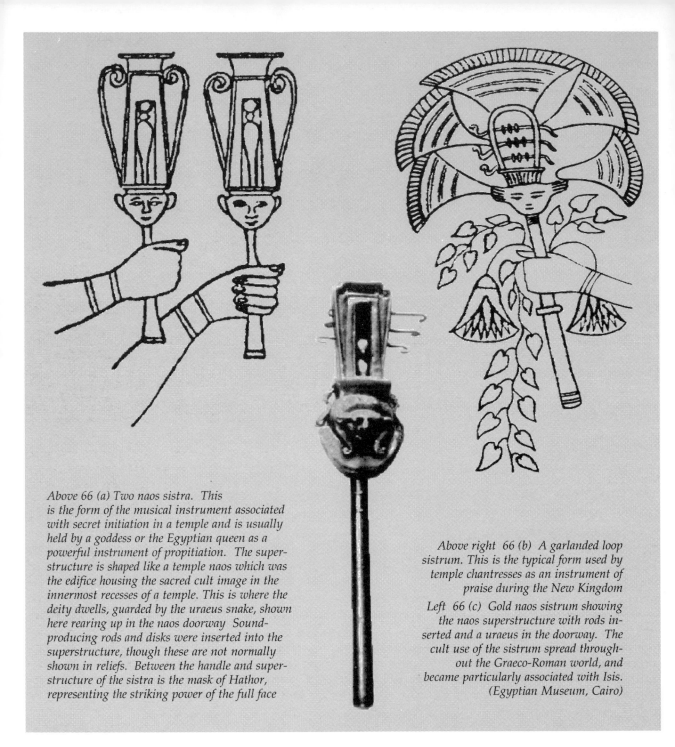

Above 66 (a) Two naos sistra. This is the form of the musical instrument associated with secret initiation in a temple and is usually held by a goddess or the Egyptian queen as a powerful instrument of propitiation. The superstructure is shaped like a temple naos which was the edifice housing the sacred cult image in the innermost recesses of a temple. This is where the deity dwells, guarded by the uraeus snake, shown here rearing up in the naos doorway Sound-producing rods and disks were inserted into the superstructure, though these are not normally shown in reliefs. Between the handle and superstructure of the sistra is the mask of Hathor, representing the striking power of the full face

Above right 66 (b) A garlanded loop sistrum. This is the typical form used by temple chantresses as an instrument of praise during the New Kingdom

Left 66 (c) Gold naos sistrum showing the naos superstructure with rods inserted and a uraeus in the doorway. The cult use of the sistrum spread throughout the Graeco-Roman world, and became particularly associated with Isis. (Egyptian Museum, Cairo)

the zenith by a daughter goddess, intently shaking her sistrum between them in an act of mediation.

The symbolic design of her instrument (pl 66), which we have already observed in the design of the sistrum pillars at Deir el-Bahri and the Speos Artemidos, is highly instructive. Most significantly, within the naos of Isis' sistrum the sound-producing bars are not visible, but rather the rearing head of a cobra is shown—an iconographic detail highlighting the fiery power rearing up within the sacred shrine.

So it is time, perhaps, to look a little more closely at this unusual musical instrument, as well as Egyptian notions of 'seeing the face' of deity, to

67 Female musicians playing loop sistra, tambourines and double pipes during a procession of Amenhotep I's cult statue at Thebes. On the right a priest turns to breathe in power from a sistrum held by one of the musicians (Relief in the tomb of Amenmose, Dra Abu-el-Naga, Thebes)

understand better its connotations for the daughter goddess and the Egyptian king.

FACING THE FATHER: ENCHANTRESS ASCENDANT

The powers of the Egyptian sistrum were remarked on by a number of classical authors in late antiquity. Juvenal tells us that Isis was able to cause blindness with her sistrum;[3] and Plutarch describes how it was used to repel and ward off Typhon, being the instrument which keeps creation in perpetual motion:

The sistrum also indicates that the things which exist should be shaken and should never stop moving ... For they say that with the sistrum they repel and ward off Typhon, meaning that when decay confines and restricts nature, the power of creation sets her free, and restores her by means of movement.[4]

However, its main significance for the Egyptians themselves was to control the excessive rage and violence of wrathful deities. By the New Kingdom the two types of sistrum known as the naos sistrum and the loop sistrum had become the standard forms of the instrument after a long process of evolution. According to an inscription in Hathor's Graeco-Roman temple at Dendara, they were played in order to drive away divine fury:

The loop-sistrum of the Powerful One
Drives away your violence,
The naos-sistrum of your ka
Obliterates your fury.[5]

Needless to say, playing a sistrum in the temple cult was a highly skilled accomplishment and specific rhythms had to be learnt by the temple musicians, who were often female. But the king was also trained in the art, and is shown in the temple of Edfu shaking sistra and running before Hathor, greeting her with the words:

I have opened your temple,
And as I enter, rage goes forth.[6]

When the king enters her temple with her musical instruments, so he brings with him the power to control the turbulent divinities residing there.

For, as the Egyptians never tired of reiterating, direct contact with the face of powerful beings is dangerous, and again and again we read in prayers to a deity, 'May your merciful face be towards me'. In the face resides the kind of power called *sekhem*, which is also one of the names of the sistrum and is obviously also linked with the name of Sekhmet 'the Powerful One'.[7] People entering the presence of the Egyptian king are sometimes shown holding their hands up before their faces, shielding themselves from his countenance, from the power which he manifests as a solar ruler, power that can strike down those who are unprotected. For as one demon boasts in an Old Kingdom *Pyramid Text*: 'He on whom my face falls, his head shall not stay in place'[8]

Not surprisingly, therefore, the frontal aspect is rarely shown in Egyptian reliefs, except in those cases where facial power is particularly emphasized as, for example, in full-face portrayals of Hathor, or of the *sekhemu*-beings shown during the journey of the sun god in the Underworld. Wisely the Egyptians guarded against revealing such a potentially blinding force too openly, a force which needed to be approached with caution and care, if its beneficent qualities were to shine.

The unpredictability of encounter with the face of Re is mentioned already in the Old Kingdom *Pyramid Texts*. King Pepi, as he ascends to the sky, implores to be granted admission to the zenithal realm of the sun god with the words, 'O Re, turn yourself about and see this Pepi'.[9] His fear that he might not be 'seen' is well-founded, though it is only in much later texts that the implacable side of the sun god is described in any detail.

This comes out most vividly in the New Kingdom story known as *The Contendings of Horus and Seth*, a text preserved on a papyrus dating from around 1150 BC, which is now in the British Museum.[10] The story deals with the contest between Horus, son of Isis and Osiris, and his uncle, the god Seth. Both believe that they are entitled to succeed Osiris, as ruler of Egypt, and the pantheon, presided over by the sun god, Re-Harakhti, have gathered to decide who should occupy the vacant throne.

Despite the fact that Horus is the eldest son of Osiris, and supported in his claim by Isis, Re is reluctant to recognize him. Far more appealing to the sun god is the violent aggression and fiery nature of Seth, who is none other than the murderer of Osiris and who has caused the confusion in the first place. Why appoint a weak child 'feeble in body . . . whose breath smells bad', Re asks dismissively? But his obstructive behaviour is challenged by the phallic god, Baba, who dares to insult the sun god, bluntly telling him,

Opposite page 68 An early association of Hathor with the Egyptian nomes occurs in this Fourth Dynasty triad of King Menkaure standing between Hathor 'Lady of the Sycamore in all her places' and the goddess of Diospolis Parva (seventh nome of Upper Egypt), who wears the nome emblem on her head. The triad was discovered with three others in the Valley Temple of Menkaure at Giza; and there may well originally have been 42 such triads, representing Hathor and the king with the different nome deities (Egyptian Museum, Cairo)

'Your shrine is empty'. To the consternation of the rest of the pantheon Re retreats, his pride wounded, and he lies sulking on his back, refusing to have anything further to do with the proceedings.

His action, or rather inaction, brings the affairs of the tribunal to an abrupt halt! Like Zeus in Greece, the supreme god of Egypt is not always a pleasant ruler, nor does he always act in accordance with the wishes of others. And as with Zeus, who blasted the unfortunate daughter of King Cadmus out of existence when she pleaded to see his undiluted magnificence, there are few equipped to approach this implacable Egyptian deity. Only his daughter, it seems, is able to do so, for in the story her help miraculously appears in the form of Hathor, 'Lady of the Southern Sycamore', the tree goddess of Memphis (pl 68) who now enters before her recumbent father. In a gesture of humorous spontaneity which only a child could bring to such a situation, she displays her genitals before him, rousing him to laughter by her playful behaviour:

She came and stood before her father, the All-Lord. She uncovered her genitals before him. And then the great god smiled at her. He got up and sat with the Great Ennead, and he said to Horus and Seth, 'Speak for yourselves'.

Re's ability to laugh here is an affirmation of life, a jovial response to the world around him, from which, but a moment ago, he had been so completely estranged. Through Hathor's cajoling intervention Re is brought back into relationship with the pantheon once again, and the rivalry between Horus and Seth, which had been so abruptly interrupted, can now continue.

What the episode also makes abundantly clear is how important the spontaneity and playfulness of a daughter, blessed with considerable

natural charm, are in the life of the sun god. Though, were it not for temple scenes showing the daughter goddess as mediatress, it might be tempting to dismiss Hathor's function here as a titillating interlude aimed at amusing listeners to the story. Yet there is more to this female self-display than merely a light-hearted striptease—the daughter goddess appears far too often in Egyptian iconography for her humorous act to be passed over too quickly.

LIBERATING LAUGHTER: MANIFESTING MERCY

In some respects the Egyptian daughter goddess has much in common with the Grecian Pallas Athene, who is said to have sprung from the head of her father Zeus in a startling birth. Certainly in Egypt, the goddess is intimately connected with the face of the sun god. And she is also a martial deity, the menacing uraeus snake, his valiant daughter, 'the Great One shining on the brow of her father, the glorious one who causes fear of her father'.[11] When Amun-Re praises Thutmose III for his deeds against the enemies of Egypt, the Theban god does not fail to mention his serpent on the king's brow, that consumer of enemies, who 'made quick booty of the evil-doers, swallowing the lowlanders with her flame.'[12]

And like Pallas Athene, the defender of cities and fortresses in Greece, the Egyptian daughter goddess is closely linked with the fate of cities. A relief in Ramesses III's temple at Karnak shows Waset, the city goddess of Thebes, incarnating the power of the serpent daughter as she shakes a sistrum and chants a propitiatory hymn of praise to her father, Amun-Re. In it she names all the daughter goddesses associated with the many cities situated between Elephantine in the south, right down to Memphis and Heliopolis at the apex of the Delta in

the north. All of them, she sings, shake sistra for the beneficent face of the Theban sun god:

Your august daughter,
Mut, the Lady of Isheru,
Propitiates you,
Satis and Anukis praise you,
Nekhbet propitiates you.[13]

So the hymn continues, in the same vein, until each Egyptian city has been placed under the protective and terrible gaze of its serpent daughter, the guarantor of its safety.

However, she is not only a martial maiden, devoted solely to overwhelming all in the path of her father. She also arouses great joy in the sun god, as mentioned already. This is also expressed in the following lines about Hathor and Re from a hymn in Hathor's temple at Philae:

Re exalts without ceasing,
His heart rejoices when he joins his daughter,
He swims in his firmament, in peace,
He turns and takes his course.[14]

Re's great love for Hathor inspires him to cross the sky each day, for it is her attraction which is the power motivating the circuit of the sun; without her there simply would not be a sunrise.

Such too seems to be the state of affairs in the royal palace on earth. A famous tale in the *Westcar Papyrus* tells how the world-weary Old Kingdom ruler Snofru, famed for his step pyramid at Saqqara, was languishing in his palace, wandering aimlessly from room to room, unable to find solace or respite from the cares of office.[15] Eventually he is advised by a wise palace magician to go on a boating party with the beautiful braided Hathorian girls

of the palace, who the story specifically states, 'had not yet given birth'. Just as Hathor soothes the heart of her father Re, so King Snofru is revived by the youthful beauty of the palace maidens, by the rocking motions of the boat as they row on the water, and by the sight of the verdant green nature along the shores of the pleasure-lake.

The episode provides a vivid picture of how a verwrought ruler at the height of his powers can all too easily become cut off from others, and how this threatens to disturb the harmony of Egypt. Such a disposition cannot be controlled by force, by rational discourse or by rigid control. For it seems that the chink in his armour can only be found by a female of youthful attraction, vital and fresh like the greenness of nature, a goddess like Isis offering her bouquet of sweet-smelling plants before Amun-Re as she shakes her sistrum (pl 65). Ever on the side of relatedness, the craft of these virginal daughters resides in their grace, their spontaneity, their rhythmic play and attraction. No wonder then that royal daughters were so sweetly praised, as in these lines from an Egyptian 'Song of Songs', dedicated by a 25th Dynasty Pharaoh to his daughter, Mutirdis, who was a priestess of Hathor:

Sweet, sweet of attraction,
* the Hathor priestess, Mutirdis,*
Sweet, sweet of attraction,
* says King Menkheperre,*
Sweet, sweet of attraction,
* say the men,*
Lady of attraction
* say the women.*
She is the royal daughter,
* sweet of attraction,*
The most beautiful of women,
* A virgin never seen before.*
Black is her hair like the blackness of night,
* Like grapes and figs . . .*
Her breasts are firm on her body [16]

Only such unsullied beauty can touch

the hearts of powerful rulers locked away in isolation, and curb destructive tendencies which may flare up at any time, separating them from those they rule.

There is a similar perception in Baubo's spontaneous act before Demeter in the Eleusinian mysteries. According to an Orphic tradition recorded by Clement of Alexandria, Demeter, at one stage in her quest for her lost daughter, sits in profound gloom beside the well of Eleusis. Lost in grief, she refuses the *kykeon*-drink of hospitality which Baubo offers her, and the young girl immediately responds by exposing her genitals before the goddess. Like the sun god in Egypt, when Hathor makes a similar gesture, Demeter's face suddenly lights up with a smile at Baubo's spontaneity and directness.[17] Unafraid to approach Demeter, the girl has been able to touch the darkened recesses of gloom into which the despondent goddess has sunk, to elicit a joyful response from her. The result is that Demeter gladly accepts the drink she is offered, and is roused to activity once more by playful humour.[18]

How highly then the spirit of laughter and humour must have been prized in these ancient cultures.[19] For in spite of overweening rage or overwhelming despair, when all seems hopeless both Re and Demeter are able to rise out of themselves for the sake of others, are restored to participation in life by the erotic young goddesses. And it is a recognition that childlike spontaneity, born out of a zest for life, is easily lost by those weighed down by the burdens of existence. Whether through

excessive pride or world weariness, they all too easily become cut off from others, hiding themselves away in darkness, no longer interested in the affairs of the world—traits which seem particularly to afflict mature rulers in middle life.

But response to the warmth and humour of the daughter dissolves fixity of mood, breathing in the scents and perfumes of her plants imbues an

overheated heart with freshness, and resonating with her sistrum's rhythms brings harmony with the dance and movement of life. And, in the case of the Theban god, Amun-Re, shown in plate 63, qualities which may not come so easily to the surface in such a magnificent and awe-inspiring god, qualities of mercy and compassion for others, now shine in meridian light as the daughter goddess leads before his

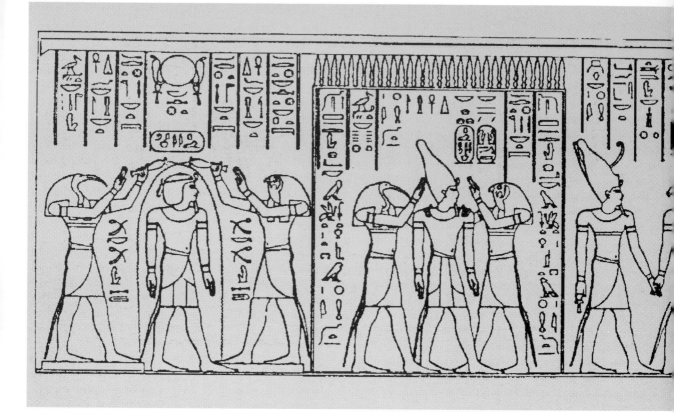

71 The Pharaoh's journey of transformation. On the left the moon god Thoth and the hawk-headed Horus purify Philip Arrhidaeus. Next Thoth and Horus bless the White Crown of Upper Egypt worn by the king, a ritual blessing encompassing all the regalia and insignia given to the king during this second phase. Then, in the third phase, he is led forth towards Thoth by Atum of Heliopolis and the Theban god Month. In the final stage (shown on the far right) the king kneels before Amun-Re, who blesses the royal crown and proclaims that the king rules upon the throne of his father, Re. Behind Amun-Re sits the goddess Amaunet suckling the king as a sign of the new sonship into which he has been reborn (Canonical coronation sequence from the fourth century BC on the shrine of Philip Arrhidaeus at Karnak)

throne the king, who seeks acknowledgement to serve as the ruler of Egypt. Here at the zenith the power to dispense great blessings manifests through the mediation of the goddess, whose mission is to bring others into the realm of providential care, to bind together king and father god.

CROWN OF ILLUMINATION: THE TRIUMPHANT KING

It remains now to place the sistrum-shaking daughter within a ritual context, and, in the lamentable absence of any Theban liturgical papyrus giving details of a crowning ceremony, we have to rely on versions of the king's *rite of passage* shown in reliefs on temple walls, and in particular, the well-known sequence of four scenes on the exterior of the granite shrine, which housed the sacred boat and cult image of Amun-Re within the temple at Karnak (pl71). The sequence shows Philip Arrhidaeus, the half-brother of Alexander the Great, who ruled Egypt at the close of the fourth century BC, passing through a series of rites designed to take him to the very zenith of solar rulership. Greek though he may have been, he nevertheless still had to be crowned according to the ways and customs of Egypt. And indeed this sequence is but a copy of an earlier one on the shrine dating from the reign of Thutmose III.

Like a number of other *rites of passage*, which Arnold van Gennep studied from a variety of cultures, the sequence follows a very recognizable ritual pattern.[20] It begins with a lustral purification. Then the king is incorporated into the realm of the sacred by being given his crowns and regalia. Having been purified, robed and adorned, he is then led forth for the final stage when he takes possession of the divine and terrestrial realms.

Nevertheless, this canonical sequence, with its concentration of

masculine deities, tells us little about the place of the daughter goddess in the royal rite of passage. To discover this we must return to the hypostyle hall at Karnak once again, this time, however, to scenes on the east wall where the first two phases of the ritual sequence are again depicted—the purification and crowning.

But there is a striking difference in the third phase. Replacing the scene of Atum and Month leading the king (here Ramesses II) is none other than Hathor, holding her sistrum aloft to shield Ramesses from the potential blast of the god's anger, as she leads him into the presence of Amun-Re and Amaunet (pl 72). The relief speaks for itself. The daughter goddess here performs what van Gennep termed a 'threshold rite', that is the rite enabling the king to cross into the realm of the Theban cosmogonic powers—a threshold rite, moreover, which van

Gennep observed is missing from the Philip Arrhidaeus' version that he used to illustrate an Egyptian *rite of passage*.[21] Had van Gennep been able to visit the hypostyle hall at Karnak and seen these scenes of the daughter goddess, his puzzlement at the apparent absence would have vanished.

Moreover, once the daughter goddess is included in the ritual sequence, some striking parallels become apparent; in particular the Tantric rite of royal consecration described in some detail by Mircea Eliade.[22]

This too involves initiation into the realm of wrathful deities. As in Egypt, the initiate first undergoes a lengthy purification performed by his guru, which includes purifying all the ritual objects to be used during the ritual.

Then he is robed in a white garment and crowned with a garland of flowers. Next, after drawing a mandala around his guru's feet to

show his reverence for him, he is accompanied by a young girl, preferably a relative, in order to experience possession by 'the angry god'. As he inhales special substances and repeats mantras, 'the angry god' takes possession of the initiate, who begins to sing and dance imitating the gestures of wrathful powers.

Only after he has experienced the full extent of their power within himself are these wrathful divinities then pacified in a series of mudras. The initiate becomes calm again, ready for the revelation of the deity who will be beneficent to him during his initiation, as blindfolded, he throws a flower into the mandala.

Then, having been prepared beforehand, he meditates upon a deep inner vision in which he sees the whole multiplicity of deities rising from and then being reabsorbed back into his heart, he experiences himself in the very

72 The daughter goddess, Hathor, shakes her sistrum to propitiate Amun-Re as she leads Ramesses II into his presence. The ritual pose reveals Hathor as the zenithal mediatress who creates harmony and channels the awesome magnificence of Amun-Re for the Pharaoh (Relief in the hypostyle hall at Karnak)

midst of the creative process of periodic birth and destruction.

Like the Egyptian ritual pattern, this pacification of wrathful divinity takes place in the company of a young girl. But leaving aside the identity of the particular deities in the Tantric ritual, as well as the specific details of ritual performance, which each culture would have expressed in its own way, there is a remarkably similar progres-

sion in the Tantric rite and the Egyptian initiatory journey involving the king and serpent goddess.

What the Tantric rite also brings home most forcibly is how important it is to understand the Egyptian temple sequence in terms of ritual experience. These scenes do not portray a series of empty gestures which deities performed for the king, belonging as one Egyptologist put it, 'to the world of imagination and make-believe'.[23] They are far more a highly charged summary of all those ritual actions—the purifications, the robings, the complex incantations, the crownings, and sacramental rites—all of which were aimed at taking the Egyptian king ultimately to the very

zenith of the sky. The scenes were not for aesthetic contemplation alone, but rather to reveal the divinities whose powers were focused, controlled and channelled during the ritual process.

Although it is not always easy to deduce from reliefs alone the actual form a royal ritual might have taken, such scenes were undoubtedly deeply rooted in the ritual life of the king and queen. Consequently, in tracing the manifestations of the attractive-destructive goddess, reference will be made, wherever possible, to papyri containing details of royal rituals. For only by interpreting the visual sources in conjunction with ritual texts, is it possible to build up a fuller picture of the Egyptian serpent goddess.

Above 74 Frontal view of 73 (previous page) Granite statue from Karnak which shows Amenhotep II, wearing the White Crown of the zenithal South, guarded by the fiery serpent goddess. Surrounding the serpent on either side are papyrus stalks, symbols of her greenness, health and propitiation (Egyptian Museum, Cairo)

THE 'FATHER' of Egyptian archaeology, Flinders Petrie—renowned for his conviction that small pottery objects, which were so often discarded as insignificant by other excavators, held important clues to the past—wrote that one of his aims had been to weave history out of 'scattered evidence using all materials of inscriptions, objects, positions and probabilities'.[1] Likewise, in order to piece together the transformational journey of Hathor and the king from the darkness of night to zenithal crowning at noon, we too have had to 'dig' and 'sift' through ancient images and scattered texts, which once belonged to a coherent serpent cult.

What conclusion can we draw so far from our study of the serpent goddess, bearing in mind also that, though it is the Pharaoh who is shown with her, the underlying paradigm for their journey is the relationship of Hathor and the sun god, Re?

Firstly, like Shakti in Hindu religion, Hathor is the dynamic partner. To her belongs that fiery, volatile power which manifests both as beneficence and destruction; and these two sides of the dangerous goddess, encapsulated by her name Hathor-Sekhmet, are the key to her nature. If her destructive impulses can become creative, and her beneficence harmonized with the unfolding rhythm of life in the solar circuit, so she becomes the *élan vital*, the energizing agent of change, the vanquisher of inertia and other threats which manifest during critical phases of the solar journey. One of the names of the uraeus is, in fact, Iaret, which is derived from the verb meaning 'to rise' (*jˁr*), itself suggestive of her upward movement. But if such a rising is to bring about positive change and transformation, it demands that her wild and dangerous power not only be actively roused, but also creatively expressed and channelled.

As the life-cycle of king and goddess unfolds from birth to death, in harmony with the passage of the sun, so her influence is brought to bear during the different phases of ascent. At night her intoxicating rhythms irrupt when the 'Child of Gold' dances and makes music for the starry goddess. Burning in anticipation for the East and new life, for release from darkness, the king seizes and takes possession of her life-giving vitality.

Only then, after her elusive power has been kindled, can the horizon doors open giving access to a realm of magnetic youthful leadership. Here the awesome Eye of Re radiates beauty and attraction for the people of Egypt, capturing affections and causing spontaneous feelings of joy to well up in their hearts. In this horizon realm, there is an intense experience of pleasure, which is gained from relationship with a shining dawn ruler.

Reluctantly, however, this phase of youthful enchantment must end, as the sun continues to climb upwards to the zenith of the sky, and the serpent goddess shifts her shape once more, this time into the graceful form of the solar daughter. Ever on the side of relatedness, she curbs the excessive qualities of the noon-day father god, calling forth his beneficent mercy and compassion, converting him to participation with the king, his son. Here, at the highest point of the cycle, lie qualities of humour, mercy and magnanimity, qualities which lie dormant and undiscovered, however, should the serpent goddess fail to appear.

It is essential to understand the polarity of Hathor and the king in this cycle of becoming. During ascent, Hathor grows ever younger as she changes from Mother-Beloved to Daughter, which means that the natural female life-cycle is essentially flowing in reverse. She is not moving towards entropy, so to speak, but rather moving towards ever more vitality and power at the zenith. Projected forth from the body of the sun god as eye or uraeus, she is the attracting, life-giving force provoking movement and unrest in the male, drawing him upwards, away from the night-time realm and dependence on the Mother.

His own progression, on the other hand, passes through the phase of night-time child of the glittering goddess, to youthful leader in the horizon, before reaching the father god and maturity at the zenith.

Thus in essence, during ascent, male and female energies are flowing in opposite, though not opposed directions; and, like a great wheel, the serpent goddess continually moves the male through the ascending cycle. Without Hathor, quite simply, there would not be any movement of the sun; like Shiva without Shakti, the sun king simply would not stir.

This upward direction, away from the Mother, marks a crucial step in the development of both male and female, as can be well judged from New Kingdom love poetry, which is pervaded by a Hathorian spirit of horizon youthful love. In some poems the presence of the Mother looms large, as the lovers long to engage fully in life and the delights of love. There is a continual oscillation between the bond with the Mother and the pull towards the 'brother' or 'sister', as the lovers affectionately call each other in the poems. All this is evocatively captured in the

following New Kingdom poem, in which a young girl of the fields, completely ensnared by love, tells how she has been diverted from the more humdrum daily task of setting traps for marsh fowl. Wracked with guilt at her failure to catch anything, she now wonders what she should tell her mother when she returns home empty-handed:

The voice of the wild goose shrills,
It is caught by its bait,
Love for you pervades me,
I cannot loosen it.
I shall retrieve my nets,
But what do I tell my mother,
To whom I go daily,
Laden with bird catch?
I have spread no snares today,
I am caught by my love for you.[2]

Yet another poem tells how the girl sees her lover standing in a doorway with his mother, and she begs Hathor—addressed here as 'Gold'—to quicken the mother's heart, so that she will release her son into the girl's waiting arms:

If only the mother knew my heart,
She would have understood by now,
O Gold put it in her heart,
Then will I hurry to my brother.[3]

Surfacing and churning in all youthful lives, Hathor is sometimes a source of conflict and tension, bringing changes not always welcome in the Mother's realm. But that is not all. Her ascending power has to be

Right 75 Three aspects of Hathor on a bronze menit counterpoise shaped like a female body. Surmounting the elaborate design is a female head in profile crowned with serpents. In the open-work frame beneath the shoulders her body opens to reveal a sistrum, which is placed on a gold sign surrounded by four serpents as a symbol of the mediating daughter.

Enclosed in the circular womb base is a solar cow within a papyrus marsh, the mother goddess in the secret place of birth where she nurtures her child. The design encapsulates the transformations of the female in the solar cycle during the New Kingdom (British Museum, London)

Above 76 Relief from the Theban tomb of Nebamun showing the tomb owner hunting birds in a papyrus thicket. His wife, dressed in a festive garment, holds lotus flowers and a loop sistrum. Their naked daughter is plucking lotus flowers from a fish-laden pool. Such attire and gestures are highly symbolic and convey the erotic proliferating power of Hathorian nature (British Museum, London)

Right 77 Ithyphallic god, crowned with the plumes of Min-Amun, raises one hand aloft as he holds his phallus with the other. His body is in the shape of the scarab beetle, Khepri, thus uniting solar and phallic regenerative themes (Vignette from Chapter 165 of the Book of the Dead)

reconciled also with other spheres, for the Sun Eye is not the sole luminary of the sky. Also shining there is another great glance—the Moon Eye—a power with which the Sun Eye needs to be balanced and harmonized.

Moreover the goddess and her father cannot remain forever at the zenith. Like all forms brought into existence, the sun god is subject to time, his body wears out with age, decline sets in, and he must descend once more into the arms of the Mother in the West, into the darkness of the Abyss for renewal. So too the daughter of the

sun must surrender her instinct for life to other, equally important goddesses, with whom she must interact in the totality of the solar circuit.

Which brings us to consideration of the Theban god, Amun-Re, 'Amun in his manifestation as Re', to whom the daughter goddess seems closely related. Who is he? And why should he be the dominant masculine deity at the zenith?

Part Two explores the implications all this has for the serpent goddess and for transformation in the solar circuit.

*Part 2 Moon and Sun:
Phallic Gods and
Solar Transformation*

7 New Age Religion: The Theban Triad

I N TRACING THE transformations of Hathor and the king we have mainly relied on evidence from Thebes, that famed 'hundred-gated city' praised by Homer in the Iliad.

What led the Greeks to use that name is unknown: among the Egyptians themselves it was known as Waset, or sometimes as 'the Upper Egyptian Heliopolis', a southern counterpart to the famous city of Heliopolis in the North where the creator god Atum and his Ennead were revered, a centre esteemed since ancient times for its cosmological wisdom, of which we shall have more to say later.

But to prepare ourselves for the immense conflict in solar religion that descended on Egypt during Akhenaten's reign, we need to breathe a little more of the religious atmosphere in New Kingdom Thebes, with its ruling divine triad of Amun-Re, Mut and their child, Khons. Whoever has visited the maze of sanctuaries at Karnak and Luxor on the east bank of the Nile must have sensed the immense influence exerted by Amun-Re, his ubiquitous figure endlessly adorning the mammoth temple walls, striding forth to bless the king, or seated to receive the manifold offerings reverently brought before him.

It was not always so. Way back in the 'pyramid age' of Old Kingdom Egypt, when Memphis reigned supreme as the state capital, Thebes was but a minor township on the eastern bank of the Nile. Little was heard of Amun—whose name means 'the Hidden One'—except as the male counterpart of Amaunet, the female 'Hidden One' in a *Pyramid Text*.[1]

Later this pair appear among the mysterious serpents and frogs brooding in the primeval swamp at Hermopolis, the 'City of the Eight', and home of the moon god, Thoth. The Ogdoad, the male-female creatures of latent existence before the coming of created life, included three other couples besides the 'hidden' pair, Amun and Amaunet: Nun and Naunet ('primordial waters' or 'inertness'), Kuk and Kauket ('darkness'), and Huh and Hauhet ('endlessness').

In later solar religion the wondrous lotus flower rises out of this seething mire, opening its petals at dawn to reveal the beautiful young sun child seated in their midst, bearer of renewed light to the world.

Around 2000 BC, however, Egypt was entering a new phase of religious development, one which saw the beginnings of Amun's extraordinary rise to supreme head of the pantheon. Shaking off his primeval slime, he emerged from the anonymity of the Abyss to appear as none other than 'Amun at the head of Karnak, Lord of the Thrones of the Two Lands'.

The rise of Amun coincided with a period during which Egypt had been reunited once again after the political chaos and distress of the First Intermediate Period. Old Kingdom centralized authority had broken down beneath the challenge of disloyal local rulers in the various nomes (districts) into which Egypt was divided for purposes of administration. The links that bound the Old Kingdom monarch and his people had been severed, unity dissolved as Egypt fragmented into a cluster of self-governing provinces at war with each other.

When the storm of this anarchic period subsided, finally brought to an end by Nebhepetre Mentuhotep, who came from a ruling family at Thebes, the mood of the country had changed radically. Gone was the divinely sanctioned visionary rule of confident kings at Memphis, close to the inspirational wisdom of the northern cosmic deities, remote from their people. These incoming Thebans were of a sterner mould, kings who carried the burden of office heavily on their shoulders, rulers close to human fate and the needs of their loyal subjects, dispensing justice and mercy as the caring shepherds of their people (pl 79).

And the deity whose star rose with these Middle Kingdom rulers was Amun-Re, whose opulent temples were eventually to rival those of Memphis and Heliopolis in splendour. Karnak itself, so Hatshepsut declares, is 'the horizon on earth, the august hill of the beginning',[2] a sacred precinct imitating in its architecture the dawn of the world.

AMUN-RE: A COSMOS COMES TO EARTH

But what kind of cosmos is involved here at Thebes and who is this Amun-Re who has so startlingly emerged from obscurity into a full-blown anthropomorphic god (pl 80), his tall plumes soaring up from his head-dress, winging through the air as if to touch the very tip of the sky? A god whose name itself suggests that the visible sun god, Re, is now also bound up with the hiddenness of existence.

Firstly, he is the source of life, order and power in a realm closely related to life on earth. It is explicitly said, albeit in a late hymn, that Amun lives in the 'atmosphere to the end of the sky's circuit'.[3] This statement is important because it suggests that it is only after the air god Shu has separated his coupling children—the sky goddess, Nut, and her partner, the earth god, Geb—that the influence of Amun-Re can be brought to bear, his power weaving through the realm arising from the separation of sky and earth. Elsewhere it is said that Amun brings with him the breath of life 'that breath which remains in all things and through which one lives forever,'[4] the life which inwardly enters into bodies.

It is important, moreover, not to confuse his appearance as a solar god with that dazzling sunrise weaving through the air at Heliopolis when Atum surges forth from the primeval waters to spit forth Shu and his female counterpart Tefenet at the very dawn of creation. Here at Thebes a different phase in the unfoldment of the cosmogonic process is involved. Sky has to be raised up and earth laid down

before Amun-Re can appear in his realm. Even his appearance seems to be less than purely solar, since his skin is sometimes painted blue in reliefs—a colour not easily reconcileable with the divine body of the sun god, which is said to be made of pure gold.[5]

Another important phenomenon associated with the rise of Amun-Re in this sun-filled environment of earth was the move towards a sense of personal inwardness on the part of the Egyptians, towards the beginnings of an individual sense of accountability and responsibility for actions, coupled with guilt for wrongdoing.

The roots of this, as we have already mentioned, lay much further back in Middle Kingdom Egypt, that period of deep disquiet and reorientation in religious consciousness which shook Egypt around 2000 BC.[6] The whole basis of the culture had been called into question by the collapse of central rule at the end of the Old Kingdom, and by the famine and wars which raged in the country.

It resulted in a whole spate of texts—lamentations, prophecies, dialogues, stories—which remarkably capture the new spirit dawning in this age. Motives were questioned, the nature of deity examined, the basis of rulership and the relationship of the king with his people re-stated. No longer could he simply command and order; rather, he had to be seen by his subjects to be a just and compassionate 'leader of his herd'.[7]

Also new was the perception that the cosmos, and more especially the solar circuit, affects human life on earth, that the world is created for human existence, that the deity (or the king who represents him on earth) is concerned for his people, caring for them like a shepherd watching over his flock. Moving and sustaining the world is not a divine power unconcerned with human fate, but rather a deity who rules with justice and

mercy, displaying anger to those who disobey him, mercy to those who are 'on his water', a personal deity who is known not only in the temple cult but also in the interior of the human heart, one who determines the fate of the land and the individual alike.

The horror that had held the Egyptians powerless during the chaotic times of the First Intermediate Period, had shocked them into a discovery that earth belonged to the cosmos, that human hurt, pain, tears, laughter, joy and suffering, all had a part to play. That there was a reason for existence which could be discovered in the human heart. Such realizations energized a whole process of development in religious consciousness, releasing new streams of creativity.

What began in the Middle Kingdom, or even before, came most fully to fruition in New Kingdom Egypt, in the cult of Amun-Re at Thebes. He, above all, was worshipped as a compassion-ate ruler, close to the one who calls to him, a god to whom the humble can pray:

You are Amun,
The Lord of him who is silent,
Who comes at the voice of the humble.
I called to you when I was sad,
And you came to save me.[8]

Not enough remains of Middle Kingdom Thebes to know how much these ethical traits belonged to Amun-Re before the New Kingdom, or how far one of the dominant Middle Kingdom images—the king as the just and caring shepherd of his people—was bound up with the emergence of Amun-Re as the royal god of Egypt.[9]

But there is every reason to believe that the Middle Kingdom sowed the seeds of the New Kingdom piety and devotion, so movingly illustrated in the scene of Isis leading King Seti I, who reverently stoops as he comes into the presence of Amun-Re (pl 65).

Certainly, it was in the reign of Hatshepsut, a ruler especially keen to link herself with Middle Kingdom traditions, that there was a veritable surge of devotion to Amun-Re in all his manifold aspects.

It was not, then, the seership and cosmic sacramental life of Heliopolis, nor the mysterious art of fabricating bodies as practised at Memphis, that were esteemed in New Kingdom Thebes but rather a just, merciful deity close to the needs of loyal subjects, a god not only of the Pharaoh but one who also listened with pity to the out-pourings of all humble supplicants.

This rise of Amun-Re represents an important development in the history of religious consciousness, the begin-ning of that long road leading towards inner personal responsibility for moral actions brought about by pious devotion to a god of the individual. In Egypt, at least until the end of the New Kingdom, this moral sense was still also strongly fostered by collective behaviour, by the experience of be-longing to a group of loyal followers who were bound to a ruler radiating attraction into the hearts of his joyful subjects, inspiring feelings of terror in those opposed to his will. He pre-served and sustained their life.[10]

A moral deity, approached through inner devotion and prayer is not, of course, confined to the ancient Egyptians. The Hebrew psalmist in Psalm 37 also puts his trust in such a god

I have been young and am now grown old,
And never have I seen the righteous forsaken . . .
For the Lord is a lover of justice
And will not forsake his loyal servants.

The difference in Egypt, however, is that this ethical deity is still entirely surrounded by powerful goddesses, who participate in divine rulership.

Such a beneficent god is bound to bestow on his faithful worshipper a reciprocal act of favour, to make a covenant with those who serve him. In the *Victory Stela* of Thutmose III from Karnak, for instance, Amun-Re warmly welcomes the victorious king, who extended the might of Egypt in a series of far-reaching military campaigns which took his armies as far as the Euphrates in northern Syria. In the following extract from the hymn, the god thanks Thutmose for the service he has rendered him in his temple:

You come to me rejoicing
  when you see my beauty,
My son, my protector,
  Menkheperre, living forever,
I shine because of you,
  and my heart is joyful
At your beautiful coming
  to my temple.
My arms have imbued your body
  with protection and life,
How pleasing is your charm
  in my breast
So will I establish you in my dwelling
  and work a wonder for you.[11]

Thutmose enriches the temple of Amun-Re through the fruits of his achievements; in exchange the deity guarantees the king's rule on earth, giving him 'might and victory' over all countries, setting his terror 'as far as the four pillars of the sky'. Nevertheless this 'quid pro quo' relationship between the Theban god and king had its drawbacks, for it meant that over the course of time the whole balance in Egypt changed radically, tipping heavily towards Thebes.

The city prospered as never before through the gifts which poured into the southern treasuries. A papyrus listing the temple donations of the 20th Dynasty King, Ramesses III, records that more than 80,000 temple personnel were employed in the service of Amun, many tens of thousands more than at either Heliopolis or Memphis.[17] And that at a time when the fortunes of Thebes were shortly to decline. How many would have been employed in the reigns of the illustrious 18th Dynasty kings?

MUT: GREAT MOTHER OF EGYPT

Mut, the female consort of Amun-Re, embodies the terrestrial character of solar rulership at Thebes and is closely linked with the cult of the serpent goddess. At first sight, the ruling triad of Thebes seems a curious family grouping (pl 81). Unlike Osiris, Isis and Horus, who are the paradigmatic family model on which Egyptian social life was founded, the 'family' at Thebes seems to be bonded together artificially.

The relationship springs not primarily from the sex-tie between husband and wife, the birth and rearing of helpless children, the succession from father to son, and the moral obligations within the family which were so important in the Osirian family triad, but rather from the welding together of sun and moon, with the mother goddess herself binding together these two great luminaries of the sky. A late text says of Mut that she is 'the mother of the mothers, who gives birth to every god, the wonderful snake who wound herself around her father Re and placed him on earth as Khons'.[13] And it is important to realize that the name Mut is nothing other than the Egyptian word for 'mother'.

Although no evidence is known of Mut as a member of the Theban triad before the New Kingdom, she displays vestiges of Nekhbet, a much more ancient and powerful mother goddess of Upper Egypt (pl 83).

Paired with Wadjet, the cobra goddess of Lower Egypt, Nekhbet belonged to an ancient stratum of sky religion before the solar cult had taken hold in Egypt, around the Fifth Dynasty (pl 82). Worshipped in the form of a gruesome, flesh-eating vulture, her most important cult centre lay at El Kab (Nekheb), across the river from Hierakonpolis (Nekhen), to the south of Thebes. And to her, originally, belonged the *Per-Wer* shrine inhabited by New Kingdom crown goddesses, described in chapter four.

83 The ancient vulture goddess of the South, Nekhbet holding the knotted loop of a Shen-ring between her talons which symbolizes her protection of the heavenly circuit (Relief in the temple of Hatshepsut at Deir el-Bahri)

It was at Hierakonpolis that the ceremonial mace heads and other objects were discovered, which give such a tantalizing, partial glimpse into the predynastic kings and early beginnings of Egyptian culture, including the finely carved palette of King Narmer, with its striking cow-eared faces of a goddess at the top.

Vivid descriptions of Nekhbet as a wild untamed sky mother are preserved in the Old Kingdom *Pyramid Texts*. To this enormous bird mother with outstretched wings the king ascends, seeking her breasts to nourish him and take him to new life in the sky. She too is associated with the cow, being hailed as:

The Great Wild Cow
Living in Nekheb,
The White Crown,
The royal headdress
With the two tall plumes,
With the two swollen breasts (PT §729)

In another she is 'the Great Wild Cow who is in Nekheb . . . with streaming hair and swollen breasts. She suckles you and never weans you' (PT §2003), a goddess from whom the king never separates, a goddess from whom he is never weaned.

She is the nourishing, intoxicating rapture, the life-giving inexhaustible

archaic mother goddess, voraciously giving and taking back life on a cosmic scale of birth and rebirth. And perhaps it is the face of this wild cow mother which stares out above King Narmer on his palette, and not, as often suggested, Hathor's (or, at least, Hathor as she manifests in the later solar cults).[14]

She is a mother goddess, moreover, who seems to have more in common with another powerful, archaic bird mother, the neolithic goddess at Çatal Hüyük in Anatolia, than with the much later solar goddesses of New Kingdom Egypt. The Anatolian shrines, which date from around 6000 BC, are decorated with such images as vultures, bulls, a female figure with long streaming hair, as well as sculpted breasts with open nipples from which animal skulls protrude.[15]

By the 18th Dynasty the life-giving, death-devouring vulture of the sky had been overshadowed by other goddesses. She may still be shown hovering above the king's head, paired with the cobra Wadjet; or protecting him with her outstretched wings, as on Tutankhamun's small Golden Shrine, with its fourteen figures of Nekhbet flying across the roof. But the truth is that to the New Kingdom Egyptians Nekhbet had become a shadow of her former self, a memory

of bygone days, her terrorizing sky traits being, by that time, utterly absorbed into the circuit of the sun. However, in typical conservative fashion, the Egyptians were loth to banish this once powerful mother goddess to complete obscurity.

Other goddesses, including the Theban Mut, now inhabit Nekhbet's sacred shrine. As befits a ruling goddess of the South, Mut wears a vulture headdress and her name too is written with the vulture hieroglyph. Moreover, she is said to inspire vulture-like dread (*nrw*) in her subjects.

Yet to call her a vulture goddess in the sense of the archaic Nekhbet, with her wild streaming hair and pendulous breasts, seems a little wide of the mark. It is hard to imagine such modern scholarly descriptions of Mut as 'colourless', 'vague' and 'ill-defined' being applied to Nekhbet, the all-devouring, all-nourishing wild cow. Relationship with Nekhbet is utterly devoid of any human earthly dimension, as the king is told in no uncertain terms in the *Pyramid Texts*:

You have no Father among the people,
You have no Mother among the people.
Your Mother is the Great Serpent,
The White Crown,
The Royal Headdress
Who dwells in Nekheb.[16]

And here perhaps lies the crux of the matter. For the New Kingdom Mother is above all a goddess of both 'people' and 'gods', a regal queen embracing both sky and earth, whom the Greeks could associate with their own Hera. Shown as an anthropomorphic figure wearing the crowns of Upper and Lower Egypt, Mut rarely appears in bird form. On the contrary, as Queen

84 Queen Nefertari-beloved-of-Mut wearing the vulture headdress and tall plumes characteristic of queens during the New Kingdom (19th Dynasty painted relief in the tomb of Nefertari at Thebes)

of Egypt she travels the land like a shimmering cult image, transforming it into 'a pleasure-garden for her delight'.[17] She is the lady of lotus flowers, shining like gold, spreading joy and sunlight in the hearts of her people.

'We are cared for. Happy are the people. Her city will exist for millions of years as the *Per Wer*', they exult joyously.[18] She is related to them, close to them like a mother caring for their needs. Moreover, through her is channelled serpent power, quickening her body with all the radiance of fiery life. She is 'the Mistress of the Uraeus', the Palace Snake, 'whose dread and awe are in the palace . . . there is no form escaping from her flame'.[19]

This vulture-mother and serpent-eye goddess is one of the crucial prototypes of queenship in the New Kingdom—truly a radical transformation of the archaic serpent-vulture pairing represented by the 'Two Ladies', Wadjet and Nekhbet.

A hymn from Karnak characterizes Queen Ahhotep (the mother of King Ahmose and Queen Ahmose-Nefertari, the founder rulers of the 18th Dynasty at Thebes) as the sovereign Mother of Egypt:

Giving praise to the Lady of the land,
The Mistress of the shores of the Hau-nebut,
Exalted of name in every foreign land . . .
The wise one who cares for Egypt,
She has cared for its army,
She has protected it,
She has brought back its fugitives,
Gathering together its exiles.
She has pacified the South,
Having driven out its rebels,
The wife of the king,
Queen Ahhotep, may she live.[20]

Queen Ahhotep is the wise mother, subduing rebels, gathering together

her people under her protective wing, the guardian of Egypt's army, spreading her influence throughout the land at a time when Egypt was being re-united once again. Similar themes also surface in hymns to Mut at Thebes during the New Kingdom. Clearly, under the influence of solar religion and through a process of long development, the old awe-inspiring vulture sky mother of the South has come right down to earth, to become a more accessible female power as the partner of Amun-Re.

Yet there is always the danger that she may break out of control and sever her bonds with Egypt. Hence, we find in the *Mut Ritual*, preserved on a papyrus dating from the Third Intermediate Period, that her cult incorporates the propitiation of Hathor-Sekhmet, the Sun Eye. Likewise, Late Period inscriptions at El Kab, Dendara, Philae and Edfu show that by this time Nekhbet had become completely solarized, an avatar of the fiery serpent Sun Eye.[21] In short, a great gulf separated this archaic mother goddess from her later successors in Egypt.

KHONS: THE FERTILIZING MOON

It might be expected that the offspring of Amun-Re and such an obviously solar queen as Mut would be a child of the sun. But this is not the case. On the contrary, their son is the moon god, Khons, whose name means 'the crosser' or 'wanderer'.

Regrettably, no-one has yet made a detailed study of Khons, and much work remains to be done on the significance of his cult at Thebes, where two temples dedicated to him still stand. One is the temple of Khons-the-Child in Mut's overgrown and strangely eerie temple complex at Karnak; the other is the well-preserved temple begun in the reign of Ramesses III, which lies to the southwest of the main temple of Amun-Re at Karnak.

Khons is by no means a typical Egyptian child, for although he wears a characteristic child's side-lock on his shorn head, there is little else in his iconography to characterize him as being in the bloom of youth (pl 85). One clue to his nature lies in his connection with male semen. As in some forms of Tantrism, male seed belongs to the essence of the moon,[22] and loss of semen is the reason given for the moon's decline in the following spell from the *Coffin Texts* aimed at possessing the power of Khons:

I am Khons . . . I am the only one,
The fruit of the gods . . .
This god who does not die on the day of rams,
When semen is taken away from this spirit[23]

According to Philippe Derchain 'the day of the rams' mentioned here is probably the 15th day of the month when the moon begins to wane, semen is lost and virility declines.[24] If a person identifies with Khons, however, this loss does not bring death, but is rather a prelude to renewal and regained fullness.

Another much later text compares these waxing and waning phases of Khons with a bull and an ox. When the moon is in its bright phase, so Khons is a heated bull provoking growth and fertility; when he is old and waning, he is emasculated, an ox of darkness, deprived of semen and vigour:

The moon is his form.
As soon as he has rejuvenated himself
He is a heated bull.
When he is old he is an ox
Because he causes only darkness.
His waxing moon, however, brings light
Causes the bulls to cover,
Brings the cows in calf,
And causes the egg to grow in the body[25]

Khons is not the moon then in the sense of time-reckoner, reconciler, restorer, all of which are functions of the ibis-headed wise moon god, Thoth of Hermopolis. Nor is he the celestial

Moon Eye which fragments into pieces each month so that its shattered parts have to be reunited and made whole during the first quarter, a fragmentation that belongs to the struggle of Horus with Seth (see chapter nine).

Khons is connected more with the flux and reflux of the ever-renewing moon, its waxing and waning through different phases of existence. His is the tumescent, swelling moon, suggested by the occurrence in medical texts of a word spelt like the god's name, used in the sense of swelling, tumour, or abscess.[26] And as a swelling god he affects germination and growth in both plants and animals.

In the *Coffin Texts* a Khons-identified person is said to be able to penetrate into 'the finger, the toe, the body, the arm, the knee and the head of Osiris' and grow like the plants, being adorned 'like the turtles'.[27] Covered with such a turtle shell, the person becomes an incarnation of the moon god, though strangely this same creature in chapter 161 of the *Book of the Dead* stands in opposition to the rising sun of the East.

'Re lives, the Turtle dies' are the words proclaimed, as the Gates of the Four Winds open at dawn, giving access to the sky. It is not descent with the backward moving old crescent moon in the eastern horizon which seems to be longed for here, but ascent to the sky with the sun.

Their cycles are not always oppositional, however, for both moon and sun belong to the same east-west heavenly circuit. Their link comes out clearly in Chapter 83 of the *Book of the Dead* when it is said that Khons too 'comes into being like Khepri'. The text also links Khons with Atum, the Old Man of the West, the sun of 'Yesterday'. He is 'this Yesterday of these four uraei who came into being in the West',[28] an association explicable by the fact that the new crescent moon is first observed in the West each month as the sun is setting. The late text from his temple at Karnak already quoted, also says that Khons takes the place of Re when he is in his Underworld dwelling, illumining the darkness for those on earth.[29]

So although solar characteristics may seem uppermost in Mut and her consort, Amun-Re, this is deceptive. For their son serves as a constant reminder that their natures are also bound up with the cycle of the moon: ruling Sun and sovereign Moon, inextricably linked together, a link also signified by the turquoise-beaded *menit*-necklace worn by Khons, which symbolically associates him with Hathor and the sun.

But there is perhaps also another, much more immediate reason, why Khons should wear this symbol of the propitiated sun goddess. He is not always a pleasant deity, as comes out most forcibly in spells aimed at taking the form of Khons in the necropolis. Under the sway of the Khons-moon, demonic forces rise up and make trouble, changing someone into a savage devourer of child victims who constantly tries to satiate evil desires by searching for hearts to feed on:

This N has bread consisting of humans.
I possess offerings consisting of children.
Fear of this N causes the gods
To pay homage to him
When he appears as Khons.
This N is one who lives on hearts.[30]

Ranged alongside the two other magical child gods—the musical Ihy and Nefertem, god of the sweet-smelling dawn lotus—the youthful moon god of Thebes can surely lay claim to being the most violent. He is:

The raging one, the Lord of Lords . . .
I am the most violent among you.
I am the double lock of hair
Which is on the bald.[31]

His cutting shadow side transforms someone into a violent force more

Above 85 The moon god Khons. As a member of the triad, his body is swathed, like that of Osiris, with only his hands visible, holding four insignia—a crook, a flail, a Djed, and a Was-sceptre. Moreover, his other attributes are those of a calendrical and royal god. Often crowned with the lunar crescent and disk, he is manifestly a moon god, but there is also the added complication that he is adorned with solar symbols—a uraeus rears up on his brow, marking him as a kingly ruler, whilst around his neck is a menit-necklace, bringing him into magical contact with the propitiated sun goddess, Hathor (Egyptian Museum, Cairo)

Left 86 View through the hypostyle hall of the huge temple dedicated to Amun-Re at Karnak

Facing page 87 Isis and Min-Amun with Ramesses II standing between them. The king is wearing the lunar crown (19th Dynasty relief in the large temple at Abu Simbel)

great healing and ward off threats from evil beings. One of the most frequently mentioned manifestations of Khons at Thebes is as Khons-Neferhotep, an epithet meaning 'the Contented One is Vital'. Perhaps here lies a clue to the *menit*-necklace over his shoulders, for how else to symbolize the benign propitiated appearance of the turbulent moon god within the Theban triad?

Nevertheless, the deeper significance of Khons within the Theban triad cannot be fully understood unless he is seen in conjunction with another, equally prominent, manifestation of Amun-Re at Thebes. For concealed within the striding solar gait of this most royal of gods is also a great daimon of earth fertility, everywhere to be seen on temple walls in ithyphallic guise, a god known to his followers as Min-Amun-Bull-of-his-Mother (Min-Amun-Kamutef). Like the moon, this phallic god also possesses the mysterious secret power of self-regeneration, living and dying in order to come again, ever-renewing himself and the royal dynastic line.

Evidently Khons, the 'Crosser', also has much to do with the phallic earth character of Amun. And it would not be far from the mark to see in his lunar movements across the sky a pattern which synchronizes most closely with the dying and regenerative gods at Thebes. His growth and decline, his swelling and subsiding, bringing increase and decrease to all living things, his loss and restoration of semen, all accord with the nature of his ithyphallic father, Min-Amun, to whom we turn in the next chapter.

powerful even than the knife-wielding executioners of the Sun Eye, Sekhmet:

'The flame of his mouth is sharper than the knives of those who go before Sekhmet'.[32]

And for those not on their guard, the lunar knife indeed pierces through to the heart.

Raging Sekhmet and violent Khons, powers of blood and semen, reveal in their own ways the destructive sides of sun and moon. Both are propitiated in

their cults by blood offerings of slaughtered animals.[33] And just as the priests of Sekhmet were renowned in Egypt as great healers, especially of diseases connected with the blood, so too Khons was able to expel demons, being venerated as a great healer in the New Kingdom and later.[34]

Paradoxically, the deities who have the power to excite and stimulate the demons of sickness and plague, are also the very same ones able to bring

8 Isis and the Bull God: Urge for Renewal

THE UNCHARACTERISTIC scene of Isis as a solar goddess leading Seti I before Amun-Re (pl 65) may have come as something of a surprise to some readers. Apart from the inscription above her, there is little proof that here before our eyes is the great goddess of the 'Throne' or 'Seat', the hieroglyphic symbol of which she often bears on her head.

But what exactly is her function? To answer this we must first go a little more deeply into the intricate web of Egyptian religion at Thebes and try to disentangle some of the threads that weave together its ruling deities.

This time, however, to a Thebes where Amun-Re has shifted his majestic solar shape into a quite different, though by no means unrelated, form. For in countless New Kingdom scenes he is portrayed as an ithyphallic figure named Min-Amun-Kamutef (Min-Amun-Bull-of-his-Mother), whose female companion is not Mut, but usually Isis (pl 87). Obviously, besides his solar manifestation, there are other dimensions to the ruling god of Thebes which involve his phallic aspect.

BULL OF HIS MOTHER: THE
REGENERATIVE CYCLE

Just as the name Amun-Re links Amun with the sun god, so too, as Amun-Min-Bull-of-his-Mother, he is united with one of the oldest Egyptian gods, Min, who was worshipped, together with Isis, at the important cult centre of Coptos in Upper Egypt. From this town the ancient Egyptians used to make their way into the desert region along the Wadi Hammamat, to the quarries which provided rich sources of gold, diorite, schist and other valuable stones; and Min himself was honoured as lord of these hill-countries.

His link with Amun can be traced back to the Middle Kingdom when

scenes show Amun in the form of the ithyphallic Min. Before this time, however, the evidence becomes hazy, and, as with so much else, we depend on New Kingdom Egypt for our knowledge of the connection between these two gods.

Yet Min was undoubtedly already known in archaic times. His symbol—which is commonly described as a thunderbolt, but in early representations looks more like a double-headed arrow—occurs already on predynastic vases dating from the fourth millennium BC (pl 88).

He, himself, is shown as a black-skinned figure with erect phallus and tightly swathed body. Always too, one of his hands, holding a flail, is raised aloft in a show of masculine strength (pl 87).

Min is a heated deity, brimming with virility, 'the most male of the gods', as it is said of him.[1] He is 'the bull covering the cows, attaching semen to the gods and goddesses', who gives abundant life and vigour to the herds—a god 'resplendent with his phallus'.[2] Constantly in reliefs, a box of cos-lettuces is also shown placed behind him, a plausible explanation for which was pointed out by Louis Keimer long ago. With his usual careful attention to every detail of Egyptian flora and fauna, he observed that these plants were the only ones cultivated in the Nile Valley that exuded a milky liquid from their leaves and stalk, fluid, resembling semen. Hence they were an appropriate natural symbol for such an obviously phallic god.

Though there is no conclusive evidence that lettuces were used as an aphrodisiac in ancient Egypt, Keimer also remarked on a persistent belief in Egyptian folklore that eating a lot of lettuces guarantees fertility and children.[3] Perhaps the ancients, in associating lettuce with Min, believed this too. We cannot be sure but one thing is certain: Min, is undoubtedly a

great bringer of fertile life, who 'creates vegetation and lets the herds live'.[4]

The unusual epithet 'Bull-of-his-Mother' (Kamutef), already associated with the ithyphallic Amun by the Middle Kingdom, also needs to be considered here, since it both encapsulates the generative fertile power of the bull god and provides a veiled hint of his incestual relationship with the mother goddess, who, at Thebes, more often than not is Isis.[5] Much more explicit is an epithet of Min-Amun naming him as 'the fecundator of his mother'.[6]

For contained in the strange name Kamutef is the paradoxical truth that the god is both Father and Son, the agent of his own rebirth, brought about by the fertilization of his own mother. And she is the matrix, the vessel of renewal, supporting and containing his fecund seed, though she herself is not to be understood as the active power engendering life. This lies in the male seed of the bull god, which she contains in her womb, seed which not only preserves the ever-recurring cycles of nature but also safeguards the generations of Egyptian kings.

The connection of Min-Amun-Bull-of-his-Mother with the recurrent cycle of royal rebirth and the renewal of vegetation is nowhere more clearly

Above 89 Festival of Min. Ramesses III is carried from the palace by his retinue which includes members of the royal family, soldiers and priests burning incense. Their destination is said to be the temple of Min, 'Lord of the snake stones'—a reference to the archaic dual shrines of Upper and Lower Egypt (Relief in the second court at Medinet Habu)

Facing page, below, 90 Photographic detail of plate 89—the king in his palanquin

seen than at the annual Harvest Festival. This began on the evening before the new moon in the ninth month of the year, Pachons, a month named after the Theban moon god, Khons. Incomplete excerpts from the festival were included in temple decoration at Thebes from the Middle Kingdom onwards, but fortunately a very detailed version is also preserved on the walls of the second court in Ramesses III's funerary temple at

Medinet Habu on the west bank at Thebes (pls 89–95).

The sequence begins with Ramesses, resplendent like a glorious cult image, being carried in state from his palace by his retinue (pl 89). After going to the temple to consecrate offerings (pl 91), the king then escorts the god forth for the main part of the ceremony (pl 92). Precisely where their destination lay is not clear from the reliefs, but Henri Frankfort suggested that the procession may have made its way to a place in the fields close to the threshing-area, where a temporary shrine had been erected to shelter the cult image.[7]

What then was enacted when the procession finally reached 'the god's stairway'? An inscription tells how the king is given a copper sickle, with which he is to cut a sheaf of emmer wheat, brought to him by a priest

(pl 94). At the same time, a *shemayt-*priestess—in all likelihood the queen herself—dances round the king, 'reciting incantations seven times' as she does so. And as she winds herself around him, so a lector priest, who stands behind the king as he cuts the sheaf of grain, intones a hymn containing a cryptic allusion to the mystery of the bull god and his mother:

Hail Min
  who fecundates his Mother,
How secret is that
  which you have done to her
In the darkness,
  O Divine One, Sole One . . .

'How secret is that which you have done to her in the darkness'. As we hear these words, our thoughts cannot help but turn to another ancient 'dancer' closely linked with fertility and nature: she who is shown with

upraised arms and turned-in hands on predynastic pottery from the fourth millennium BC (pl 88). Even if her pose is not that of a dancer—and such an interpretation has indeed been questioned by some—she seems more at home in nature, more abandoned to life, than anything we may associate with Bull-of-his-Mother's female companion in New Kingdom Egypt, by which period the female has become the vessel through which the god fulfils his regenerative urge.

Is she a votary of Min? Or is she perhaps an ancient Lady of Beasts, the Great Mother, sustainer and nourisher of all life whose cult was so widespread in neolithic communities? Whoever she is, she seems totally at one with nature, as if she too is an active source and renewer of life, so much so that hunters propitiate and bring offerings to her. Perhaps in this

New Kingdom ritual for the phallic Bull-of-his-Mother, with all its emphasis on masculine self-renewal, we have a faint echo, some two and a half thousand years later, of a more ancient fertility rite.

However, all this has taken us far away from the Harvest Festival of Ramesses III. For after the king has cut the first sheaf and inhaled its freshness, a priest then places an ear of grain before the god—the grain which contains the seed for the next year's cycle. Watching too are some of the royal ancestors, whose cult statues have also been carried in the procession and are shown beneath the white bull in the lowest register (pl 94).

In the version of the festival shown in Ramesses II's funerary temple at Thebes (the Ramesseum), these statues include King Menes, honoured by tradition as the founder of the First Dynasty. And it means that the whole dynastic line of Egyptian kings reaching right back to 3000 BC is involved in this Harvest Ritual. As the ear of grain is offered to the god of undying vigour, a symbol perhaps of the grain which he will revivify in the coming year, so too these royal ancestors, though seemingly 'cut down' are, in reality, alive and present with their son, Ramesses. The rampant fertility of the Bull-of-his-Mother is immune to death in the violent act of reaping. Like the grain and the moon, he renews himself again and again. So too all these ancestral kings, who partake in his mystery as he sows and re-sows his seed in the mother goddess, are reborn again, reappearing as the reigning king of Egypt.[8]

One final point before leaving this festival. Was the white bull shown in the procession at Medinet Habu sacrificed during the Harvest Festival, or was he being driven before the god to be dedicated as the sacred new bull of the year, to be set apart as a guarantor of crops and fertility? It is not stated in the inscriptions, but one small detail speaks for the former. As the procession returns four birds are released to the four corners of Egypt, proclaiming the triumphant rulership of Ramesses III (pl 93). Also included is a priest, who holds a bull's tail beside a processional standard of Nefertem, the child god of Memphis. Perhaps he holds it as a sign that he enjoys the privilege of returning with that portion of the sacrificial beast which the Pharaoh is often shown wearing, hanging down between his legs at the back.

SOLAR RIGHT AND FEMALE MIGHT: TALE OF THE TWO BROTHERS

The New Kingdom tale of *The Two Brothers*, preserved on a papyrus in the British Museum, also throws some interesting light on the regenerative powers of 'Bull-of-his-Mother, and on his relationship with kingship.[9] It is a strange story, not least because of its very negative characterization of the female, evidently fuelled by a deep-seated masculine fear of the Mother.

Moreover, certain themes also recall cults known from Syria-Palestine and Anatolia. Most striking of all is the frenzied self-castration of the hero,

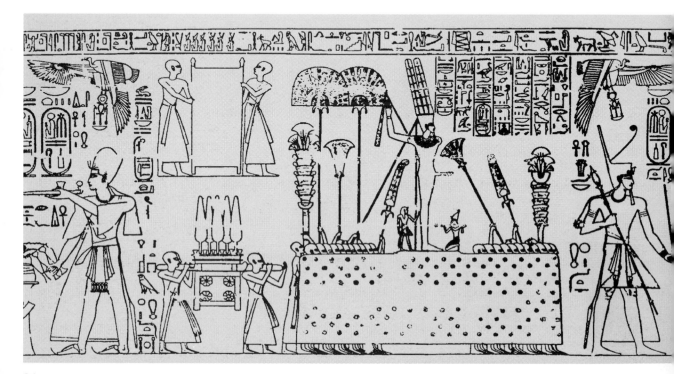

Bata, who places his torn-out heart at the top of a pine tree, after being betrayed by a vengeful Mother—a self-immolation recalling that of Attis, who, according to one version of the Phrygian myth, emasculates himself beneath a pine tree on account of Cybele's jealousy.[10]

Yet even though certain themes may reflect the wider Near Eastern religious milieu, it would be a mistake to see the story as purely 'foreign'. The regenerative process through the

Right 91 The king consecrates offerings for the ithyphallic Min-Amun before escorting him forth from his sanctuary for the main part of the festival called 'the Beautiful Festival for Min of the Steps'

Below 92 The great spectacle of ritual splendour as the priests carry aloft the god's statue. The priestly bearers are completely hidden from view except for their heads and feet, peeping out from a red hanging worked with metal studs, which is draped over the poles they carry. Behind them come other priests who fan the heated god with huge ostrich-feathered fans, whilst other priests carry Min's sacred lettuce plants. At their head strides the king, accompanied by a white bull and standard-bearers. Included in the procession too is an unnamed queen, her cartouche for some reason having been left empty, who is shown with her arms tightly pressed to her body between her breasts. Before her strides a lector-priest holding an unfurled papyrus scroll, chanting a hymn as accompaniment for a dance performed in honour of the bull god.

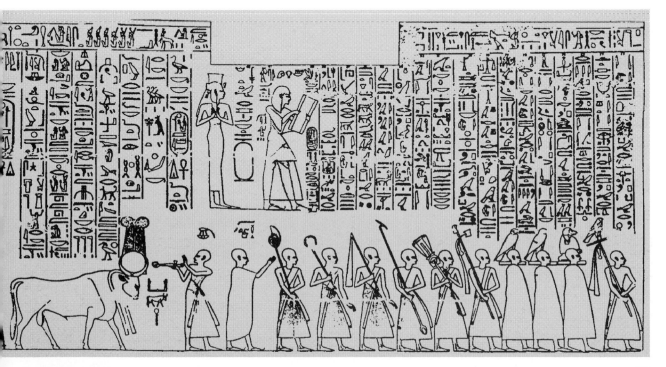

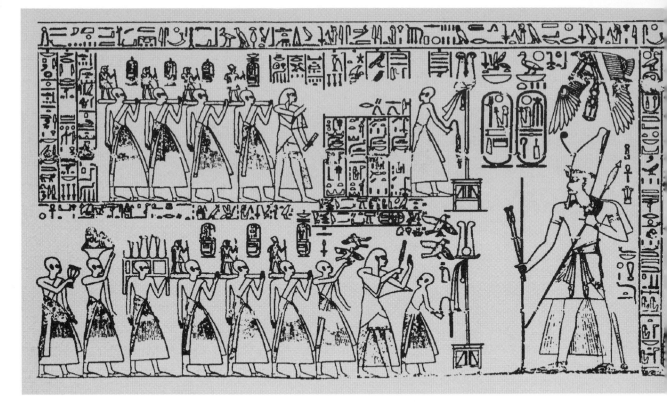

Above 93 Releasing four birds to the four corners of Egypt at the close of the festival in order to proclaim the Pharaoh's triumph. A priest holding a bull's tail stands beside the standard of Nefertem in front of the king.

Facing page, above 94 A priest holds the first sheaf of the harvest grain which the Pharaoh cuts as an offering to Min, the harvest god who forever seeds the mother goddess. Above is the queen standing with her hands tightly pressed to her breasts. Her sacred chants and the dances during the ceremony had binding magical significance. In the bottom register are nine statues of royal ancestors and above them, the white bull sacred to Min

Facing page, below 95 The king offers to Min at the close of the celebration

heart, which is initiated by a powerful destructive-seductive female belongs firmly within the religion of New Kingdom Egypt.

Consequently, despite its undeniably negative attitude to the female, the story is quoted at some length here because it evocatively captures the vegetative qualities of Kamutef and his phallic cycle.

Its hero is a strong and vigorous herdsman named Bata, who dwells with his brother Anubis and his brother's unnamed wife. The name chosen for Bata's brother is in itself significant, since it relates him to the god Anubis, who guides those entering the West on their journey of renewal. Anubis and his wife are said to be 'like a father and mother' to Bata, who lives in complete harmony with the world around him, bringing the produce of the field to the familial home each night, speaking the language of his exceedingly fine cattle and listening to their advice about where the best pastureland lies.

Yet Bata's doom is fast approaching. One day he is busily helping Anubis with the ploughing and seeding of the fields when they run out of seed. Anubis sends Bata to fetch more from the village and he goes to his brother's wife to ask her to give him seed from the storehouse. He interrupts this female guardian of seed as she is combing her hair—a coded hint that she is making herself ready to be sexually approached. Too busy to fetch the seed herself, she tells Bata to go to the storeroom instead, and when he returns laden with seed, she is filled with desire for the virile young hero, whom she has secretly long admired. She tries to seduce him: 'Come let us spend an hour lying together, it will be good for you'. But Bata, horrified by this approach from a woman who is 'like a mother' to him, rejects her advances—so sealing his unhappy fate.

Filled with rage the woman smears herself with fat and grease to make it seem as if she has been attacked. When Anubis returns, she convincingly denounces Bata, saying that he has tried to seduce her and beaten her. But warned by his cattle of Anubis's intention to kill him, Bata flees, appealing to the sun god, Re-Harakhti, for justice. The god responds by placing a river

full of crocodiles between Bata and his brother, who has come in search of him. When the two brothers finally confront each other, Bata, in a frenzy about the woman's lies, castrates himself and throws his phallus into the water.

He tells Anubis he is going to live in the Valley of the Pine, where he will remove his heart (which in Egyptian belief was held to be the real spermatic organ) and place it at the top of a pine tree. Moreover, Anubis can make amends for the wrong that has been done to him by searching for his heart should the pine tree ever be cut down. He will know when this happens because his beer will begin to ferment. If he finds the heart, he should place it in a jar of cool water so that it will revive, for it is from this living heart that Bata will be regenerated. Like Dionysus Zagreus in Orphic religion, who is cut to pieces by the Titans after Hera has stirred up hatred against him, and whose heart is rescued by Pallas

96–97 Braiding the hair of the Egyptian queen. In the scene above (96) the hairdresser pins a lock to the queen's hair and twists another into a braid. In the scene below (97) a hairdresser holds three braids (Sunk reliefs from the 11th Dynasty tomb of Queen Neferu at Deir el-Bahri, Brooklyn Museum, New York)

Athene so that he can be regenerated, Bata will be reborn if his brother saves this vital organ.

Having learned from Bata about his wife's treachery, Anubis then returns home in great distress and kills his wife. Thus, the first half ends with a deadly blow struck against the female, and implicitly against all those cults in which a vengeful female demands the sacrifice of her son-lover. Not only has Bata become a mutilated victim of her jealous instincts, but she too has also perished under the gaze of the masculine sun of justice.

But the story does not end here. For Bata is not one of the son-lovers whose vitality begins and ends with the mother goddess. He is himself a possessor of life and self-renewal, and this is the theme of the story's second part.

Once again, Re-Harakhti intervenes. Having taken pity on Bata's plight, he orders the potter god, Khnum, to fashion a beautiful female companion to console him during his exile in the Valley of the Pine. Deprived of his phallus, however, Bata is condemned to live a celibate relationship with her. As he mournfully tells her 'I too am a woman like you', and he warns her of his inability to protect her from the sea. Apart from its allusion to Bata's lack of virility, this mention of the sea provides an effective lead-in to the second half, bringing into play the power which will shortly separate Bata from his wife.

For one day, as she is walking near the pine tree where Bata's heart lies, the sea billows up to try to embrace her and, as she flees the wave, a tress of her hair is snatched away by the tree's branches. The sea carries it to the place in Egypt where the Pharaoh's servants wash the royal garments. Hair in Egypt, particularly the hair of Hathor, was held to be a source of great attraction and power (pl 96). And so it is in this story. Scenting the presence of this beautiful female in his clothes, the king immediately desires her and sends his envoys to the Valley of the Pine in search of her. Helped by a woman bringing gifts of fine Egyptian jewellery, the envoys manage to entice Bata's wife back to Egypt where she then reigns as queen.

And now, once again, a female threatens Bata's life. One day the Pharaoh asks his new queen about Bata and, stung by the threat which Bata might pose to her new-found existence, she begs him to cut down the pine tree where Bata has placed his heart and he agrees. Soldiers are sent to fell it, and as they do so, Bata falls dead.

Far away, however, his brother Anubis realizes what has happened when his beer begins to ferment. Then he starts out on his quest to save his brother and, after searching several years, eventually finds his brother's

heart lying on the ground, like a fallen tree-fruit. Remembering his brother's words, he places it in a bowl of water and as it swells, so the lifeless body of his brother begins to twitch and shudder into new life.

Bata, having transformed himself into a splendid bull, sets out for Egypt with Anubis upon his back in order to find the wife who had sought to kill him. On their arrival the Pharaoh can but marvel at such a magnificent animal, and persuades Anubis to give him the bull in exchange for gold and silver. So Bata becomes the much admired bull of the palace, who is allowed to roam freely round the royal residence, marking time, and waiting for the moment to confront his wife. The opportunity arises when the queen enters the palace kitchens one day and Bata reveals his identity to his terrified wife.

That night, as the queen feasts with Pharaoh, she persuades him to sacrifice his prized bull, on the grounds that she desires to eat the liver as sacrificial meat. Reluctantly, the king is bound to fulfill his promise to her. But even this ritual slaughter cannot destroy Bata, for as he is killed, drops of his blood

spatter the pillars on either side of the palace gate, and from his blood new life springs forth in the form of two Persea trees.[11] Bata's life is still not over, and he continues to haunt the Egyptian queen. As she sits with the Pharaoh one day beneath the persea trees, so she hears Bata's voice speaking to her from within the tree-trunk:

Ha, you false one! I am Bata! I am alive [in spite of you]. I know that when you had the pine felled for Pharaoh it was because of me. And when I became a bull you had me killed.

In desperation she asks the king to fell the trees. But in so doing, she seals her own fate for, as she watches the felling, a splinter of wood flies into her mouth, which she unwittingly swallows. In this way she becomes pregnant, an unwilling victim of Bata's urge for self-renewal. For the child she gives birth to is none other than Bata himself, whom the reigning king takes upon his knee before the assembled Egyptian court as a sign that he will one day be his chosen successor.

And on the king's death, this indeed happens. Bata becomes the ruler of Egypt, assisted by his brother Anubis. Although Bata now summons the court

98 Four launderers washing linen on the banks of the Nile (Relief in the tomb of Ipuy at Thebes)

in order to tell them everything that has happened, we are not explicitly told what happens to the queen, who has now become both Bata's wife and mother. But, since at her birth earlier in the story the seven Hathors predicted that 'she will die by the knife', we can but assume that she is judged and killed.

Thus the second half of the story—with its strong assertion of masculine regenerative power and a female transgressor, who is judged according to the laws and customs of Egypt—completely reverses the themes of the first half in which Bata, castrated and wronged, falls victim to feminine jealousy. It would seem that for some Egyptians the cycle of renewal in which the male fertilizes and enters the mother goddess was deeply troubling, arousing male fears of engulfment, incest and castration. As one solar hymn says about the all-embracing mother 'She loves entering, she hates going forth'.[12]

There seems to be a strong need in this story to stress the masculine urge

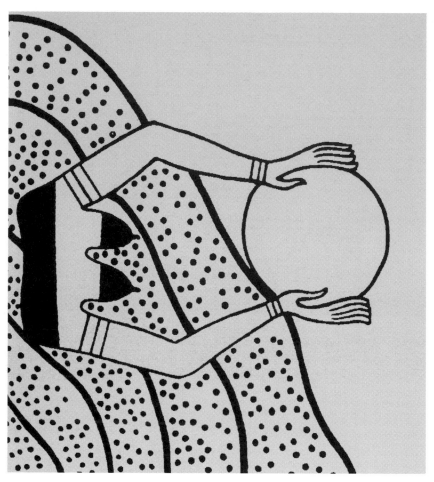

of the day in order to give birth to the next cycle, the dying god sinks into the protective arms of Isis to be born anew at dawn. Through her lies the hope of ever-repeating life as the god returns to his origins, to be taken care of in the maternal embrace (pl 99). Then at dawn her womb gives birth again in the East, light comes forth when the dawn mother bears life anew.

This solar-seed rhythm of renewal also involves Isis with Hathor and the Pharaoh, as seen in two different groups of scenes in the 19th Dynasty temple of Seti I at Abydos.

The first scene is in King Seti I's chapel off the second hypostyle hall, and shows masked priests, wearing jackal and hawk masks, bearing the king aloft in a carrying-chair (pl 100). They represent the collective body of ancestral rulers associated with the ancient cities of Pe (Buto) in the North and Nekhen (Hierakonpolis) in the South, the old capitals of Lower and Upper Egypt. And as these representatives of the royal ancestors carry King Seti, so he learns from them about his sonship with the Bull-of-his-Mother and Isis. In short, they are initiating Seti into the secret customs of Egypt, and he, a devout king who was especially filled with a deep sense of the past and his own responsibility to

as the potent source of regeneration—potency which the female is powerless to destroy. Through the bizarre way in which Bata accomplishes his own re-birth, namely by entering the mouth of the unwilling female in the form of a splinter of wood, masculine power in the vegetal way of renewal is vindicated. It is the Bull-of-his-Mother who forever gives birth to himself through the Mother, an act which also brings about an ever-repeating cycle of regeneration and continuity in the royal line of kings.

SPARKS FLY UPWARDS: REPEATING PATTERNS

We have focused almost exclusively on the masculine role of Bull-of-his-Mother. But what about his relevance

for the solar cycle and his relationship with Isis, the mother of Egypt's dynastic line? The urge for renewal, which drives Kamutef to beget himself anew through the mother goddess, is inexorably wedded to the cycle of the sun, although the Egyptians, reticent as ever, refrain from explicitly describing their union in evening hymns to the sun god. That Isis is involved can be deduced from the naming of her in the same breath as the Theban god, as in the following lines from an evening hymn:

Hail to you, O Amun-Re,
When you set in the western horizon,
The West greets you . . .
Your mother Isis protects your body . . .
They say, 'May you reach her in peace'.[13]

Seeding the mother goddess at the end

ensure dynastic succession, listens as he is told:

You are established on the throne like the Son of Isis, O Lord of the Two Lands, Menmaatre. You are the seed of Bull-of-his-Mother, who created you in the likeness of his body. The womb of Isis has made him to be the heir upon the throne of Atum.[14]

The preservation of the royal line involves many generations of kings, all of whom in their turn have been sons of the bull god and Isis; and all, too, have impregnated the Mother for self-regeneration. Now Seti, the reigning king, is counted among these mighty ones of the past, known as 'the living Kas', who live in him by virtue of the royal seed, carried in the womb of Isis, that courses through the generations. All have partaken in the mystery of Isis and the Bull (ka), through whom this perpetual cycle of reincarnation continues without ceasing.

Because the nature of the royal Ka is the key to understanding this mysterious regenerative cycle, it merits closer examination. The ancient Egyptians considered that every person has a number of subtle elements of being besides the physical body. Although there are varying accounts, all articulate a view of human reality much more complex than mind-body dualism or a simple mind-body-spirit framework – and all include the Ka, which is closely linked with the physical body, and is represented in reliefs as well as statues by two arms extending upwards (pl 103).

Everyone is born together with his or her Ka, and it might be said that the Ka is the inherent capacity to live possessed by every living creature. So, to put one's arms around another person means to imbue and surround that person with existence and life. But the Ka also gives nourishment. For it is closely associated with food, one of the

name of the Theban Bull/*Ka*-of-his-Mother, characterizing him not only as a regenerative god but also as a food-giver.

This is abundantly clear in the Harvest Festival at Thebes, which brought together the food cycles of nature and the regenerative cycle of kingship. It was the duty of every Egyptian king to safeguard the food of Egypt for his people, and he did so at the Harvest Festival as a ruler supported and surrounded by the whole corporate body of the ancestor kings Sustained by these mighty figures of the past, he was the son belonging to the generation of the *Kas*. Both food and kingship were perpetuated through the *Ka*, and it can hardly be emphasized strongly enough how deeply the Egyptian Pharaoh experienced himself to be the living reincarnation of his predecessors. They were forever present with him and in him, supporting him and participating with him in the rulership of Egypt.

On one level, then, the Bull-of-his-Mother and Isis lived a closed, obsessive relationship, governed by male seed, ancestral ties and repetitive incest, which by its very nature excluded any notion of rising to life, of transformation in a manifest solar world. But although the importance of

words for food being the plural *Kas*. It is said in the *Pyramid Texts*:

Wash yourself and your Ka washes itself,
Your Ka sits down and eats bread with you,
Without ceasing for ever and ever. (PT §789)

Thus the *Ka* is a nutritive force, continually sustaining and preserving the body through life—and also in the afterlife, since the bread, beer and other food offerings, which were placed in tombs, were given for the *Ka* of the tomb-owner.

Moreover, by virtue of being written with the same hieroglyph as the word for bull, the *Ka* is also associated with

male generative power. Like other ancient cultures, the Egyptians made great use of wordplay to express significant connections, and much was made of this link between the bull, (an animal especially associated with masculine virility), the royal *Ka* and male potency. For example, the king is said to be a 'mighty bull', an epithet which frequently occurs in the Horus name of New Kingdom rulers—the name which was also equivalent to the *Ka*-name. And reliefs often show *Ka*-arms supporting this name of the king.

Furthermore, both the bull and the *Ka* are implicitly incorporated into the

103 Wooden Ka-statue of the 13th Dynasty king, Auibre-Hor, bearing the hieroglyph for 'Ka' on his head. The statue had been robbed of its necklace, loincloth and sceptres when it was discovered in a wooden shrine in a Middle Kingdom tomb at Dahshur (Egyptian Museum, Cairo)

this repetitive cycle should not be underestimated—both for the stability of Egypt and the provision of food and nourishment—it cannot, by itself, have been the whole story.

Also necessary was that solar serpent rearing up within the arms of the *Ka*, as we have already seen her in images from Hatshepsut's reign (pls 46, 55), that aggressive-erotic power who coils around the sun god, bringing enhanced possibilities of life to the *Ka*-realm.

Hathor's interweaving with Isis in the royal cult is strikingly conveyed in a group of three reliefs in the temple of Seti at Abydos, which date from the reign of Seti's successor, Ramesses II (pl 102). The scene above shows Isis, crowned with a solar headdress, seated calmly on her throne suckling her child, Ramesses II. According to the inscription behind her, she nurtures the king with her milk so that he may 'spend a lifetime like Re in the sky' and be 'rejuvenated like Atum' All seems solar in these figures of mother and child, living their lives together in harmony with the phases of the sun. That is until we turn to the hawk-headed god, Horus-Son-of-Isis, shown seated directly across from them in the same scene. He holds out a crook and flail towards Ramesses, telling him that these insignia mark his sonship with the Bull-of-his Mother and the Lord of Abydos, Osiris:

Receive the crook of your Father and the flail of Bull-of-his-Mother. You are the seed of the Lord of Abydos. May he give strength entirely.

The milk of Isis flows not only for a solar ruler, but also for the young royal

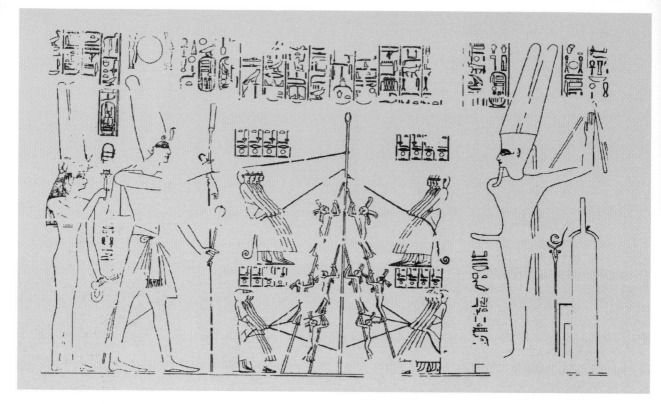

104 Ramesses II and Queen Nefertari participate in a ritual for Min. Naked men wearing feathered headdresses swarm up a pole raised by men called 'companions of the king'. This rite of 'raising the pole' may have taken place during the Harvest Festival, or possibly during another celebration for the fertility god (Relief in the first court of Luxor Temple)

seed engendered in her womb both by the bull god and by Osiris. Quite explicitly, in this scene of Isis, the solar circuit and the cycle of reincarnation are woven together, as the Bull's seed is sown and resown over and over again in the womb of the mother goddess.

But that is not all. Beneath this scene is a very different figure of Isis, this time offering a uraeus snake, coiled upon a basket, to Ramesses (pl 102). An *Ankh*-sign of life extends from the uraeus to the king's nostrils, as he breathes in her fiery life-giving power. In her other hand, this serpent daughter holds a naos sistrum and

menit-necklace, betokening Hathor's involvement with royal investiture. Seed Mother above, Solar Daughter below, together this functional identity of Isis and Hathor encompasses a complex cycle of death and renewal. And it helps to explain why Isis appears as a solarized goddess leading Seti I before Amun-Re at Karnak (pl 65). Solar ascent and zenithal crowning, by themselves, are not sufficient for rulership at Thebes, but need to be earthed in that regenerative urge for renewal which binds together Isis and the Theban father god.

There is, however, a third scene placed immediately to the right of Isis and Ramesses in the lower register. It too is connected with the bestowal of insignia, though neither the symbols of the Theban bull god nor those of the serpent goddess are relevant here. Now Ramesses raises one hand to the Double Crown of Upper and Lower Egypt, touching the power residing in this crucial regalia, which is given to

him by the hawk-headed Horus (pl 102). This particular gesture brings us on to another god who is closely involved with Isis. A god, moreover, whose tumultuous energy is equally bound up with his phallus, but one whose heated sexuality is not, of its own accord, channelled into fertility or procreative life.

This god is Seth. A turbulent deity whose struggle with Horus for the crowns of Egypt is bound up with the cycle of the moon in its monthly fragmentation and restoration. Their conflict needs to be understood if we are to piece together the mosaic of deities connected with ascent to new life.

For the Moon Eye of Horus must be balanced with the raging-beneficent Eye of the Sun; both must be restored and propitiated in their different ways within the cosmic order. In other words, rising to new life in the solar circuit must be synchronized with the birth of the moon.

9 Light and Sexuality: The Struggle for the Kingdom

A CHALLENGING and disruptive force entered creation on the three hundred and sixty third day of the year (the third of the five so-called epagomenal days added at the end of the 360-day calendar of the Egyptian civil year). On that day Seth is said to have broken out violently from the womb of the Heliopolitan sky goddess, Nut, a birth which marked both 'the beginning of confusion' and future suffering for his elder brother, Osiris.

Like his modern counterpart, Don Juan, Seth struts and swaggers across the Egyptian stage, drinking and lechering in order to gratify his lustful desires. His insatiable appetite for both beer and women is well described in the following magical spell for beer-drinking, which was prescribed as a cure for illness:

Hail to you, lady of the vulva.
* When he has set his heart on it,*
There is no restraining Seth.
* Let him carry out his desire*
To capture a heart
* In that name 'beer' of his.*
To confuse a heart,
* And to capture the heart of an enemy*[1]

Seth's influence in the beer drunk by the sick person is so great that tormenting demons become confused and are borne away, leaving the person restored to health.

Driven by his 'phallus of fire' the Sethian man, who is prone to drinking and quarrelling, is said to be much loved by women 'because of the greatness of his loving them', though there is also a disparaging remark later in the same text to the effect that it matters little to him whether a woman is married or not.[2] All are fair game in his eyes, and he stalks his prey with the easy confidence of a man well used to conquest. So, for example, in *The Contendings of Horus and Seth* we find him lurking behind a tree as he ogles Isis, calling to her with the words: 'I am here with you, beautiful girl!' But as we shall see, his self-confidence on this occasion is sadly misplaced.

Great lover of women though he may be, there is little emotion or feeling involved in coitus with Seth. Yet another text tells how Seth leaps like a ram upon the Seed Goddess, whom he espies bathing in the water and 'covers her like a bull'. He is then described as having 'copulated with her with fire after raping her with a chisel'. It has to be said, however, that his exploits only caused him suffering, for, after leaping on the Seed Goddess, his seed (which in Egyptian also means 'poison') went to his forehead and he became ill. It implies that his attempt at sexual gratification had been singularly misdirected, and that his sexuality had not been fruitful.[3]

Indeed, in contrast to the god Min, Seth's sexuality, if left to itself, is rarely, if ever, channelled into any kind of fertility. According to Plutarch, Seth was deserted by his concubine, Taweret, the pregnant hippopotamus goddess who protects women in childbirth.[4] She had perhaps good reason to leave him, for other sources tell of Seth's power to endanger birth and, not surprisingly, pregnant women—like Isis carrying Horus—lived in fear of an attack from the god.

Wherever brute force is uppermost Seth is in his element. His curious animal form (with its dog-like body, long curved snout, truncated square ears and stiffly raised tail—features which so far have defied any precise zoological classification) is used in the script to determine words for atmospheric disturbances, quarrelling and illness (pl 106). He is a god of redness, heat and dryness, and to him belong the inhospitable desert regions as well as foreign lands. Consequently in his company a person goes far beyond the bounds of acceptable behaviour and ordered existence.

According to a book of dreams, which was once the property of a scribe living in the tombmakers' village at Deir el-Medina, Seth causes bad dreams or 'evil filthy things', disturbing people whilst asleep. After such dreams a person must seek protection and say on waking, 'Come to me, come to me, my mother Isis; behold I have seen what is far from me in my city', thereby identifying with Horus in order to regain composure.[5] The dreamer has entered strange regions under Seth's influence, a god whom Herman te Velde describes as 'the spirit of disorder' and 'lord of the unbridled forces in nature and in civilisation'.[6]

Yet however disreputable Seth may be, he cannot simply be exiled to the inhospitable desert and thrown on the scrap-heap of existence. His brutish elementary urges, however unpleasant, are a part of creation. He is, after all, the brother of Isis, Osiris and Nephthys and, like them, a child of the Heliopolitan sky mother, Nut, and earth god, Geb. Moreover, his confusion and disorder, if harnessed, have an important function within the cosmic scheme.

This was true of Egyptian religion until the end of the New Kingdom, at least. Subsequently, however, when a more xenophobic attitude towards foreigners prevailed in Egypt as Egyptian influence abroad waned, there was increasing emphasis on the demoniacal side of Seth. He became the scapegoat, the foreigner, for whom no place could be found within the pantheon. In Graeco-Roman temple inscriptions at Edfu and Esna, the birthdays of Osiris, Horus, Isis and Nephthys on the first, second, fourth and fifth epagomenal days are all mentioned, but Seth's birthday on the third day is passed over in silence. By the Graeco-Roman period his murderous and lustful tendencies aroused only horror and abhorrence; and he was cast out and condemned as an evil force serving no useful function whatsoever.

But this was not always so. The very ancient tradition about Seth's quarrel with his nephew Horus over who should succeed to the throne of Egypt after the death of Osiris provides an alternative, much less damnatory approach to this instigator of confusion. Though Seth may be the murderer of his brother, Osiris, his turbulent qualities are necessary, if Horus is to

grow into manhood and rule Egypt. There are scattered references to this quarrel already in Old Kingdom *Pyramid Texts*, as in the following lines describing the paradisial circumstances which prevailed in the cosmos before the conflict between uncle and nephew had begun:

> When no anger had yet arisen
>> When no noise had yet arisen
> When no conflict had yet arisen
>> When no confusion had yet arisen
> When the Eye of Horus
>> Had not yet been injured
> When the testicles of Seth
>> Had not yet been made impotent. (PT §1463)

Until Horus and Seth came into being all lived in peace and harmony.

By far the fullest account of their quarrel is contained in the humorous and sometimes bawdy story known as *The Contendings of Horus and Seth*, which was mentioned already in chapter five in connection with the episode when Hathor displays her genitals before the sulking sun god.[7] Although the story is full of humour and ridicule, it also contains profound truths about the nature of the pantheon and rulership, truths which could usefully be transmitted and disclosed, as in so many cultures, through the art of the story-teller. And to this particular story, with its multiple layers of meaning, there are many possible approaches.

On one level it is obviously concerned with rightful inheritance to the throne of Egypt—with the claim of Horus to rule as successor of his father Osiris, a claim which is challenged by his uncle, Seth. These two conflicting claims between the mother's brother, on one side, and the father's son on the other, have somehow to be reconciled, a drama which is played out against the backdrop of Egypt's geographical landscape. It is an ideal natural setting for such an oppositional conflict, since Egypt itself is a place of vivid contrasts

and sharp distinctions—a long strip of black cultivatable land, bounded on either side by mountain chains, with little else than the red desert hills beyond. Through its midst flows the life-bringing stream of the Nile, clearly separating the country into right and left, West and East. Overhead the hot sun sails triumphantly across a cloudless sky by day, only to disappear in a red blaze of glory at sunset, bringing darkness and night. All these natural contrasts and oppositions could be associated with the struggle between the two gods.

It has been suggested, moreover, that the mythical conflict reflects a historical memory of actual events leading up to the founding of the First Dynasty by King Menes at Memphis. Under this scenario, predynastic Egypt was originally split into two rival camps (the followers of Horus and the followers of Seth), until finally the rulers of Upper Egypt, who were nomadic in origin, were able to gain ascendancy over the settlers in the more cultivated Delta area, and so unite Egypt for the first time. Such an explanation of the myth seems far too narrow and reductionist, not least because the antagonism between the two rivals, the balancing of their warring forces, the reconciliation of opposites, and finally the uniting of the country under one king, wearing the Red and White Crowns as a symbol of the united country, would have been valid throughout the whole of Egypt's long history.

On more than one occasion disputing factions split the country apart with devastating social consequences. And to keep control of such a geographically distinct land as Upper and Lower Egypt, as well as maintain safety in the border regions, was no easy task for the Pharaoh. There were permanent threats needing a permanent response, so that, if the myth is related to the historical plane, the

conflict would have been a relevant archetypal reality in every historical period.

Another approach to the struggle is to see it as a royal ordeal, a sexual initiation aimed at bringing Horus, the future King of Egypt, to manhood. We know practically nothing about adolescent initiation rites in ancient Egypt; but the story has all the hallmarks of an obligatory contest designed to test and bring the future king through the crisis of puberty to adulthood. That the opponent with whom Horus does battle should be the very one who has also wrested life from Osiris is perhaps inevitable. For Seth seems to contain within himself the drive for both life and death, being that spirit of uncontrolled raw excitation and raging violence which surges up in youth, and which, by its very nature becomes a dismembering force, demanding the death of an older victim.

Finally, there is also the important strand of religious physiology running through the conflict, based on the 'eye' of Horus, and the 'testicles' of Seth. In essence, therefore, it is a conflict between light and sexuality (semen), and brings to mind, as Herman te Velde points out in his study of Seth, a similar oppositional conflict in Tibetan Tantric religion involving light and semen.[8] Moreover, this light or 'Eye of Horus' is bound up with the fragmentation and restoration of the moon in its monthly cycle, the restoration of the Eye being associated with the reappearance of the waxing moon.

It would be a mistake, however, to interpret the struggle simply as a masculine ordeal or solely as a lunar initiation. The goddesses Isis and Hathor are also deeply involved. And, as with all things Egyptian (excluding Amarna religion), the moon must be balanced with the sun, the appearances of these two heavenly bodies and their different phases brought into

harmony. Consequently, we find both in this story and related cult rituals, a constant interweaving of themes connecting the king with the deities of the rising sun and waxing moon. For both Moon Eye and Sun Eye shine resplendent in the sky and in the face of the Egyptian king, as Hathor herself makes perfectly clear in a scene at Karnak, when she opens her arms to the sweet-lipped Ramesses II, whose eyes 'are the sun and moon' (page 46). So it remains now to see how these different light rays are woven together in the New Kingdom story.

TRICKING LECHERY AND TEASING PRIDE:
FEMININE ENCOUNTERS

The story opens with proceedings taking place in the court of the Heliopolitan Ennead (presided over by the sun god, Re-Harakhti), and the judgement that the throne of Egypt should be given to Horus, son of Osiris—a decision which his mother, Isis, greets with great joy.

However, the choice displeases the sun god, who much prefers Seth, 'the great of strength, the son of Nut', his claim to the throne being made on the grounds that Osiris is his brother. A powerful deity like Re feels little natural empathy with the feeble-bodied Horus, whom he considers unfit to occupy such an exalted office; and, as happens so often in life, the claims of the weak and innocent, however legitimate, are in danger of going unheeded by the strong and powerful in authority.

This alliance between Re and the violent Seth naturally plunges the Ennead into disarray, and, as we have already seen in chapter five, the baboon god Baba insults Re who then refuses to take any further part in the proceedings. It is at this point in the narrative that the goddesses Hathor and Isis begin to intervene as both, in their different ways, seek to curb the potentially anarchic forces of Re and Seth.

By humorously exposing her genitals before the sun god, Hathor succeeds in dissolving his rage, so bringing Re once more into relationship with the Ennead. But her action is by no means the end of the story. For on the sun god's return, Seth then

108 *Relief showing paired figures of Seth holding out symbols of life and power to the Horus hawk. The bird is perched on a serekh (palace facade) enclosing the Horus name of Thutmose I (Egyptian Museum, Cairo)*

makes another outrageous bid for the throne, this time claiming it because of his great strength in the sun-boat as protector of Re. Moreover, he also demands that the court should sit without Isis being present, and they agree to cross the river to hear the case on the Island-in-the-Midst. In order to prevent Isis from intervening, the ferryman is also instructed not to take across any female resembling the goddess.

Seth has good reason to fear this wily mother seeking justice for Horus. Although Re may have poured scorn on her young, weak son, Isis knows how to expose the limitations of the sun god's favourite.

Renowned for her great magical gifts, Isis possesses the cunning and skill needed to challenge Seth's lustful passions, which now threaten to cut her (and Egypt) off from all tradition, custom, and ancestry by his claim to

109 Terracotta of Isis seated on a pig

the throne of Osiris. Is she not, after all, the cold-blooded calculating goddess, who once formed a snake out of the saliva dribbling from the mouth of the ageing sun god, and then mercilessly extracted his secret name, as he endured the pangs of death after the snake had bitten him?[9]

Isis showed no hesitation whatsoever about carrying this out at a time when Re was a weak, slobbering old man, unable to control his bodily movements. Such a time of weakness was precisely the time to strike in order to discover his 'Great Secret Name', the name which gave her a hold over the sun god. For knowledge of names played an important part in Egyptian magical practice. Encapsulated in the name is a person's essence and, of all Egyptian deities, it is Isis who weaves spells over others by means of her skilful words and knowledge.

Moreover, in pursuit of her quarry, Isis knows how to turn herself into a shape-shifting goddess, manifesting in this particular story the triple aspects of Mother, Virgin, Crone, which are often associated with moon goddesses in other cultures.

First she changes herself into an old hag, carrying food which, she tells the ferryman, is for a young herdsman

tending cattle on the Island-in-the-Midst Remembering his promise to the Ennead, he is reluctant to take her across but finally succumbs when she bribes him with a gold ring. Having landed safely on the island, Isis then spies Seth feasting and drinking with the Ennead in the Pavilion of Re, and immediately changes her shape yet again, this time into a beautiful young girl. Ever on the watch for ways of gratifying his desires, Seth notices her in the distance, and abandons the Ennead to give chase. When they meet, however, clever-tongued Isis launches into a sad tale about a wicked stranger who has entered her farm after her husband's death, and seized her son's cattle—an act which Seth indignantly condemns, so unwittingly condemning himself as a claimant to the Egyptian throne. The episode gives a good insight into Isiac cunning:

Let me tell my Lord: As for me, I was the wife of a herdsman, and I bore him a son. My husband died, and the boy began to tend the cattle of his father. But then a stranger came. He sat down in my stable and spoke thus to my child: 'I shall beat you, I shall take your father's cattle, and I shall throw you out!' So she spoke to him. Now I wish to make you his defender. Then Seth said to her. 'Shall one give the cattle to the stranger while the man's son is here?' Thereupon Isis changed herself into a kite, flew up, and sat on top of an acacia tree. She called to Seth and said to him, 'Weep for yourself! Your own mouth has said it. Your own cleverness has judged you! What do you want?'

Armed with her alluring appearance and clever words, the goddess has forced Seth to admit that his own claim to the throne is invalid, and, realizing his foolishness, the humiliated god returns in tears to the sun god. He would have done well to heed the words of the scribe Ani

writing about the perils of drunkenness in New Kingdom *Wisdom Literature*:

Do not indulge in drinking beer lest you utter evil speech and don't know what you are saying.

Or again warning about talking to strangers:

Do not reveal your heart to a stranger, He might use your words against you.[10]

Such warnings could have been written for Seth himself in the story. For, having left the feasting Ennead, he lays himself open to Isis who well knows his weak points, and uses them to accomplish her own ends. Just as she took the saliva from Re's mouth to work her magic against the sun god, so here she uses Seth's innate lustfulness to turn the tables against him.

According to a passage in the much later *Papyrus Jumilhac*, dating from the end of the Ptolemaic period, Isis humiliates Seth by changing herself into a bitch and running in front of him.[11] He is unable to catch her and ejaculates his semen as he runs after her whereupon she taunts him because of his lack of self-control.

Plate 109 shows a well-known terracotta of a female, with outspread legs and genitals exposed, sitting on the back of a pig, which was one of the animals associated with Seth in Egypt. A link with Baubo and the Eleusinian Mysteries has been suggested for the object, but it may well be that this is an image of Isis displaying the sexual power which she uses to trick and humiliate her archenemy.[12]

In contrast to Hathor's playful exposure of her genitals before Re, the sexuality of Isis displays little warmth, feeling or relatedness with the male, at least in the context within which this terracotta probably belongs. Her purpose is a merciless curbing of those destructive impulses lurking in uncontrolled male sexuality. So too Apuleius, in *The Golden Ass*, writing about the Isis

110 Horus, watched by Isis, spears a hippopotamus, one of the Sethian animals (Relief on the girdle wall in the Temple of Edfu)

mysteries of the second century AD, tells how Lucian has to impersonate Typhon, the Ass, in order to experience the full range and extent of his frustrated hunger and sex. Only after much suffering and humiliation is he finally granted a wondrous vision of Isis and then initiated into her temple. Like the pig, the ass also counts as a Sethian animal, epitomizing lust incarnate, as is drily observed in one of the maxims in the wisdom book, *The Instruction of Ankhsheshonq*, written in the late Ptolemaic period:

Man is even more inclined to sex than an ass; only his purse prevents him.[13]

Besides money, the scribe might well have added the name of Isis as another restraint on lustful male appetites which, if left unchecked, may disrupt the whole fabric of the social order.

ISIS BEHEADED: BREAKING TIES, TRANSFORMING AGGRESSION

According to our New Kingdom story, however, this thwarting of Seth's ambitions does not deter him from continuing to seek the throne. However the time for talking is at an end. He now declares his intention to fight Horus, who has yet to prove himself as a potential ruler of Egypt. Then the two gods change themselves into fierce hippopotami and plunge down into the depths of the water. Now for the first time Horus is locked in fierce combat with his violent uncle, and Isis fears for his life (pl 110).

In an attempt to save Horus she makes, and then throws, a harpoon into the water; but this strikes her son's body. Hearing his cry of distress she immediately releases the weapon and throws it again and this time 'it bit into the body of Seth'. But he has profited

a little from his previous encounter with Isis. For now he cunningly appeals to his sister's familial ties, cleverly reversing and twisting the words from the sad story she had previously concocted to trick him. Cunningly he asks her:

Do you love the stranger more than your maternal brother Seth?

Torn by conflicting loyalties, Isis is now forced to release the harpoon

from Seth's body, who is after all her brother, a child of Nut, as she herself is.

Her action enrages Horus. Thwarted by his mother, he now comes towards her with 'his face fierce like that of a leopard', and savagely beheads her with his knife. Then, carrying her head under his arm, he flees to the mountainous regions to escape the wrath of the Ennead.

Alone in this desert realm, the realm of Seth, he is an easy prey for his

103

111 Youths participate in a stick fight during a festival for Ptah-Sokar-Osiris. Their fighting is associated with the inhabitants of the twin cities Pe and Dep [Buto] in the Delta. Stick fighting still persists in modern Egyptian village life (Relief in the tomb of Kheruef, Thebes)

enemy. And indeed Seth now finds his nephew, throws him on his back, and tears out his eyes, which he buries in the earth. These then flower at dawn as lotus bulbs:

He removed his eyes from their places and buried them on the mountain. Towards morning his two eyes became two bulbs and they grew into lotus flowers.

The brutality of Horus towards Isis has led to his light being extinguished, to his eyes being buried deep in the earth; he has become like the eyeless celestial hawk god worshipped in Letopolis, whose blindness meant that neither the moon nor the sun shone. Now Horus has been forced to embody the kind of frenzied violence for which Seth is notorious. No longer can he be described as an uncorrupted child, his state of innocence is at an end.

There is an interesting passage in chapter 112 of the *Book of the Dead*, describing a premonition Horus has about his blindness. According to this version, Re asks to look into the eyes of Horus in order to see the future, which materializes in the form of Seth as a black pig, who then proceeds to injure the Eye. When Horus sees the horror of his impending fate, he faints and has to be taken to his room to recover:

Re said to Horus, 'Let me see what is coming into existence in your eye', and he looked thereat. Then Re said to Horus, 'Look at that black pig', and he looked, and immediately his Eye was injured, (namely) a mighty storm. Then said Horus to Re, 'Indeed my Eye feels like that blow which Seth has done to my Eye'. And he ate his heart. Then said Re to those gods, 'Place him on his bed, and he shall be well'.

Apart from its obvious relevance to the blinding of Horus in the New Kingdom story, the strange way in which Horus is shown his future fate by Re seems to hint at a technique of divination widely practised in Graeco-Roman Egypt. This involved a priest and a young boy assistant, gifted with clairvoyant sight, who acted as a medium. For example, a bowl was sometimes filled with water covered with a thin film of oil before which the child knelt. Such a spreading of oil on water has a strange iridescent affect, because the oil first spreads in a rainbow of colours, but as the film thins out, so the colours disappear into the ultraviolet taking the watcher into invisible realms. The priest used to order the boy to open his eyes and look into this film of oil. If he saw special light mirrored there, contact could be established with the deities and the future revealed through the child. [14]

Ancient cultures seem to have attached special significance to the divinatory powers of pre-pubescent young boys, a gift which diminished, however, once puberty was reached: and Egypt was no exception, at least in the Graeco-Roman period. Plutarch remarked on an Egyptian belief that children were able to foretell the future,[15] though it has been argued that such practices never occurred in Egypt before the Graeco-Roman period, and only then as a result of foreign influence.[16] But it may well be that one way of understanding the loss of sight suffered by Horus in his struggle with Seth is precisely in connection with this loss of clairvoyant vision at puberty—a gift particularly associated by the ancients with a young medium untouched by sexuality. The *Book of the Dead* passage quoted above certainly suggests familiarity with a magical practice using the vision of a young boy. And, as with so much else, it may simply be the lack of evidence from papyri that tempts one to conclude otherwise. Certainly, clairvoyant sight was important in ancient Egyptian rituals. In the archaic *Opening of the Mouth Ritual*, for example, a priest, as Horus, had to sleep beside a statue of the Osirian deceased, and seek out the person in a dream. Only when the person was 'found' could the redemptive part of the ritual then proceed.[17]

Be that as it may, the action which leads to this blinding of Horus—his beheading of Isis—seemed so monstrous to the gentle Plutarch, writing in the second century AD, that he had to soften the blow and could only record lamely that Horus had removed the crown from his mother's head.[18] No such inhibition is observable on the

part of the usually reticent Egyptians, however, who never shrank from mentioning this horrendous violence. Moreover, beheading Isis is only one aspect of her son's violent reaction; other texts state that Horus rapes his distraught mother, as in the following extract from a magical spell on a papyrus in the British Museum:

Isis became weary on the water,
Isis arose on the water:
  her tears fall into the water.

See, Horus has copulated
with his mother, Isis:
  her tears fall in the water.[19]

Contact with Seth has radically changed her son; he has become possessed with a tumultuous force which transforms him, like Ares in Greece, into an embodiment of blind aggression and sexual violence. At a much later date Herodotus records an annual festival celebrated in the Delta city of Papremis during the month of Epiphi, involving the god Ares (Horus) who comes to Egypt as a young man from the distance in order to visit Isis.[20] Though it is unknown whether such a festival was celebrated in Pharaonic Egypt, the description given by Herodotus seems to be connected with the painful episode between Isis and her son known from New Kingdom sources.

At the beginning of the ritual the priests removed the cult image of Ares from the main temple, and when it was brought back again towards the evening, armed priests wielding clubs, assisted by some of the local inhabitants, tried to prevent the procession of Ares from approaching the temple. Help had to be brought from a neighbouring town, and eventually the god managed to force his way in

113 *Cow-headed Isis pours water for the Ba of Osiris perched on plants* (Detail of a relief on Hadrian's gateway at Philae)

from restrictive maternal bonds. And amidst all the pain and tears, it is she who is able to heal Horus, connecting him for the first time to the solar realm of feeling and desire, before leading him into the presence of the sun god, Re-Harakhti. Nor is that all. According to a New Kingdom calendar of lucky and unlucky days, Hathor also brings healing to the abused, beheaded Isis, for it is said that Thoth gives Isis a cow's head in place of her own:

Horus cut off the head of Isis. But Thoth transformed it through magic and restored it to her again, so that she was 'first of the cows' [ie like Hathor, Lady of Atfih].[21]

The necessary, if brutal, rupture between Isis and her raging beast of a son means that Isis too is transformed (pls 112,113). She is no longer solely a 'Mother' concerned with the needs of her son, but is reconnected with Hathorian solar life. She has been made to relinquish that part of her maternal instinct which prevents growth in her son, and in doing so, both mother and son have been given the possibility of new life.

It should not be imagined, however, that we are dealing here with some kind of fiction, far removed from the ritual life of the Egyptian Pharaoh. Despite the fact that we cannot be sure whether anything like the Papremis Festival, described by Herodotus, occurred in more ancient times, there is much other evidence to show that such mythical narratives are closely linked with actual cult practices. So, for example, at the beginning of the annual New Year ritual, *The Confirmation of the King's Power*, the king is given special regalia and anointed with sacred oils. As he receives the *Was* and *Ankh* amulets symbolizing

to Isis by violence. Evidently, at this late date, an aspect of the relationship between Isis and her tempestuous son had to be enacted each year in a ritual.

But to return to the New Kingdom story. In the midst of all this blinding rage and horror there is also redemption at hand for Horus in the guise of the lovely Hathor. A hint of this has already been provided when Seth buries the two eyes in the ground and they grow again as beautiful lotus flowers—those fragrant plants from which Re rises forth at dawn. This symbolic rooting of light in earth means that Horus can now be approached by other deities, ones who connect him with youthful erotic love and the rising sun at dawn.

For it is Hathor, in her manifestation as 'Lady of the Southern Sycamore', who now comes to his aid, finding the young blind god weeping in the desert. This Hathor is the tree goddess of Memphis, who is shown in reliefs dwelling in the branches of the much loved sycamore fig tree, dispelling her

milky juices to worshippers, a liquid which Egyptian doctors used to heal wounds and abscesses. And it is she who now seeks to restore the dripping eyes of the young god. First she finds a gazelle in the desert, which she milks and then returns to Horus with this healing liquid, saying:

'Open your eyes, so that I can put this milk in'. He opened his eyes, and she put the milk in. She put it in the right eye, she put it in the left eye. She said to him, 'Open your eyes!' He opened his eyes. She looked at them, she found them healed. Then she went to tell Re-Harakhti: 'I found Horus had lost his eyes because of Seth, but I restored them. Now here he comes.'

Hathor's intervention is important here and a sure sign that the conflict between the two gods is not without significance for the Egyptian goddess of love. Indeed, as we have already seen in the love poems quoted in chapter six, her erotic power, surfacing in adolescent life, compels the youth to leave the mother, to break free

114 *The union of opposites. Horus and Seth bind together the heraldic plants of Upper and Lower Egypt. Each places one foot on the base of a sm3-hieroglyph which supports a cartouche containing the name of King Senwosret. This hieroglyph means 'unite' and it represents a lung and windpipe. Thus, through the binding movement of the reconciled gods, the royal name, placed here at the top of the windpipe, can be 'voiced' or creatively uttered (12th Dynasty relief on the side of a throne from el-Lisht supporting a statue of Senwosret I, Egyptian Museum, Cairo)*

royal dominion and life, so the chant which is sung to accompany this ritual bestowal, refers to the beheading of Isis:

Come, see Horus
  who has been given his Eye . . .
Isis is in peace
  because of her son Ihy.
Hail to you , O Isis!
  your head has been reconnected,
You have taken possession again
  of this your face of life.
Pharaoh lives with you
  because he is this your Horus.[22]

Reconciled with his mother Isis, the Pharaoh – the living incarnation of Horus – has regained his Eye, and Isis, too, has been given her head. The king is now hailed as Ihy, the child of Hathor, showing that this restoration of mother and son cannot occur without Hathor's healing intervention.

BIRTH OF THE MOON: HORUS, THE SHINING LORD

The drama in *The Contendings of Horus and Seth* is still not at an end. Horus has indeed succumbed to Seth, and seen his own brutality surface from the depths when his mother wavers in her family loyalties. This episode marks a significant phase in his adolescent development: the weakling Re derided at the beginning of the story no longer exists. Gone for ever is his innocent childlike dependence on Isis; and his

new-found strength also means that he is ready for a final encounter with Seth, an encounter in which Seth must also be brought to heel. If there is to be any possibility of a reconciliation between these warring gods, such an equalization of their powers is crucial. Moreover, a solution is urgently needed, as Re and the Ennead have long grown weary of the struggle.

The decisive contest involves a homosexual meeting between uncle and nephew, in which the loser will be the one who is penetrated by the semen of the other. Seth invites Horus to feast with him and, at nightfall, they lie down together on a bed where Seth makes a sexual advance to his nephew. Once again, however, Seth is about to

fall victim to Isis, for Horus manages to catch Seth's semen between his thighs, which he then carries in his hand to the horrified Isis:

At night Seth let his member become stiff, and he inserted it between the thighs of Horus. Horus placed his hands between his thighs and caught the semen of Seth. Then Horus went to tell his mother, Isis: 'Come, Isis, my mother, come and see what Seth did to me'. He opened his hand and let her see the semen of Seth. She cried out, took her knife, cut off his hand, and threw it in the water. Then she made a new hand for him.

Again, a sexual approach on the part of Seth has led to his downfall. This time, however, it is Horus, aided by Isis, who has caused Seth to waste his misfortunes of Horus. But their laughter is short-lived. For now Horus demands that both his semen and Seth's semen should be called by the moon god, Thoth, who steps forward as arbitrator. Thoth begins to call:

'Come forth, semen of Seth!' And it answered him from the water in the midst of the ditch. Then Thoth laid his hand on Seth's arm and said : 'Come out semen of Horus!' And it said to him: 'Where shall I come out?' Thoth said to it, 'Come out of his ear'. It said to him: 'Should I come out of his ear, I who am a divine seed?' Then Thoth said to it: 'Come out from the top of his head'. Then it came out as a shining disk on Seth's head. Seth became exceedingly angry, and he stretched out his hand to seize the disk. Thereupon Thoth took it away from him and placed it as a crown upon his own head.

Seth has been duped into becoming a pregnant being, a 'container' for the seed of Horus. In reality, he has not done 'a man's deed' to Horus, but rather he has been made to give birth, bringing forth the semen of Horus in the form of the lunar disk, which bursts forth from his head. Humiliated and angry, he tries to harm the disk, but it is saved by the moon god, Thoth, who snatches the disk away from Seth and places it upon his own head (pl 115).

A much later text in the temple of Horus at Edfu—a temple especially linked with Horus's victory over his rival—refers to Seth's effeminacy in swallowing the seed of Horus:

I bring you the beautiful green plants on which you have emitted your seed, which is hidden there, which the effeminate one has swallowed. Your seed belongs to him, and he will conceive for you a son, who will come forth from his forehead.[23]

Horus has not only stolen Seth's semen, but has also deprived him of his masculinity. Seth has been forced to succumb and to give birth. Now both gods have been made to suffer:

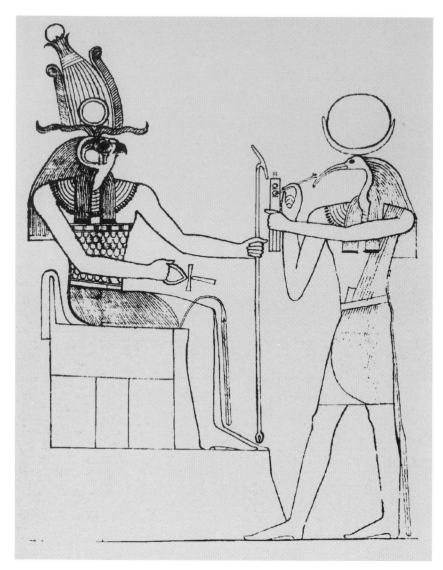

Above 115 The moon god Thoth as divine scribe, holding his writing palette and reed pen before Re-Harakhti (Greenfield Papyrus, British Museum, London)

Facing page 116 Bronze statuette of the triumphant Horus hawk wearing the crowns of Upper and Lower Egypt (Detroit Institute of Arts)

seed by not allowing it to enter his body. The semen is thrown by Isis into a ditch, and she then proceeds to masturbate her son until his semen falls into her jar—a hint perhaps that there is about to be some kind of containment, birth and generation. Next, Isis learns from Seth's gardener that he eats only lettuce plants, as might be expected of a god displaying such voracious sexual appetites— these being after all the vegetable sacred to Min. She spreads her son's semen over some of these lettuces, which Seth then unwittingly eats.

Over-confident as ever, and not suspecting the trickery, Seth persuades Horus to go to court with him for judgement. Addressing the divine tribunal, he demands that the throne be given to him, because, as he boastfully declares: 'I have done a man's deed to him'. The Ennead immediately dissolve into laughter at the

'Horus has groaned because of his eyes', but Seth too 'has groaned because of his testicles'.[24] Both have temporarily lost their essential power in the course of the conflict. The two oppositional forces have been compelled to concede the reality of the other, and both have been forced to experience the other in the depths of their being.

This victory of Horus over Seth has profound meaning within the cosmic order. The re-emergence of light from Seth's head, in the form of the crescent moon-disk, is interpreted in texts as the birth both of Thoth, 'the cutter', and of each month's new moon. It is also the rebirth of the sound Eye of Horus—the *Wedjat*-Eye—which has passed through Seth's body and been restored into a new and fuller life.

The Moon Eye had to be shattered, to go to pieces in the struggle, before it could be recreated and made whole again. Importantly, too, its loss and subsequent restoration were extended to other fragmentations in which an equalization of parts was relevant, notably the counting of grain in the *hekat*-measure. Each part of the Eye of Horus was used to write down the fractional parts of the measure (pl 118), though when these individual fractions were added together they made 63/64ths, falling just short

118 The sound Eye of Horus. The various separate elements of the Moon Eye were used by the ancient Egyptians for writing the fractional parts of the grain measure. When the individual fractions were added together they made up 63/64ths falling just short of unity. However, when they are set in 'the sound eye' (the Wedjat-eye) they form a totality in which nothing is missing. In other words, the whole is shown to be greater than the sum of the individual parts.

that 'Horus, Son of Isis be summoned, and let him be given the office of his father Osiris'.

Yet despite all the confusion he has wrought, this troublesome god, who is after all 'the chosen of Re', still has a creative role to play. For the sun god now demands that he be given Seth

To dwell with me and be my son. He shall thunder in the sky and be feared'.

Plate 117 shows Seth at the prow of the sun-boat, aggressively defending Re against Apophis, the evil serpent and cosmic enemy, who constantly seeks to retard the passage of the solar boat.

But it is Horus who appears as the new and noble ruler of Egypt, whom the moon mother, Isis, acclaims at the end of the story with the words:

You are the perfect King.
  My heart rejoices
When you brighten earth
  With your lustre.

Tested and extended by his rival, Horus has, in the words of te Velde 'had to learn and win adult divine life through sad experience'.[27] But his ordeal has also brought him into contact with the turbulent sexual power he needs if he is to manifest as a shining influence in Egypt. His reconciliation with his erstwhile opponent means that both the Red Crown of Lower Egypt and the White Crown of Upper

of unity. Set in the sound *Wedjat*-Eye, however, they formed a whole.[25]

The ritual of *Filling the Eye* was also celebrated in the temple cult on the sixth or seventh day of the month in connection with the waxing moon; it is then that the crescent moon begins to take its shape, making this a time of great significance in ancient Egypt. Likewise, on the fifteenth day of the month when the moon reached fullness, a ritual of *Counting the Eye* was again performed.[26]

And what of Seth? Reconciliation occurs at the end of the story when,

bound and fettered, he is led by Isis as a prisoner before Atum, the creator god of Heliopolis. The beast of untamed lust has finally been overcome, his strength and energy harnessed for the benefit of the kingdom. And he, himself, is reconciled to the failure of his claim. Of his own volition he asks

119 The two sacred Eyes with hands raised in praise towards Nefer-signs meaning 'vitality' (Detail of a relief in the tomb of Amenemonet at Thebes)

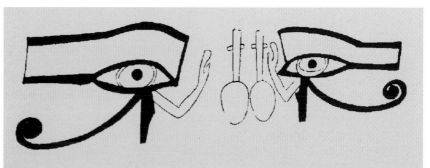

Egypt are now assuredly his (pl 116).
Moreover, not only has he proved his
right to inherit the throne of Osiris, but
also, in the course of his struggle, he
has through the saving grace of Hathor
joined the circuit of the sun.

Now two sacred Eyes illumine the
sky of Egypt: the left eye—the waxing
moon and Eye of Horus—and the right
eye associated with the raging goddess
Hathor-Sekhmet (pls 120, 121). For as
the initiate in chapter 17 of the *Book of
the Dead* well knew, both must be
restored and propitiated in their
different ways within the cosmic order:

*I have filled the Eye after it was injured
  On that night of conflict
  Between the two men.
What does that mean?*

*That is the time of the conflict
  Between Horus and Seth.
  When Seth caused a discharge
  In the face of Horus.
  When Horus seized
  The testicles of Seth.
It was Thoth who did this
  With his fingers.*

*I raised the hair of the Wedjat-Eye
  At the time of the storm.
What does that mean?
It is the right Eye of Re
  When it became enraged against him
  After he had sent it forth.
It was Thoth, indeed,
  Who raised the hair from it,
  Bringing it back alive,
  Whole and healthy,
  Without any harm.*

Facing page 122 Hatshepsut— dressed as a male sovereign—kneels at the feet of her divine father, Amun-Re. The god's gesture of empowerment forms the hieroglyph ka *meaning 'life','vital force', 'bull'. The name and figure of the god were chiselled out during the reign of Akhenaten and although they were restored by a later ruler, signs of the damage are still visible (Tip of the fallen pink granite obelisk of Hatshepsut, one of two she erected between the fourth and fifth pylons at Karnak Temple)*

114

Part 3   Hatshepsut and Akhenaten:
The Trinitarian Revolution

10 Hatshepsut: The Temple Builder

THE MORTUARY TEMPLE of Queen Hatshepsut, anciently known as *Djeser-Djeseru*, 'Holiest of the Holy', is one of the most striking monuments to have survived from ancient Egypt. Built beneath the towering cliffs of Deir el-Bahri on the west bank at Luxor, a locality where Hathor had long been worshipped, the temple stands directly opposite the great temple of Amun-Re at Karnak on the east bank of the river. From the height of the temple's upper terraces there is a wonderful view of the Theban plain, its fields woven into a green and black tapestry of fertile cultivation, with the ribbon of the Nile glinting in the distance and the eastern desert hills lying beyond.

Hatshepsut chose well the location for her temple, as did Thutmose III who built his own temple high on the hill immediately to the south of Hatshepsut's monument.

Not surprisingly, as a temple located in one of Hathor's holy places, there is an abundance of Hathorian imagery decorating its walls, including the well-preserved reliefs in the Hathor shrine showing Hathor as cow suckling Hatshepsut. These important scenes encapsulate Hatshepsut's power of attraction as ruler of Egypt, although when we discussed them in chapter four their significance within the temple's overall design was not considered. As will be seen below, they also belong within a very carefully thought out threefold scheme incorporating the temple's three terraces and notions of Amun-Re as a threefold god.

Before looking at Hatshepsut's innovatory monument in more detail, however, there is another person whose presence cannot be ignored at Deir el-Bahri, namely the influential chief steward Senenmut, who was also tutor of Hatshepsut's daughter Neferure. There are numerous portrayals of Senenmut in the Deir el-Bahri temple, discreetly hidden away in secret niches and behind doors (pl 124). Given that officials were never included in royal temple reliefs, this suggests that Senenmut had a close link both with Hatshepsut and the temple.

Indeed, Senenmut has often been identified as the temple's designer, even though the title 'architect' is not included amongst his many functions. His secret unfinished tomb, located in a small quarry near the temple, is tunnelled in such a way that it ends beneath the temple precincts.[1] Again, like the temple, his tomb includes features not previously seen in Egyptian architecture, notably the beautiful astronomical ceiling with its depiction of the heavenly constellations. Inscribed in the tomb also is the earliest known version of Chapter 145 of the *Book of the Dead*, which details the journey of renewal through the 21 gates of the fiery goddess, 'the great Powerful One with red hair who comes forth in the night'. Whatever Senenmut's ultimate fate might have been—and no satisfactory conclusions can be drawn from the surviving evidence—it is clear that he was deeply committed to religious developments in Hatshepsut's reign.[2]

What were these developments? We have already seen how a more earth-related, heart-centred religion had been taking root in Egyptian consciousness since the Middle Kingdom. This was also connected with the rise of Amun-Re and a more inward experience of the deities (chapter seven). It was, to quote Jan Assmann, a religious movement characterized by a 'more personal conception of deity, of gods intervening in life and history, manifesting a personal will, intention and purpose' and Assmann notes the importance of Hatshepsut in the development of these new ideas about divine intentionality.[3] The new religious mood is certainly reflected in reliefs and inscriptions at Deir el-Bahri. Moreover, Assmann also draws attention to the importance of Hatshepsut's reign for the emergence of Amun-Re as a threefold god, a development which is crucial for interpreting the Deir el-Bahri temple's three terraces.[4]

AMUN-RE: THE TRIPLE GOD

Drawing primarily on written sources, Assmann's careful work shows how there was a move towards clarifying Amun-Re's threefold nature during Hatshepsut's reign by the addition of specific epithets to the god's name.[5] These define him as

1 *Ruler and King of the gods appearing with the insignia of the Theban cult image;*

2 *Solar Life Deity and Preserver; and*

3 *Primordial Creator God.*

Taking Assmann's work further, it can also be applied to interpreting sacred architecture, for this threefold conception of Amun-Re coincided with the

Right 125 Hatshepsut, the female Pharaoh of Egypt (Granite statue in the National Museum of Antiquities, Leiden including a cast of the original head which is in the Metropolitan Museum, New York)

emergence of new temple forms at Thebes, which were appropriate for the worship of a threefold god.

The temple Hatshepsut built at Deir el-Bahri is composed of three ascending terraces and the decoration on each level was evidently chosen to reveal the three different manifestations of Amun-Re. The temple shows Amun-Re interacting with Hatshepsut within three different dimensions of divine existence corresponding—as in the later Hermetic tradition—to 'three worlds'

1 *Image (terrestrial) realm .... first terrace*

2 *Life sphere .... middle terrace*

3 *Primordial realm .... upper terrace*

Equally significant, as a temple located in a place long sacred to Hathor, its decoration gives great prominence to Hathor's power within this intricate threefold existence. It would be a mistake, however, to see the 'three worlds' view as separate from the solar cycle. The different manifestations of the goddesses within the solar cycle (Part 1) also belong within the 'three worlds' conception, although it is not until the Ramessid temples that the interrelationship can be traced in any detail.

DEIR EL-BAHRI: A CHANGE OF HEART

To appreciate fully the innovatory design of Hatshepsut's temple, it is essential to compare it with the neighbouring Middle Kingdom funerary temple, built in the reign of Nebhepetre Mentuhotep who founded the 11th Dynasty (pls 126-7). The temple—which was also the burial place of the king and female members of the royal family—is now in a ruinous condition but was evidently planned in a sequence of terraces. Unlike Hatshepsut's temple, however,

Above 126 Possible reconstruction of the Middle Kingdom temple at Deir el-Bahri. The central flat roof and mass continue the tradition of the primeval hill in Old Kingdom architecture

Left 127 View from the cliffs looking down on the Middle Kingdom temple at Deir el-Bahri. The remains of the solid central core and surrounding colonnade are clearly visible

Below 128 The three terraces of Hatshepsut's temple; the Hathor shrine at the left end of the middle terrace is paired with the Anubis shrine at its right end

there are the remains of a solid core at its centre, which archaeologists think was probably a solid structure similar to Old Kingdom mastaba tombs in the north of Egypt.

Obviously the idea of building a terraced temple across from Amun-Re's temple at Karnak was not new. But nothing in the Middle Kingdom design has been discovered which compares with the middle terrace of Hatshepsut's temple, with its paired shrines at each end of the terrace dedicated to Hathor and Anubis; nor with Hatshepsut's processional way leading straight through the temple to the sanctuary above. And it is precisely the shift in design on the second level which is so crucial for understanding Hatshepsut's contribution to New Kingdom religion.

Indeed Zygmunt Wysocki makes the telling point that it seems to have been Hatshepsut's husband, Thutmose II, who first started building the Deir el-Bahri temple, adopting an architectural plan similar to the earlier Middle Kingdom design. However, work in his reign only progressed as far as excavating the central sanctuary in the

cliffside and part of the upper terrace. After a meticulous study of the building design, Wysocki concludes that Thutmose II must have planned the temple with the same sort of central core surrounded by porticos as the neighbouring Middle Kingdom building (pl 127).

It was only after her husband's death that Hatshepsut 'rearranged the original conception and extended it according to her plans'.[6] And how different these plans of Egypt's female Pharaoh proved to be. For, if Wysocki's careful observations are accepted, they throw even more light on Hatshepsut's achievements, marking her reign as the crucial turning-point in New Kingdom sacred architecture.

FIRST TERRACE: THE CULT RULER OF EGYPT

The temple's central axis is oriented northwest to southeast, being designed as a long open-air processional way leading up from a valley temple to the innermost sanctuary carved out of the cliffside, high in 'The Holy Place'. In the spacious courtyard before the lowest portico there were once two

pools and trees individually planted in containers, providing greenness and shade in this part of the temple.

Although the scenes along the left (southwest) colonnade are now very

damaged, enough remains to confirm that their theme is Hatshepsut's renewal of Amun-Re's temple at Karnak where his holy cult image was housed. Two great granite obelisks are shown being transported by river from Aswan.

Whether these represent the pair of obelisks that Hatshepsut had erected on the east side of the Karnak temple, or whether they are the pair which she placed between her father's fourth and fifth pylon before the sanctuary is not known.

But it is interesting to read what Hatshepsut has to say about her adornment of Amun's temple in an inscription carved on the base of the northern obelisk that still stands at Karnak.[7]

She proclaims that she has brought the two great obelisks 'as a monument for her father Amun' which can be seen from both sides of the river. Moreover, she says that Karnak becomes the horizon on earth when the sun shines between these two great towering pillars:

Their rays flood the Two Lands
When the sun rises between them,
Like at sunrise in the horizon of the sky.

Heaven has been enshrined here on earth in the Karnak temple. Musing on her mood when she accomplished this for Amun, Hatshepsut declares:

I have done this with a loving heart
* for my father, Amun,*
When I entered before
* his primordial cult image.*

And again:

My heart directed me to make for him
* two obelisks in electrum,*
Their pyramidions merged with the sky
* in the august pillared hall*
Between the great pylons
* of King Thutmose I.*

She, the 'Gold of Rulership', is in truth 'his daughter who glorifies him'. The tone of the inscriptions is entirely devotional, emphasizing Hatshepsut's heart as the motivating power in her cult activity.

Such a devotional service of the heart pervades the later Ramessid era but here is evidence enough that it was already present in Hatshepsut's cult of Amun at Karnak. Near the Deir el-Bahri reliefs of transporting obelisks, Hatshepsut appears before Amun-Re, the 'Image Ruler' of Egypt. She offers obelisks to him, she offers him his temple.

In short, the first terrace of this three-fold temple includes—in the southwest colonnade—a variety of scenes revealing her devoted service for Amun-Re in his cult realm on earth.

Though little remains of the decoration in the northeast colonnade across on the other side of the courtyard, there is a relief showing Hatshepsut as a fearsome sphinx, trampling her enemies underfoot, so maintaining Egypt's order and boundaries. Another scene shows her fowling and fishing in

canoes, again activities symbolizing defence of Egypt from hostile forces. All these themes on the lowest terrace relate to Hatshepsut as a terrestrial ruler: she protects Egypt from enemies, she enlarges Amun-Re's cult temple at Karnak. Together with Amun-Re, she is the Crown of Egypt functioning within the terrestrial realm.

SECOND TERRACE: THE LIFE SPHERE

Ascending the processional way to the next level, the mediating zone of the Deir el-Bahri temple is reached, which also gives access to the uppermost

terrace and the central sanctuary beyond. Here on this second level Hatshepsut located the Hathor shrine discussed in chapter four, with its sistrum-shaped columns and scenes of Hathor as cow nurturing Hatshepsut with her life-giving milk, embracing the youthful dawn ruler with her *menit*-necklace of attraction (pls 54-55). These scenes reveal Hathor as a nurturing goddess who sustains the warmth and flow of life for the Egyptian Pharaoh.

The corresponding shrine at the other end of the middle terrace is dedicated to Anubis—the jackal-headed god who preserves the dead from decay and assists those in the transitional realm between life and death in the West. Hathor is also included in the shrine's decoration (pl 129). Other scenes include the Goddess of the West and Hatshepsut, standing with her *Ka*

before Anubis. Hence the two end shrines on the middle terrace are dedicated to a nurturing goddess who promotes growth and vitality, and a god who prevents dissolution at the close of life. Their life-enhancing and death-defying powers enclose the temple's 'life' sphere.

Within the colonnade, close to the Anubis shrine, scenes show Hatshepsut's divine conception and birth as the child of Amun-Re and Queen Ahmose, conceived and born within the intimacy of the palace, a ruler destined for the throne of Egypt.[8] Whether the birth cycle was included in earlier temples is unknown and it is possible that the cycle represents an older myth related to rulership. Nevertheless, Hatshepsut is the first Pharaoh known to have enunciated her conception and birth, with all its

details of the sexual pleasure, fragrance and joy surrounding her arrival in the palace. Amenhotep III followed her example by including similar scenes in the Luxor Temple, no doubt inspired by this striking temple on the other side of the Nile.

Though both Hatshepsut and Amenhotep are born to Amun-Re and the Egyptian queen, their birth in the royal palace is presented not as a remote event far removed from mortal concerns, but as one profoundly invested with all the emotional pleasure and pain which surround the entry of new life into the world. Significantly too, it is not a sky goddess who appears as mother of the future Pharaoh, but rather the queen in the palace, reflecting yet again the shift towards a more human, earthly religion characteristic of the Theban deities.

This shift is also reflected at the beginning of the drama at Deir el-Bahri when Amun-Re announces to a heavenly gathering his intention to engender an heir; the god here manifests a personal will as he prepares to intervene in the rulership of Egypt. The child's conception is portrayed in a delicately carved relief showing Amun-Re seated with the queen on the royal bed. Nothing in this discreet portrayal, however, betrays the deep emotion surrounding the event, though much more is told in the text inscribed beside them. It is said that Amun takes the form of Thutmose I, Hatshepsut's father, as he comes to the queen in the middle of the night, flooding the palace

with his perfumes. Aroused by his presence, the queen joyfully wakes and their union is consummated as 'he gives his heart to her'.

She woke because of the god's fragrance.
She smiled at His Majesty.
  He came to her immediately
  His phallus erect before her
  He gave his heart to her.
He let her see him in his form of a god
After he had come to her.
  She was filled with joy
  At the sight of his beauty
  His attraction entered into her body
The palace was flooded with the god's fragrance
And all his perfumes were from Punt.[9]

The pleasurable excitement of sensual love shared by the divine lover and Hathorian queen pulses through these lines. The richness of perfumes, the attraction of sexual aromas, surround their marriage bed deep within the palace where they mingle with each other to conceive a child in an ecstatic embrace. As they melt into each other's arms in the heavily scented air, so these odours of the god, whose 'perfumes were from Punt' take them to that paradisial land, to the place of spices, of sweet odours and exotic plants, of gold. To the place of sunrise.

After this erotic conception, the theme shifts to the mysterious realm of embryological growth, as Amun orders the ram-headed god, Khnum, to mould the newly conceived Hatshepsut and her *Ka* on his potter's wheel. In the Luxor version Hathor, giver of vitality to the forms shaped by the Memphite craftsmen god, sits across from Khnum as he forms the king's two bodies, holding out an *Ankh*-sign of life to them; at Deir el-Bahri the frog goddess Heket is Khnum's companion. The appointed time for delivery is at hand, the days of waiting over, heralded by Thoth, god of measurements, time and numbers, who appears before the pregnant queen to confer a royal titulary on her. He has measured out the time-span of her pregnancy and now the queen is led to the birth room, where she is helped by her birth attendants and numerous protective deities all holding 'life' signs.

A new light has appeared in the world, greeted with jubilation by the hawk-headed souls of Pe (Buto) and the jackal-headed souls of Nekhen (Hierakonpolis). The collective body of ancestral rulers, dwelling in the ancient cities of North and South, gathers together to welcome this new ruler who will continue the royal traditions of Egypt. Each bends one knee and beats his chest with his fist to give a whooping sound of jubilation, greeting the royal arrival at Luxor with the words:

Give her a flame...
O come forth,
  Lord of strength. The flame.

Near these ancestral presences stand the dwarf god, Bes, and the hippopotamus goddess, Taweret, who watch over all Egyptian women during their time of child-bearing. Next Hathor brings the child to Amun, who kisses and embraces his newly-born infant. Then the child is returned to feminine care as cow-headed goddesses nourish the future Pharaoh with their milk. Then the child is taken for a ritual purification in the 'House of Purification' and finally the royal fate is ordained, as four kneeling women hold Hatshepsut and her *Ka* before Seshat, goddess of writing, who records the duration of Hatshepsut's reign.

Patently, different levels of birth and ritual passage are interwoven in these scenes at Deir el-Bahri and Luxor. On one level the sequence unfolds according to rites which must have been practised whenever a child was born in Egypt, culminating in the name-giving. On another level it relates to the coronation rites—to birth and vitalization by the crown goddesses, purification in the realm of Horus and Seth, and finally the zenithal proclamation of royal names. Near the birth scenes are others showing Hatshepsut's coronation, legitimizing her as the crowned successor of her father, Thutmose I. Moreover, by placing these scenes close to the Anubis shrine at the far end of the birth colonnade, it suggests that her *Ka*-rulership of Egypt is also connected with those dwelling in the West.

Nowhere is the birth and making of a future king portrayed so clearly during the New Kingdom as in these birth scenes at Deir el-Bahri and Luxor. So much of what is shown here touches a human chord, is of perennial concern, deeply involving life as it exists right here on earth. The life lived by the Pharaoh and royal mother, exalted though they undoubtedly may be, is on an earthly scale, has a human dimension; and the deities surrounding them are those to whom every Egyptian woman could call in her anxious hour of need to protect her through the pangs of birth. Hathor, Khnum, Isis, the frog goddess, Heket, the birth goddess, Meskhenet, Bes,

Taweret, all are also invoked in magical spells for a safe delivery in childbirth.

Across in the colonnade on the other side of the terrace are the famous reliefs of the expedition to Punt, the land of sunrise over which Hathor presided as 'Lady of Punt', with its exotic products and beehive houses on piles which were reached by ladders (pl 132). Ships are shown being loaded for their return to Egypt, laden with sweet-smelling incense trees, apes, gold ingots and even a giraffe—all the wonderful treasures of the 'Land of the God' which beautified, vitalized and enhanced life on earth.

It may seem as if the inclusion of these scenes is simply a historical record of Hatshepsut's expedition. Yet, if interpreted within the temple's overall threefold conception, their inclusion on the middle terrace close to the Hathor shrine clearly has religious significance. For the precious substances brought from Punt all symbolized 'life'

to the Egyptians. Moreover, when Amun-Re comes to the queen in the birth cycle he manifests, like Min, as a sweet-smelling palace god imbued with the aromas of Punt.

Here on the second terrace, with its emphasis on birth, nurture and growth, on gold, greenness and vitality, the expedition is part of a carefully chosen decorative scheme which reveals the essence of 'life'.

And when Hatshepsut appears before her subjects at the return of the Punt expedition, she appears to her people solarized and transfigured like the sun shining over Egypt, a fragrant golden being, who has been empowered by the great life-bearing goddess, Hathor:

Her perfume mingled with (that of) Punt,
  Her skin being fashioned in electrum,
Shining as the stars do in the festival hall,
  Before the land in its entirety.[10]

Furthermore, a special Chamber of Appearance seems to have been

constructed in a corner of the temple on the upper terrace directly above the Punt colonnade. Like the later 'window of appearance' where Akhenaten and Nefertiti loved to appear before their people, so here in Hatshepsut's temple there is a special place for her to appear in all her exalted glory as a life-giving ruler.

On this mediating second terrace Hatshepsut's glorified existence is glimpsed as she manifests in the 'life' sphere; and it is significant that great prominence is given to her *Ka* on this level, for the *Ka* is, above all, the vehicle of life for the body (chapter eight). Moreover, even more than Amun-Re, Hathor appears as the source of life here. The food on which life depends flows from the great Lady of Punt, and it is her vitality which energizes the heart of the temple.

THIRD TERRACE: THE PRIMORDIAL REALM

From this 'life' space of the temple the processional way leads still further upwards—towards the Osirian realm. Originally the pillars fronting the upper terrace supported huge statues of Hatshepsut in Osirian form; and a large granite doorway flanked by statues of Hatshepsut once sealed the central entrance. This is not the place for a detailed analysis of the upper terrace, with its open court surrounded on all sides by colonnades and niches cut into the walls for Osirian and royal statues. But enough of the decoration needs to be described to highlight the temple's overall design.

On the left (southwest) side of the court are two chambers dedicated to the funerary cult of Hatshepsut and her father, Thutmose I, where food offerings were brought and placed before the false doors in each room. Across on the northeast side is a Helio-politan style sanctuary, open to the sky, with a huge altar in its midst for burning offerings in the rays of the

133 Map showing the northwest-southeast axis of Thebes. Hatshepsut's temple at Deir el-Bahri lies across from the temple complex of Amun-Re at Karnak. Rising up high behind the temple are the cliffs of Deir el-Bahri and beyond these, in the Valley of the Kings, are the royal tombs

sun. Within these Heliopolitan walls is a small chapel dedicated to Anubis and Hatshepsut's family. One relief shows Hatshepsut and her mother Queen Ahmose offering to Amun; in another Thutmose I, accompanied by his mother, Seniseneb, offer to Anubis —three generations of the women associated with Thutmose I and the royal line are present on this upper Heliopolitan terrace at Thebes.

Also portrayed on one of the walls in the court is the annual boat procession from Karnak to Deir el-Bahri. Each year Amun-Re made this journey to Deir el-Bahri during the annual 'Beautiful Feast of the Valley' celebrated for two days during the second month of *Shemou* (or the tenth month of the year called *Paoni*) when his boat, accompanied by priests, musicians and dancers, was brought from Karnak in a festive procession across to the west bank. Its destination was the sanctu-ary at Deir el-Bahri, but before arriving there the procession visited other sacred places along the way.

Following in the wake of Amun-Re were numerous families who had come to celebrate a nocturnal festival of feasting and revelry in the tombs of their loved ones whilst Amun-Re so-journed with Hathor in the Deir el-Bahri temple. In this way humans

and deities together shared in a glorious feast of renewal uniting the Living and the Dead, the climax of which was the coming forth from tem-ple and tomb at dawn to behold the rising sun in the East alighting upon a regenerated world.

This connection of the Living and the Dead is taken up in the decoration of the sanctuary itself. In one scene Hat-shepsut and her daughter, Neferure, offer to the boat of Amun-Re behind which stand her father, Thutmose I her mother, Queen Ahmose, and Princess Neferubiti. Carved into the walls are niches for statues of the royal family. Further within the New Kingdom part of the sanctuary, the Heliopolitan creator Atum receives offerings from Thutmose III. In another scene Hatshepsut offers to that great bringer of life, Hathor. Every-thing in the decoration here points to Hatshepsut united for eternity with her ancestors in the West.

Carved on the base of the south wall of the sanctuary's first chamber are representations of four basins depict-ing the containers for milk originally placed around the room. It was in milk that the torchbearers—who appear as fecundity figures beneath the boat of Amun—extinguished the flames of their candles at dawn when Amun's

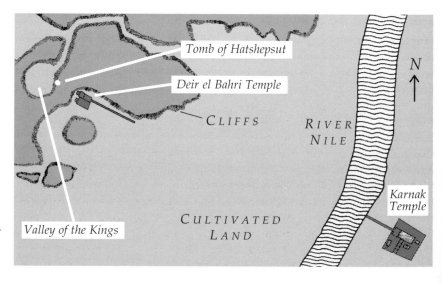

boat was taken forth again from the sanctuary after his nocturnal sojourn in the temple.

During this night of jubilation, when the sanctuary was transformed into an illumined room of light and renewal, the intoxicating power of Hathor dissolved the barriers separating the Living and the Dead. There was a return to the chaos of pre-creation, to an experience of primordial unity as the night-time power of the goddess erupted to renew the exhausted cosmic order. Then at dawn, as the flames were extinguished in milk, Amun-Re's boat was taken forth again from the interior of the mountain. Emerging from the darkness of night towards Karnak in the southeast, the primordial god of Egypt manifested anew in a regenerated world.

It has to be remembered, moreover, that Hatshepsut's father was probably the first Pharaoh to have built his tomb in the Valley of the Kings on the other side of the mountain from the Deir el-Bahri temple. Also the tomb in which

Hatshepsut planned her own burial after she became ruler was cut into the western mountain directly on the other side of the cliff from the Deir el-Bahri temple.

Whether this was Thutmose I's original tomb is unclear, but what is known is that at some point in Hatshepsut's reign her father must have been buried there, lying deep in the earth behind the Deir el-Bahri temple. Two empty sarcophagi were discovered in the tomb, one for Hatshepsut and the other also originally bearing her name but subsequently recarved with that of Thutmose I.[11]

Here then lay the Ancestor King, deep within the realm of Ptah-Sokar-Osiris close to the temple of his daughter where rituals for the Osirian dead and Amun-Re were reverently performed. Enacted in a holy place, which had long been sacred to Hathor, such rituals were inevitably deeply charged with the power of the solar goddess. But, as importantly too, because of the Deir el-Bahri temple's

134 Hatshepsut (centre)—accompanied by Thutmose III—performs the cult for Amun-Re, whose sacred boat is being carried from the left (Relief on a block from Hatshepsut's dismantled quartzite shrine at Karnak)

location directly across from Karnak, the Osirian realm in the Valley of the Kings was also linked with the Karnak temple and Amun-Re, the Crown of Egypt ruling on the east bank of the Nile.

Each year when Amun-Re, the compassionate god of justice and mercy, travelled from his sanctuary across in the southeast to Hatshepsut's beautiful threefold temple in the northwest, so a great subtle pathway of connection was traced out in the landscape of Thebes, uniting his complex realm with Hathor the life-bringing goddess of the West, and with the Osirian dead. Here, in this creative holy place of Hathor, Amun-Re appears in three worlds.

He is the Ruler of Egypt appearing in the 'Image Realm' on the first terrace;

Left 135 View of the Valley of the Kings at Thebes. The doorway in the centre is the entrance to the tomb of Ramesses VI

Opposite page 136 Senenmut cradles Hatshepsut's daughter, Neferure, in his arms. His tender pose exemplifies the spirit of Hatshepsut's reign when there was a concerted move towards realizing a 'human' heart-centred religion in sacred art and architecture (Egyptian Museum, Cairo)

he appears in the realm of 'Life' and sexual generation on the second terrace; then on the uppermost level of the temple he reaches the northwestern 'Primordial Realm' of renewal and the Osirian ancestral dead.

Hatshepsut's ascending pathway, along which Amun's sacred boat was brought, had given new meaning to Egyptian temple design. For at the temple's heart was not a solid core (as in the neighbouring Middle Kingdom temple), but rather a terrace celebrating sexuality and generation, growth and nurture with the mother goddesses, coronation and transfigured life—a terrace encompassing Hatshepsut's *Ka*-lifetime as lived in the light of the sun related to the life of her people on earth.

The New Kingdom move towards a more 'human', heart-centred religion not only needed new temple designs but also demanded new forms of sculpture appropriate for a threefold temple world. Statues of royal officials holding cult objects before them, such as a naos sistrum or an open naos containing a cult image, now began to appear from Hatshepsut's reign onwards. These private statues were placed in the open courts of temples, and reflected officialdom's increasing access to the temple sphere. Senenmut himself is shown holding a solar serpent named as the food-giving harvest goddess, Renenutet, who is enclosed by *Ka*-arms (pl 46)—a motif devised by Senenmut so that it could be read cryptographically as Hatshepsut's name (*Maatkare*).

All this is not to say that we are dealing with completely new religious phenomena which suddenly sprang up in Hatshepsut's reign, for ever since the Middle Kingdom, or even before, a gradual shift towards a more earth-oriented religion had been underway (chapter seven).

However, this change needed to be earthed in ritual and architecture, the new experiences and insights needed to be expressed in worship. New forms of sacred buildings were essential to reflect the wisdom of the time.

The Middle Kingdom rulers began to move in this direction, for the dawning of the new consciousness is very noticeable in their texts—and Karnak itself was emerging as an important cult centre. But the Middle Kingdom architectural forms still relied heavily on the 'pyramid age' of Old Kingdom Egypt, the 12th Dynasty kings themselves being buried in pyramids in the North.

In a very real sense the Middle Kingdom was the crucial bridge between the old and new, providing the inspiration on which Hatshepsut and those surrounding her could draw to create the innovations of her reign. Yet it took 500 years or so from the Middle Kingdom to Hatshepsut's reign for the new religious mood to mature and find expression.

Something new was needed in Egypt, and Hatshepsut was the innovator. Perhaps too, such startlingly new architecture as the threefold Deir el-Bahri temple, with the beating heart of the Mothers vitalizing and nurturing its centre, could only have come into being in the reign of a woman.

And no wonder that Hatshepsut granted Senenmut a special dispensation allowing him to be shown as a worshipper within her temple. For surely he, with his deep star knowledge and such evident devotion to Hatshepsut and her daughter, had been instrumental in bringing the temple to fruition (pl 136). And long after both Mentuhotep's temple and the temple subsequently built by Thutmose III had fallen into ruin at Deir el-Bahri, Hatshepsut's magnificent creation remained a magnetic centre at Thebes, becoming a place of healing in the Ptolemaic period where pilgrims came for incubatory restorative sleep or to hear oracular advice in dreams from the resident temple healers.

Nevertheless, not all who witnessed the emergence of this threefold temple were in sympathy with religious developments at Thebes. This is most clearly seen in Luxor Temple where, on the orders of King Akhenaten, to whom we turn in the following chapters, its reliefs suffered the most dreadful mutilation, especially those involving Amun-Re. Similar damage occurred at Deir el-Bahri. Yet, however zealous Akhenaten may have been in his attempts to eradicate Theban religion, it seems that even he was influenced by Hatshepsut's remarkable reign. For, though he was to follow a very different spiritual path from that of Hatshepsut, her insights into the threefold nature of Amun-Re were deeply important for his own cult worship of the Aten.

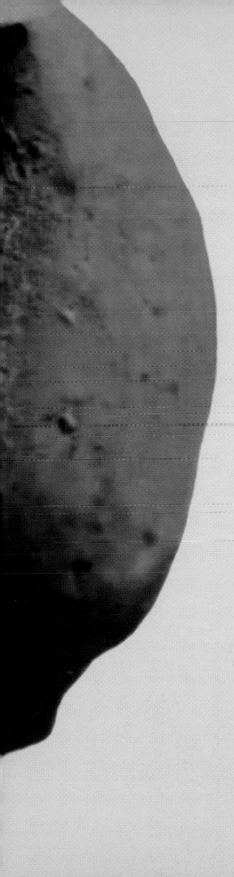

11 The Challenge to Thebes

AROUND 1350 BC one of the most unusual and radical rulers Egypt was ever to experience came to the throne—the Pharaoh Amenhotep IV or, as he was later to call himself, Akhenaten. Branded a 'criminal' by his successors and omitted from the 19th Dynasty king lists, opinions about his real motivation and character are still sharply divided even today.

To some he seems nothing but a religious fanatic, obsessed with devotion to the one God. To others he appears as a repressive monarch ruling in the mode of a contemporary dictator. Canadian archaeologist Donald Redford, for instance, who has worked extensively as director of the Akhenaten Temple Project at Karnak, displays little sympathy for the king, ending his book on Akhenaten with the words:

For all that can be said in his favor, Akhenaten in spirit remains to the end totalitarian . . . He was the champion of a universal, celestial power who demanded universal submission, claimed universal truth, and from whom no further revelation could be expected. I cannot conceive a more tiresome regime under which to be fated to live.[2]

Alternatively, Freud saw Akhenaten as the first monotheist, the mentor of Moses.[3] Much less sublime, however, are descriptions of the king as a

This beauty is first of all eternal; it neither comes into being nor passes away, neither waxes nor wanes; next, it is not beautiful in part and ugly in part, nor beautiful at one time and ugly at another, nor beautiful in this relation and ugly in that, nor beautiful here and ugly there, as varying according to its beholders; nor again will this beauty appear to him like the beauty of a face or hands or anything else corporeal . . . he will see it as absolute, existing alone with itself, unique, eternal, and all other beautiful things as partaking of it, yet in such a manner that, while they come into being and pass away, it neither undergoes any increase or diminution nor suffers any change . . . Do you not see that in that region alone where he sees beauty with the faculty capable of seeing it, will he be able to bring forth not mere reflected images of goodness but true goodness, because he will be in contact not with a reflection but with the truth? (From the speech of Diotima, the woman from Mantinea, in Plato, The Symposium[1])

physical freak, suffering from a pathological illness, which some have deduced from his strange appearance in reliefs and sculpture. Yet another approach is to be heard in the opera *Akhnaten* by the American composer, Philip Glass; in this an unconventional Oedipal figure haunts the stage, torn between his powerful mother, Queen Teye, and playful wife, Nefertiti.

Some of the facts may have become blurred with the passing of time, but it cannot be doubted that fascination with Akhenaten's short-lived revolution lives on. For a revolution indeed it was, characterized both by the king's uncompromising worship of the celestial sun god and by his exclusion of the traditional pantheon.

In one short reign of seventeen years Egyptian pluralism and religious tolerance were shattered as, step by step, the king swept away the gods and goddesses from the royal cult, dedicating himself entirely to the cosmic creator, whose life-giving power streamed down to earth in the rays of the sun.

But it would be a mistake to regard Akhenaten as an isolated visionary, completely outside the main stream of Egyptian religion. Even before he came to the throne there were traces of what Jan Assmann has termed 'the new solar religion'—and long after his death these were to continue in religious texts.[4]

Only a few instances need be mentioned here, such as the following lines from an 18th Dynasty hymn on a stela of the brothers Suti and Hor, which praise the

*Aten of daytime
who creates all,
who makes them live . . .
who lights the Two Lands with his disk . . .
who sees all that he has made, being alone,
who reaches the borders every day.[5]*

Another later hymn acclaims the primordial sun god who 'has distanced himself afar, his form is not known'.[6] Yet another hymn says:

You cross the sky and everyone sees you,
But your movement is hidden from their faces.[7]

Moreover, a version of the Aten, the great solar orb with embracing arms which was to become such a dominant motif in Amarna iconography, had already appeared as early as the reign of Amenhotep II (pl 138).

Evidently, alongside the traditional solar cycle of death and rebirth, new perceptions were dawning during the 18th Dynasty, ones which comprehended the sun god as a cosmic power alone in his circuit in the sky, animating and preserving the external world with his rays. This is no longer Re continually transforming himself each day, together with his beloved Hathor and other goddesses, with whom he shares all the vicissitudes of life and death. But a celestial solitary Being, whose power is revealed to human eyes in the great orb of the sun, whose effects are known through the medium of light and movement.

From whence came the inspiration for these new insights? Some have suggested foreign influences, perhaps from the Indo-European kingdom of Mitanni, situated between the upper reaches of the Tigris-Euphrates rivers. It was ruled by a military elite, who had brought with them a pantheon which included deities in the Indo-European mould.

But whether foreign elements played any part or not—and there is little

concrete evidence to prove this one way or another—it is highly unlikely that such a major step in new consciousness could ever have occurred without a long preparation beforehand in the country itself. Neither the new solar religion, nor the revolution that Akhenaten attempted to carry through to such a startling conclusion, can be understood without taking into account also the rise of Amun-Re, the marked shift towards an inwardness of religious experience and the sense of personal accountability and devotion to a god of the individual which had been surfacing in Egypt since the Middle Kingdom. Indeed it was Amun who became the main focus of persecution during Akhenaten's iconoclastic outburst against the other cults towards the end of his reign.

For such a move inwards must, by its very nature, also have implied the eventual possibility of a split between the 'outer' and the 'inner', of personal separateness from what was gradually to be perceived as an external object world. So it is understandable that there also came more and more sharply into focus during the 18th Dynasty—in contrast with the deities known through the human heart, who were approached through feelings of both fear and devotion—knowledge of the eternal deity of radiant life, the spirit of the cosmos who is revealed to the physical senses through the medium of the sun dwelling alone in the exteriority of the heavens. It was a development, however, that ultimately carried with it the problem of reconciliation, though in hymns associated with the new solar religion before Akhenaten's reign, it is worth noting that the pantheon still continue to be mentioned along with the celestial sole creator.[8]

However, it is for the devastating impact that Akhenaten's revolution had on the female powers, especially on our goddess of dreadful-desire, Hathor-Sekhmet, that the Egyptian Sun King must be included in this book. And there can be little doubt that Akhenaten himself played a central role. For although there must have been influential groups in Egypt supporting the king, Akhenaten's own part in all this should not be underestimated. Indeed artists declare in inscriptions that they were personally taught by him. The great achievement of his reign lay in giving artistic, literary and cult expression to the new solar vision which had been emerging during the 18th Dynasty. Its radicalism lay in the fact that Akhenaten tried to base Egyptian kingship entirely on a relationship with the trinitarian solar creator. Its failure probably lay in Akhenaten's unwillingness to reconcile this vision with the rest of the pantheon and other dimensions of existence.

Perhaps under the gaze of eternity, once the veil had been lifted to reveal the glorious unity of creation, transformation and renewal paled into insignificance, making return to a

Left 140 Plaster head of Akhenaten from el-Amarna (Egyptian Museum, Berlin)

Facing page 141 Sandstone head of Amenhotep IV (Akhenaten) from Karnak (Luxor Museum)

fragmented, restless world of change impossible. Moreover, amidst such a prolific flow of creative activity, it would scarcely have been possible to undertake the mammoth task of reconciliation in the short space of one king's reign.

Had Akhenaten's elder brother Thutmose, high priest of Memphis, lived to succeed Amenhotep III on the throne of Egypt, events might well have taken a different course. But that was not to be. Akhenaten was the one who took over from his father, doing so at a time when Egypt enjoyed great material prosperity, buttressed by the military campaigns of earlier 18th Dynasty rulers.

Traded goods and presents flowed into Egypt, exchanged from as far away as Mycenae and Crete, from Libya, Nubia and Punt. And Egypt herself had ample gold to secure her influence abroad, not least with the kings of Babylon and Mitanni. Their clamouring for the precious metal is recorded in a lively correspondence with the Egyptian court preserved on hundreds of clay tablets discovered at el-Amarna, where Akhenaten founded his new capital. Amenhotep III's tolerance, his taste for luxury and openness to the neighbouring world had resulted in a flurry of diplomatic activity during his long reign lasting nearly forty years. The stage had been set. For this cosmopolitanism was completely in tune with the spirit of the new religion which flowered in Akhenaten's reign.[9]

We know little about Akhenaten's early upbringing before he came to the throne. He may well have spent his youth at Memphis where it was customary for Egyptian princes to be educated during the New Kingdom and where from the reign of Thutmose III onwards the court may well have resided more often than at Thebes. If this was the case, he would also have been close to Heliopolis, the

135

religious centre which seems to have been particularly linked with the dissemination of the 'new solar religion' in Egypt.

Certainly, as we shall see, there is a distinctly Heliopolitan orientation in the cult practised by Akhenaten, at least in the earlier phase of his reign. So we must pause here briefly to consider Heliopolis and its Ennead in order to appreciate better Akhenaten's extraordinary spiritual journey.

HELIOPOLIS: ORIGINAL CREATION

Only a solitary obelisk of the Middle Kingdom ruler, Senwosret I, now stands in a northern suburb of Cairo as a monument to this once esteemed religious centre, called 'the Pillar City' (*jwnw*) by the Egyptians, and known as On in the Bible. And for clues to the cult and character of Heliopolitan solar religion we must first look to the

142 Reconstruction of the Fifth Dynasty sun temple built by King Niuserre at Abu Ghurob showing its open-air court

open-air sun temples built by the Fifth Dynasty kings near their pyramid complexes on the western desert edge in the north of Egypt. Though even here it has to be remembered that these were sun temples associated with the West, and not necessarily imitations of the solar sanctuary at Heliopolis itself.

It was under these Fifth Dynasty kings that solar religion really began to take root in Egypt. They were the first to adopt the title 'Son of Re' as a regular part of royal titulary, and, according to a later folk tale in the *Westcar Papyrus*, the first three kings of the Dynasty were the Sons of Re by the wife of a priest in Heliopolis.

The best preserved sun temple, belonged to King Niuserre (c 2450 BC), and it is true to say that nothing faintly resembling its remarkable structure has survived from later Egypt. It is built on the edge of the desert at Abu Ghurob, about two kilometres to the north of the king's pyramid at Abusir. From a valley building at the edge of the Nile a covered causeway slopes

upwards to a natural desert mound, which has been transformed into an open-air court some 100 metres long and 80 metres wide.

Rising up within its midst was once a squat obelisk placed on a high podium, which, in shape, looks rather like the mastaba tombs of Old Kingdom officials. At the base of this podium was an alabaster altar for sacrificial offerings. Beyond the enclosure wall, to the south, lay a great sun-brick solar boat, a model of the boat used by the sun god, Re-Harakhti, in his daily crossing of the sky from East to West (pl 142).

Those privileged enough to enter into the podium would have passed along a covered corridor on the east and south sides of the court, which led to the podium's entrance. There, adorning the 'Room of the Seasons', they would have seen a dazzling sequence of reliefs showing the different flora and fauna throughout the three seasons of the Egyptian year. The blossoming of plants, the seasonal work in the fields, the increase of animals, the migrations of birds and Nile fishes, all carefully observed and recorded by highly skilled artists, working with obvious delight and with an eye for every detail of the seasonal pattern.

These three seasons of earth are guarded and guided by the sun god, his is the power which enables earth to bring forth increase. This is made abundantly clear in an inscription close to a scene of pelicans:

When the sun goes to rest
  At night in the temple,
    Then there is no copulation.
When day dawns,
  Then the divine command takes its course,
    Then he rules again every phallus and vulva.[10]

The sun god is the source of sexual delight and fertility. Nevertheless, before he can be the source of life, health and salvation, the cosmos must arise

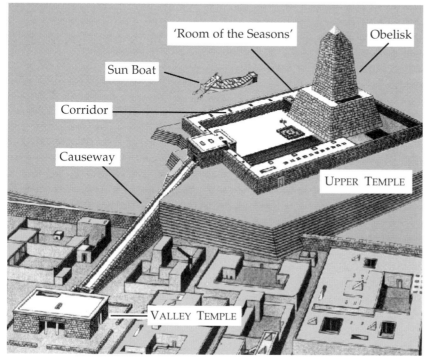

'Room of the Seasons' Obelisk

Sun Boat

Corridor

Causeway

UPPER TEMPLE

VALLEY TEMPLE

in the first place and be brought into existence. This is the work of Atum, whose name means both 'the Complete One' and 'The Not Yet Existent One', the creator who ruled in Heliopolis long before the solar cult had been established there (pl 148).

According to the *Pyramid Texts* Atum reveals himself upon the primordial mound, rising up from the primal waters of Nun, to bring the first pair into being—the air god, Shu, and his female counterpart, Tefenet.

In one version Atum fulfils his pleasurable urge for creation by masturbating, letting his seed fall into the waters so causing the birth of Shu and Tefenet:

It is Atum who came into being as the masturbator of Heliopolis. He put his phallus in his fist and he achieved the pleasure of orgasm with it, giving birth to the son and daughter, brother and sister, Shu and Tefenet. (PT §1248 a-d)

In another version Atum spits out the

first pair from his mouth in the *Benben* temple of Heliopolis:

Atum-Khepri, You are high on the hill,
You shine forth as Benben,
In the Benben temple in Heliopolis.
You eject Shu, you spit out Tefenet,
You put your arms around them with your ka,
So that your ka is in them (PT §1652-3)

Spitting or ejaculating, Atum rises forth from water and darkness to create the first sexually differentiated cosmic pair through his semen or saliva. Though how the name of Shu's female twin should be understood is uncertain. Sometimes it is translated as 'heat', sometimes as 'moisture', but so far there is no scholarly consensus as to the derivation of Tefenet's name.

But she, along with the air god, emanates from 'the fiery blast' of the creator, and as they come forth, so too a realm of radiant light comes into being. Khepri, 'he who becomes' appears in the eastern horizon. After this initial beginning, 'the first time' as

143 The bipartition of the world as the sky goddess Nut arches her body over the earth god Geb after their father, Shu, has interrupted their primeval coition (Papyrus of Tameniu, British Museum, London)

the Egyptians called it, the cosmos unfolds further.

To Shu and Tefenet are born the sky goddess, Nut, and the earth god, Geb (pl 143). Shu ends his children's primal coupling by lifting up the body of his daughter. This separation of sky and earth from the delight of sexual union has to happen so that Osiris, Isis, Seth and Nephthys can in turn be born from the womb of the star-strewn sky mother.

Sometimes Atum seems to be an androgynous creator, 'the He-She', according to one *Coffin Text*.[11] But, for reasons which will become more obvious after we have looked at Akhenaten's revolution, greater prominence is given to the female companions of the Heliopolitan onanist

137

Above 144 Sistrum of Nebet Hetepet, the 'hand of Atum', showing a hand holding a phallus combined with a naos sistrum (Relief in the Temple of Hibis founded in the fifth century BC)

Right 145 Limestone bust of Nefertiti from a sculptor's studio at el-Amarna (Egyptian Museum, Berlin)

from the 19th Dynasty onwards. One is the goddess Iusaas, whose name can be translated as 'She comes and she grows' and is probably connected with an epithet of Atum as 'masturbator' *(jws3w)*. The other is Nebet Hetepet, 'Lady of the Vulva', or alternatively 'Lady of Food Offerings' *(Hetepet* having both meanings in Egyptian), who is known also as 'Hand of Atum' and frequently associated with Hathor.

Plate 144 graphically illustrates the sexual power of these Heliopolitan goddesses as partners of Atum. It shows a hand holding a phallus combined with a naos sistrum, Hathor's musical instrument. The conclusion

to be drawn from such a juxtaposition is clear enough. The goddesses of attraction both rouse Atum to ejaculatory activity and, as the Hand, the Lady of the Vulva associated with the female sexual organ, receive the semen of creation. Together they represent the dual feminine principle, the Mother and Daughter, associated with Atum's creative act—a duality ensuring the continuum of cosmos, the transformation from nothingness to the fullness of being, from darkness to light, the emanation of existence from inchoate primeval beginnings. Here at Heliopolis the beginnings of the world are expressed by patterns of sexual activity. Atum's seed is emitted in a great blast, spewing forth the world in sexual delight, but at the same time there would be neither cosmos nor seed without the goddesses who give Atum the whole possibility of being.

Whether the obelisk and podium towering above Niuserre's sacred enclosure at Abu Ghurob architecturally symbolize Atum's sexual activity on the primeval mound is open to speculation. Is the obelisk a pillar of light for catching and focusing the rays of the sun? Or is it essentially phallic in nature, the ancient stone at the centre of the primeval hill where cosmos dynamically began, a great conductor for channelling cosmic creative energy? Or are we looking at a grave mound, shaped like the mastaba tombs of Old Kingdom Egypt, intended for the renewal of life? Who can say, when so little is known about the cults practised in third millennium Egypt. But in the temple at Heliopolis itself there was indeed a sacred stone named the *Benben*-stone which, in origin at least, may be safely described as the stone of Atum. That is, of course, if we follow Henri Frankfort's convincing suggestion that *benben* derived from a root *bn(n)*, which has a number of meanings including 'to swell', 'pour

out', 'become erect', and 'ejaculate'.[12] Such a holy stone connected with the myth of creation by masturbation belonged in the Heliopolitan sanctuary. Later, under the influence of solar religion, this stone of origins becomes a stone of light, and much play is made between the word 'to shine' *(wbn)* and the name of the stone *(bnbn)*.

So, we have to imagine the temples of Heliopolis as vast mounds, open to the air, with everything in the sacred architecture designed to take the Heliopolitan king, and his high priest, 'the Greatest of Seers', into contact with these dynamic beginnings of cosmos, to the source of creative energy. His appearance within the Heliopolitan temenos is vividly encapsulated in the following lines from a *Pyramid Text*:

Rise upon it,
  This land which came forth as Atum,
  The spittle which came forth as Khepri,
Take your form upon it,
Rise high upon it,
  That your father may see you,
  That Re may see you. (PT §199)

And very much part of this Heliopolitan spitting, emanating world of creation is the sistrum, with its snake rhythms and bars crashing against the frame of the superstructure, compelling the gaze of the sun god towards the king.

Indeed, scenes on blocks from Akhenaten's open-air temples at Thebes show his wife, Nefertiti, rattling her sistrum in the cult of the Aten. Long since dismantled and used as filling in the huge pylons of the Karnak temple, these solar sanctuaries originally lay to the east of the Amun temple at Karnak; and it is patently clear that the open-air cult for which they were designed had its roots in Heliopolis. One temple is even named 'the Mansion of the *Benben* Stone', its walls being once adorned with reliefs of Nefertiti raising offerings to the solar orb.

12
'Beauty is come': Akhenaten and Nefertiti

Left 146 Amenhotep IV (Akhenaten) (Statue from his temple at Karnak now in the Egyptian Museum, Cairo)

Right 147 Head of a young queen (probably Nefertiti) from el-Amarna (State Museum, Berlin)

influence her son. Indeed scenes at el-Amarna show her feasting with Akhenaten and his family (pl 163) or accompanied by him to one of the sun temples.

NEFERTITI: THE BEAUTIFUL ONE IS COME

Whether Akhenaten and Nefertiti ever lived at Thebes is unknown. But certainly from the early years of the king's reign onwards, Nefertiti, whose name means 'the Beautiful One is come', appears alongside Akhenaten as the radiant feminine influence in the land (pl 145).

Where she came from or who she was remains a mystery. Her parents are never mentioned on the monuments, which may indicate that she was of non-royal birth or perhaps even a foreigner.[3]

But whatever her origins, her share in rulership was considerable. Like the Pharaoh she appears in active aggressive roles, smiting enemies with her scimitar, or as a raging lioness in the form of a combative sphinx. Bound captives are also shown in the decoration at the base of her throne. None of this is strictly new, however, since Akhenaten's mother, Queen Teye, had also been depicted as a female sphinx trampling enemies in the previous reign.

But what is interesting is that Nefertiti, for some unknown reason, seems to have aroused particular hatred and become an object of vilification in later years. So, for example, in contrast to the face of Akhenaten which is usually left untouched on monuments at Karnak, the features of Nefertiti's face have often been

I T HAS BEEN SUGGESTED that Akhenaten may have been in his late twenties when he succeeded to the throne of Egypt. This is on the grounds that the Jubilee Festival he celebrated early in his reign may have been to mark his thirtieth birthday. Usually a king celebrated his first Sed Festival after a thirty year period on the throne, and it seems a plausible explanation as to why Akhenaten, ever the radical, may have chosen to celebrate such a festival so early in his reign.[1]

A little of his wayward character may also be gleaned from letters written by Tushratta, king of Mitanni, to Akhenaten's mother Queen Teye.

Tushratta was not a little put out by Akhenaten's gifts of gilded statues in place of the high quality ones he had been accustomed to receive from Amenhotep III. In one letter to Teye he writes: 'The words which you have spoken to me with your own mouth, why have you not raised the matter with Napkhururiya (Akhenaten)?'[2] And he continues by saying that if Teye fails to discuss this with Akhenaten no one else will do so.

Apart from the intriguing glimpse it gives into Queen Teye's standing both in Egypt and abroad, it also suggests that she was especially close to Akhenaten, being the only one able to

hacked out with a hammer and chisel, as if she were the greater villain of the reign.

Initially, however, the royal couple were content to keep a connection with Thebes, where they dedicated a number of sun temples to the Aten. The remains of these have been discovered in some of the massive pylons in the Amun temple at Karnak, in the form of thousands of sandstone blocks called *talatat* which were used by later kings as filling for the pylons after the sun temples had been dismantled. The painstaking reconstruction by the Akhenaten Temple Project of the contexts in which these individual blocks originally belonged, has brought to light a vivid picture of these early years. A picture showing Akhenaten and Nefertiti already set on a course doomed to bring them into conflict with the powerful Theban priesthood.[4]

For there is no trace on these blocks of the realm ruled by the Theban deities, nothing whatsoever to suggest cults in the secret hidden interiors of temples. All is solar, though it is true to say that Akhenaten had not yet become the complete iconoclast of his later years.

Such features as the hawk-headed figure of Re-Harakhti are still to be seen, as well as the striking face of

Hathor on the handles of the sistra which Queen Teye or Nefertiti shake in the cult. Also, on blocks recovered from the Ninth Pylon at Karnak, there are the same dance scenes for Hathor as in Kheruef's tomb (chapter three). Evidently the journey to dawn with the night-time goddess of Gold was still meaningful enough to be shown on Theban Aten temple walls at the beginning of Akhenaten's reign.[5]

But portrayals of the couple embracing, like Hathor and Re, as they ride in a chariot from the palace to the temple beneath the solar orb; or officiating before open-air altars laden with blazing offerings, their flames licking the

rays of the sun, provide a foretaste of what was to come.

At this stage Akhenaten was still calling himself Amenhotep—'Amun-is-Content'—so retaining a token relationship with the Theban god. Moreover, the group of some thirty colossal statues, which originally stood in one or another of the solar temples at Karnak, still show the king holding the traditional crook and flail of rulership.

Yet at the same time all artistic conventions have been flouted in these statues. Gone is the classical royal physique of broad chest and shoulders, flat stomach, and taut hips. Instead the statues portray Akhenaten's refined intelligent face, elongated in shape and broad-lipped, supported by a body displaying a naked swollen abdomen and bulbous thighs that taper into slender limbs—details taken almost to the point of caricature in some examples from the beginning of his reign.

Somehow Egyptian artists had to come to terms with this radical new image of the Pharaoh; and clearly too Akhenaten had lost no time in instructing particular sculptors as to how he wished to be depicted in Theban temples. Nor can there be any mistake about the nature of his kingship on these Theban statues. Cartouches, containing the new names of the trinitarian sun god, have been moulded in such a way that they stand out on his body, branding him eternally with the mark of his solar kingship. A conflict was bound to come with the Theban clergy, and events soon began to take a more dramatic turn.

Nowhere are the abrupt changes more startlingly revealed than in Ramose's tomb on the west bank at Thebes. Ramose is usually thought to

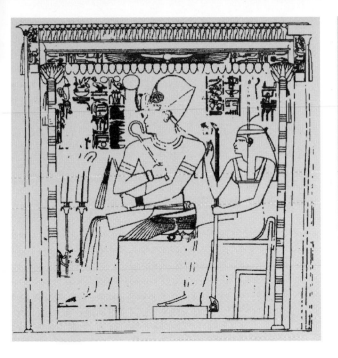

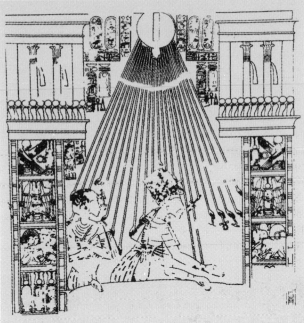

have been vizier of the South under Amenhotep III as well as during the early phase of Akhenaten's reign—a post which meant he was in charge of all the government offices in the southern part of the country. In contrast to the usual scenes painted directly onto suitably smoothed walls in Theban tombs, those in Ramose's tomb have been carved into the limestone, with the result that delicate reliefs of great beauty adorn the walls of the hall. They are typical of the high artistic quality achieved at Thebes during Amenhotep III's reign, another example being Kheruef's tomb with its scenes of Amenhotep III's Sed Festival (chapter three). They may well have been executed by skilful Memphite artists from the North accustomed to working in limestone, especially as Ramose himself came from a family having strong links with Memphis.

Tradition still holds in the scenes on the east wall of the hall, which portray Ramose and his wife and family at a banquet, the performance of funerary rites, and also chantresses bringing the blessings of Amun and Hathor, probably in connection with the annual Feast of the Valley celebrated at Thebes (pl 17).

Across from these scenes on the west wall of Ramose's hall, Akhenaten (or Amenhotep as he is still named) is shown enthroned impassively together with the goddess Maat in conventional style (pl 152).

Then suddenly new instructions must have been given to the artists working on the tomb—or perhaps even new artists brought in—for, on the other side of the doorway here on the western side, Akhenaten and Nefertiti appear in the new style, leaning over a palace balcony as they reward Ramose with gold necklaces (pl 153). But that is not all. Ramose, himself, and the other court officials, are no longer shown as vigorous well-proportioned Egyptians, but rather with the long thin skull, thin neck and arms, typical of Amarna figures. And all bow low in deference to their ruler. What became of Ramose we do not know. His tomb at Thebes was never finished, and he is nowhere

Left 152 Amenhotep IV (Akhenaten) seated in a kiosk with the goddess Maat in traditional Theban style (Relief in the tomb of Ramose at Thebes)

Right 153 Akhenaten and Nefertiti stand on a palace balcony beneath the raying hands of the Aten depicted in the new Amarna style (Relief in the tomb of Ramose at Thebes)

Facing page 151 A group of weeping women taking part in Ramose's funeral procession (Relief in the tomb of Ramose at Thebes)

to be seen in the new capital shortly to be built in Middle Egypt. But these scenes in his tomb leave little doubt that the storm clouds must have been gathering over the southern capital, that a major upheaval was imminent in the country.

SHATTERING IMAGES: CONSECRATING FIRE

Sometime in the fifth year of his reign Akhenaten's burning zeal seems to have made it impossible to keep up any pretence of traditional kingship or links with the Theban Amun-Re. He dropped the name of Amun and

took a new name, calling himself Akhenaten (which can be translated as 'The-Beneficial-One-for-the-Aten' or perhaps as 'Emanation-of-Aten'), a name evoking the shining, exalted state in which the king perpetually walked during his lifetime on earth. He is an *Akh*, a 'transfigured one', who stands in the horizon between heaven and earth, mediating the radiance and power of the eternal sun god through his effective deeds on earth. Henceforth he was to be known as:

The Living Horus:
Mighty Bull, beloved of Aten:
Two Ladies:
Great of Kingship in the Light-Land-of-Aten:
Horus of Gold, who exalts the name of Aten:
The King of Upper and Lower Egypt
who lives by Maat,
The Lord of the Two Lands:
Beautiful-of-Transformations-is-Re,
Sole-One-of-Re:
The Son of the Sun who lives by Maat:
Lord of Diadems: Akhenaten,
Great in his lifetime, given life forever.[6]

Nefertiti too added a new name, Nefer-Neferu-Aten 'Beautiful-are-the-Beauties-of-Aten', to her own, as together they set out on a path of fire to found a new royal capital called Akhetaten or 'Light-Land-of-Aten', which they dedicated to the Sole God of Egypt.

The site chosen for Akhetaten (which is generally referred to by its modern name of el-Amarna) was a largely uncultivated territory in Middle Egypt, on the east bank of the river across from Hermopolis, the city sacred to the moon god, Thoth.

Here, rugged steep cliffs form an immense protective semi-circle around a hot sandy bay, about thirteen kilometres long and five kilometres broad, the plain of el-Amarna. Tunnelled into the sides of the cliffs are tombs of officials who served Akhenaten, which contain so much of the information about these extraordinary events.

Also hewn out of the cliffs are eleven majestic stelae, each inscribed with a text in which Akhenaten defines the sacred space of his city and vows never to extend its boundaries.[7] Across on the other bank of the Nile, three more stelae hewn in the lime-stone of the Libyan mountain chain

Right 156 Nefertiti, accompanied by her daughter, worships the Aten. The absence of the Pharaoh in such scenes highlights the unique importance of Nefertiti in the solar cult at Karnak (Reconstructed scenes on a gateway of the Benben temple at Karnak)

mark the western boundaries of the city (pl 155). It is instructive that Akhenaten also records on the stelae that he ordered a tomb to be made in Akhetaten for the holy Mnevis Bull of Heliopolis—a sure sign indeed that the traditions of Heliopolis had been transferred to new royal territory in Middle Egypt.

Why did Akhenaten choose this site? Why go to such lengths to build a new city? Why could he not simply have based himself at Heliopolis?

Almost certainly because he was too radical even for Heliopolis, as he strove to provide an entirely different basis for Egyptian kingship, one which needed fresh territory if it were to grow and flourish. Though Heliopolis might provide the foundation for the new religion, untried ways needed to be found if it were to bloom and flower.

There must have been a mass exodus from Egyptian cities in order to build a city from scratch—artists, sculptors, craftsmen, brewers, bakers, farmers, bricklayers, soldiers and generals—all were needed in the new city. The scribes came too, taking with them official documents, including the famous diplomatic correspondence written in cuneiform script on clay tablets, which were found by a local Egyptian farmer digging for fertilizer in 1887.

The same fervour and energy that built the cathedrals in the Middle Ages seems to have flowed at el-Amarna, for in an incredibly short space of time, a city complete with sun temples, mud-brick palaces decorated with exquisite murals and painted floors, villas with gardens,

military barracks and living quarters for the work-force, all sprang up out of nowhere as miraculously as the dawning of Aten each day.

This cannot have been the work of a weak, effete individual, as some have claimed Akhenaten to be. Besides his spiritual qualities, a certain ruthlessness and driving will must have been needed to carry through such a revolutionary step.

Nor was this achieved without the help of the military, who are everywhere to be seen in Amarna reliefs; and the king himself is saluted by his soldiers as 'the one who trains the groups eligible for the military'.[8]

Akhenaten was certainly extreme, as we can glean in the following passage from an intriguing letter, which was found in the Amarna correspondence, sent by Ashuruballit I, the king of Assyria, to the Egyptian court. He complains bitterly to the Egyptian

Right 158 View of the largely ruined smaller Aten temple at el-Amarna. The main entrance was between two pylon towers and a large altar stood in the centre of the first courtyard. It has been suggested that the temple's axis was deliberately oriented towards the royal wadi in the desert hills where the royal tomb was located

king that his messengers have been made to stand in the fierce heat of the sun when they came to Egypt:

Why are my messengers kept standing in the open sun? They will die in the open sun. If standing in the open sun is profitable for the king, then let the king stand there and die in the open sun. Then will there be profit for the king! But really, why should they die in the open sun? . . . They will be killed in the open sun.[9]

Like his father before him, Akhenaten seems to have cared little about any rules of hospitality for visitors to Egypt. Amenhotep III had also been

Above 157 Wild ducks flying in the papyrus marshes. Floor painting from a royal palace at el-Amarna (Egyptian Museum, Cairo)

Facing page 159 The uraeus rears up on the brow of Akhenaten who wears the Blue Crown (Relief in the Royal Scottish Museum, Edinburgh)

reprimanded, in his case by the king of Babylon, for the way he treated the Babylonian envoys in Egypt—an accusation which he hotly denied, however, replying that the Babylonian messengers were untruthful about their stay in Egypt: 'Whether I give them something or whether I do

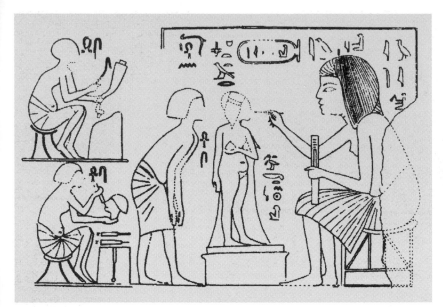

not give them, they speak so . . . Do not listen to them, your messengers whom you send here, whose mouths are hateful.'[10]

WINDOW OF APPEARANCES: THE ART OF JOY

Yet however intolerable Akhenaten may have been in pursuit of his vision, the lyrical hymns he composed are deeply moving in their eloquent universal praise of life, reaching out as they do to embrace all races and countries. The following lines from the famous *Great Hymn to the Aten*—a hymn which has often been compared to the Biblical Psalm 104—serve to illustrate this. It is inscribed in the tomb of Ay, one of the king's most trusted counsellors at el-Amarna:

Above 160 Yuti, the chief sculptor of Queen Teye, finishes a statue of princess Baketaten in his studio. In contrast with traditional Egyptian art, the names of the Amarna artists are mentioned in inscriptions (Relief in the tomb of Huya at el-Amarna)

Below 161 Painting from a royal palace showing two small princesses affectionately embracing as they sit together on cushions (Ashmolean Museum, Oxford)

Right 162 Unfinished quartzite head of a queen from el-Amarna (Egyptian Museum, Cairo)

How manifold are your deeds,
Though hidden from sight,
O Sole God,
Beside whom there is no other.
You have created the earth
As you desired, being alone,
With people, herds and flocks,
All upon earth that walk on legs,
All on high that fly with wings,
The lands of Khor and Kush,
The land of Egypt,
You set all in their places,
You supply their needs,
Everyone has food,
His lifetime is counted.
Their tongues differ in speech,
Their characters likewise,
Their skins are distinct,
For you differentiated
The foreign people.[11]

Such lyrical poeticism, which is a feature of all the hymns, can only have arisen from experience deeply felt. Moreover, there is a strangely contemporary ring about this acceptance of a diverse, multi-cultural world. No longer are foreigners to be pitied for not being Egyptian. On the contrary, cultural differences are

Left 163 Akhenaten, Nefertiti and their family entertain Queen Teye at a lavish banquet. The names of the Aten within cartouches are in the later form (Scene in the tomb of Huya, who was Queen Teye's steward at el-Amarna)

Below left 164 Akhenaten and Nefertiti embrace as they ride together in a chariot (Sketch in the tomb of Ahmose at el-Amarna)

usual anonymity of Egyptian artists (pl 160); and according to Bak, whose father, Men, was a sculptor working in Amenhotep III's reign, he was instructed by Akhenaten himself, being 'under the supervision of his Majesty'.[12]

Despite the fact that Akhetaten was subsequently dismantled (probably in the 19th Dynasty), we can tell from the remaining fragments how the floors and walls of the mud-brick palaces must once have been adorned with beautiful mural paintings and glazed tiles, showing the plenitude of nature—pied kingfishers diving down into the water for fish, brightly coloured plants with flights of wild birds, frisking calves leaping in the sun, all painted with a freshness of colour and movement which characterizes so much of Amarna art, and brings to mind the liveliness of Cretan work (pl 157).

Now too artists were permitted to convey the spontaneity of human feelings on a scale never imagined hitherto, indeed the expression of such affection seems to have been positively encouraged.

So we see Akhenaten and Nefertiti kissing and embracing each other as they ride in their chariot through the streets of Akhetaten (pl 164); or they lounge together in one of the palaces, idly playing with their daughters, surrounding them with love and affection (pl 165).

On another occasion they appear at a banquet, feasting together on roast duck, meat on skewers, and other

affirmed as revelations of the richness and multiplicity of a diverse world, spawned forth by the beneficent Creator. A connectedness weaves through the whole of life, a unity flows through everything.

All this continuous flow of solar life is also captured in the art of the period. Ever the radical, Akhenaten changed the traditional artistic canon to accommodate the elongated figures so characteristic of Amarna art. Likewise, the surfaces of sculpture and stelae, the latter often heavily incised, were specially designed for the play of light and shade when they were placed in outdoor settings.

Moreover, the identities of the people who bequeathed so much beauty were no longer cloaked in the

delicacies as they lavishly entertain Akhenaten's mother, Queen Teye (pl 163). Another delightful fragment shows two princesses squatting together on cushions, tenderly embracing each other (pl 161). Their faces are painted reddish-brown rather than the yellow customary for females in traditional art, perhaps because this red colour represents vital energy, a sign that their bodies carry solar life.

For the first time in the history of Egypt a royal couple and their children are consistently portrayed in the intimate, unmistakable setting of Akhetaten, a city bathed and transfigured by light. And it is also noteworthy that in this radical shift, attempts were made for the first time to convey three-dimensionality in art, to portray external images as they were actually seen. So, for example, hands and feet were now 'correctly' drawn. Moreover, the classical written language too was updated to reproduce more closely the spoken idioms of the time, a development which led to the creation of the Late Egyptian language which continued after Akhenaten's death.

Egypt was being wrenched into a completely new contemporary world, and the scale of what the king was trying to achieve is breathtaking. Yet it was also a world in which no decay or death—no dissolution, diminution or wearing out of forms—could be

allowed to disturb the flow of solar radiance and life welling up in the midst of creation.

But here and there we also catch a glimpse reminding us of another side to this seemingly unending happiness. Scenes in the royal tomb (pl 166), which is located in a remote desert ravine behind el-Amarna, convey a rare moment of sorrow in the palace as the grief-stricken king and queen mourn the death of Meketaten, one of their six daughters.[13] It has been suggested that the princess died in childbirth (the fate of many women

in ancient Egypt) since amongst the mourners in this chamber of death, is a woman holding a baby, presumably the child to whom the princess had just given birth so shortly before.

Much weeping and wailing surround the royal couple as they stand before the funerary bier on which their daughter lies, drained of all life, her stiff inert body making a chilling contrast to the usual mobile forms in the City of the Sun. Pierced by grief, Akhenaten, Nefertiti and the other mourners hold up a hand before their faces in the gesture of all who lament

166 *Akhenaten and Nefertiti and others in the royal circle mourn a mother who has died in childbirth. In a similar scene depicted in another chamber of the royal tomb the mother is named as their second daughter, princess Meketaten. Weeping women are shown accompanying the royal couple, including a woman holding a child in her arms (Relief in the royal tomb at el-Amarna)*

Right 167 *The royal family worship the Aten, the outward manifestation of divinity in Amarna religion (Egyptian Museum, Cairo)*

the dead in Egypt. And somehow the rays of the Aten shining above seem strangely untouched by the pain and suffering of mortal existence, distant and unconsoling at such a moment of profound sadness. Where can comfort be sought when everything relating to change and death, to the cult of the dead, had been so drastically abandoned?

For a brief moment, the rays of the Aten appear a little brittle over such a scene of pathos, serving to remind us

of one important reason why Akhenaten's successors drew back from following in his footsteps. One reason why they felt compelled to return to the pantheon, to a deity 'who hears pleas', who takes pity on the poor and suffering.

But we need to look a little more closely at the expression of these universal insights in Amarna religion, at the inspiration guiding and shaping events in Akhetaten, and at its implications for the serpent goddess.

13 The Cosmic Gaze: A Rapturous Celebration

WHILST MUSING ON 'the eye' as a cosmic principle, the French author Gaston Bachelard wrote: 'Everything that shines sees, and there is nothing in the world which shines more than a look'.[1]

He might well have been reflecting about Amarna religion, at least in its earlier phase, for the all-seeing celestial 'gaze' looking down on a radiant world is constantly praised in Amarna hymns. The *Great Hymn to the Aten*, for example, says

Your rays nurse all fields,
  When you shine they live, they grow for you,
You make the seasons
  To nurture all that you engender,
Springtime to cool them,
  Heat that they may taste you,
You made the distant sky to shine therein,
  To behold all that you make.
Being alone, you have appeared
  In your manifestation as living Aten,
Risen and radiant,
  Distant and near.[2]

Like a gigantic eye in the sky, the Aten watches over earth, sustaining all the conditions needed for life, including the changing seasons of the year —'springtime to cool them, heat that they may taste you'. This mention of the seasons brings to mind once more

the influence of Heliopolis on Akhenaten, not least the lovely 'Room of the Seasons' in King Niuserre's Old Kingdom sun temple at Abu Ghurob (pl 142) with its once dazzling wall paintings illustrating the different flora and fauna throughout the three seasons of the Egyptian year. Here at Akhetaten we find similar themes in Akhenaten's hymns.

But not only is the celestial deity all-seeing. Living creatures too have been blessed with eyes, so that they may delight in this warmth and flow of solar life. When earth brightens at dawn, all eyes open to behold the manifold beauty of the world, made manifest in the light.

Earth erupts in spontaneous praise, as all gaze fixedly, rapt in joy, upon this manifestation of their creator, upon whom they depend for their life and existence:

When you have dawned they live,
  When you set they die,
You yourself are lifetime,
  One lives through you,
And all eyes are on beauty
  Until you set.[3]

THE SNAKE IN THE SUN: SEEING UNITY

From the standpoint of our goddess Hathor, who after all is also the 'Sun Eye', it is of interest that the same affective qualities she radiates also emanate from the Aten.

In one sense the goddess *is* still there, the uraeus serpent is not forgotten, its rearing head being always visible at the base of the celestial solar orb in Amarna iconography and also on the brow of the Pharaoh. Moreover, Nefertiti embraces Akhenaten exactly as if she is Hathor-Maat uniting with the sun god, manifesting for all to see the mysteries of solar rulership (pl 164). What had once been veiled in the secrecy of the temple cult is now openly revealed. Likewise, hymns praise the attraction and beauty

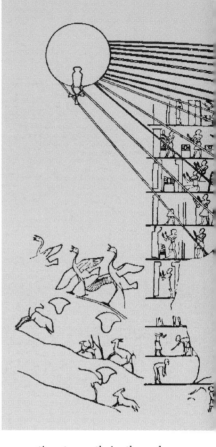

emanating to earth in the solar rays, touching hearts, eliciting joyous responses:

You are glittering, beauteous, mighty,
  Your attraction is great, immense,
Your rays light up all faces,
  Your bright hues give life to hearts,
When you fill the Two Lands
  With your attraction.[4]

The intoxicating, dynamic power we have come to associate with Hathor is everywhere in Akhetaten:

All living plants which grow on earth
  Flourish when you shine,
They are drunk at your face.
  All herds dance.[5]

Fructifying warmth, light and desire flow through the whole of creation. And there is great rejoicing as all peoples, herds, flocks, fowl, fish and feathered creatures join together in the

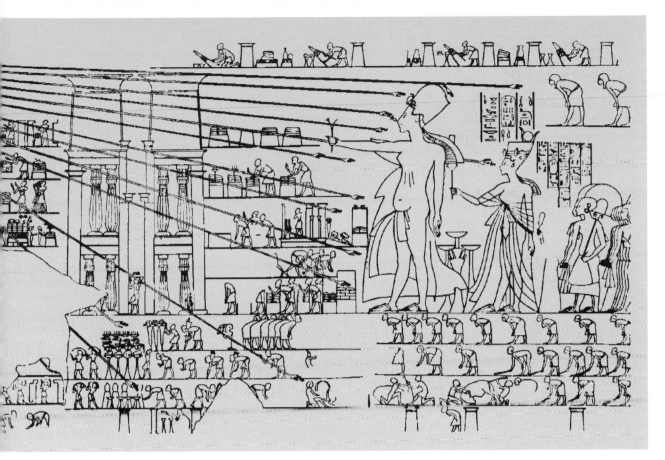

dance of life, growing, moving, frisking, flying, darting and leaping, all at one beneath the life-giving shining Aten. Flowing garments, flags and streamers fluttering in the breeze—all add to the movement, colour and gaiety in 'The Lightland of the Sun'. Music, too, rings out from the *Benben* temple in the city:

Musicians and chantresses
  Shout for joy
In the court of the Benben temple,
  And every temple in Akhetaten.[6]

Indeed, female members of the royal family are shown as musical leaders of this praise, rattling their sistra in the cult of the Aten.

But there is a crucial difference. No longer is the cow-eared face of Hathor shown on the handles of their musical instruments, which are almost invariably the loop sistrum. For this type

does not have any connotations of dark temple interiors, of the naos-shrine with its cult image, as is the case with the naos sistrum type.

Nor are there any traces of Hathor's numerous other manifestations in Amarna iconography. And in this respect the goddess we have known with Re no longer exists, since she has shed all semblances of her tree, animal or human forms. The heavy cumbersome body of the Hathor cow, wearing her *menit*-necklace, has gone; so too has the mediating graceful figure of the goddess shaking her sistrum. No longer is the serpent goddess differentiated and projected forth from the sun god as a beneficent-destructive force in the ceaseless world of change and becoming, the goddess with whom he experiences the whole course of human life in the unfolding of a day. Now her serpentine female energy is

coiled back, fused with the Aten. And her solar attraction manifests in another dimension ruled by the celestial 'eye of light', a dimension in which the vast energy of the sun streams forth each day at dawn, replenishing the myriad creatures of the world, bestowing on them the gift of radiant life.

She is not the goddess of traditional religion, reconcilable with endless cycles of transformations, associated with a god who sinks into the regenerative waters of Nun each night, returning as a radiant child at dawn, just as the moon is reborn each month again at the time of the new moon. A

170, 171 Paired scenes on a block from Hermopolis showing different functions of Nefertiti. On the left both queen and Akhenaten hold a sekhem-sceptre as an authoritative symbol of their power in the cult of the celestial Aten. Behind them is the small figure of their eldest daughter, Meretaten, shaking a loop sistrum. On the right Nefertiti and Meretaten appear as praisers of the Aten, shaking loop sistra behind Akhenaten. Note the absence of the traditional Hathor face between the handle and frame of the sistra. Here the queen's ritual action associates her with her daughter. Both females appear as members of the royal family within the social hierarchy of Egypt ruled by Akhenaten as described in Amarna royal inscriptions. Such iconographic details were obviously carefully chosen to reveal different aspects of Nefertiti's queenship (Egyptian Museum, Cairo)

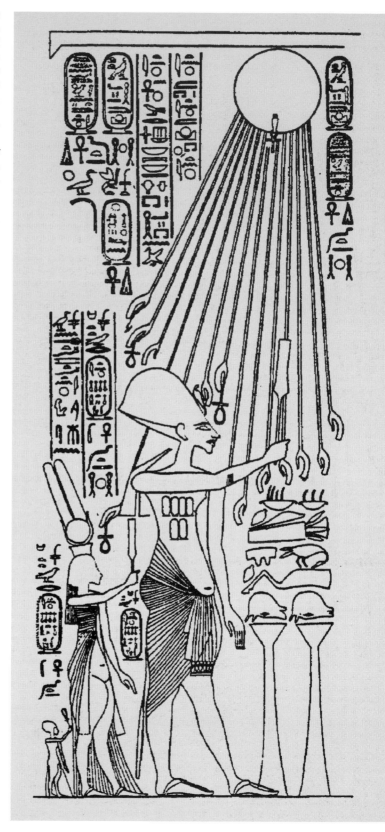

sun god who traverses through the phases of life as child, youth, mature ruler and old man with the goddesses, a god who journeys through the divisions of both night and day, a sun in time regulated by the moon god, Thoth, a sun in fragmented time, time in which there is 'Yesterday' and 'Tomorrow', and a whole host of manifestations, births and rebirths, endless appearances and disappearances, processions and epiphanies, changes and renewals.

All this was not for Akhenaten, with his eyes firmly fixed on the celestial sun. In the city of Akhetaten, the moon is sundered from the sun. And time is no longer regulated by Thoth, the god of neighbouring Hermopolis across the water, with all his days, nights, months and years, his manifold measurements and divisions. Time belongs utterly and entirely to the sun, and nothing but the sun.

Life in the cult exists in the stream and current of time called *neheh*, sometimes translated as 'eternity'. It is the rhythm of day and night, light and darkness, the streaming forth of creation at sunrise, the vanishing of the world at sunset, a ceaseless pulsating

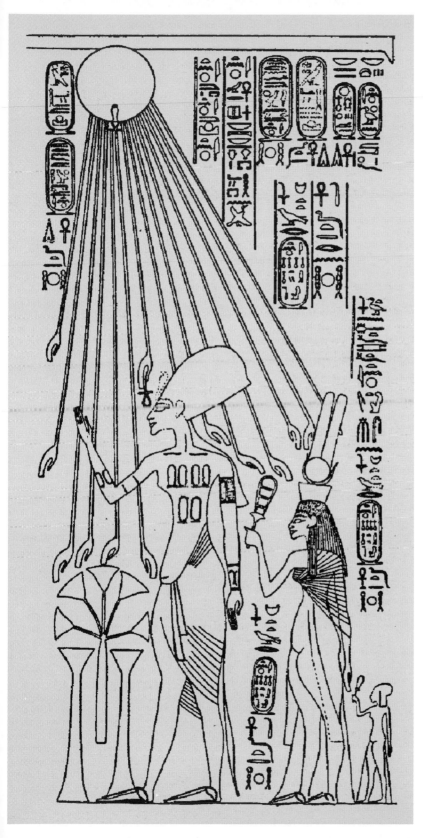

flow of light, constantly replenishing the myriad creatures of existence, then withdrawing again at night to leave all in rest and sleep.

In such time Akhenaten lives, moves and has his being as the Son of the Aten. And he celebrates this great cosmic rhythm in his chant of praise which begins with the words

Beautiful your rising in the lightland of sky,
*   O living Aten, Creator of life,*
When you have dawned in eastern lightland,
*   You fill every land with your beauty.*
You are beauteous, great, glittering,
*   High over every land,*
Your rays embrace the lands,
*   To the limits of all that you have made.*

When darkness falls it is the time of the deity's absence, the time when evil creatures emerge to trouble the world as the deity rests. The hymn continues

When you set in western lightland,
*   Earth is in darkness, as if in death.*
They sleep in chambers, heads covered,
*   One eye does not see another,*
If robbed of goods from under their heads,
*   They would not notice it.*
Every lion comes from its den,
*   All snakes bite,*
Darkness is a tomb, earth is silent,
*   As their Maker rests in his lightland.*[7]

This is the sun in the time of eternity. There is no journey through the divisions of the night in the Underworld, no raising up of the sun in the East and drawing down into the West, with all the attendant dangers traditional sun religion seeks to keep at bay. As in the Sufi metaphysical experience of subsistence and light alternating with annihilation and darkness, so too in Amarna religion there is a similar expanding and contracting movement within creation.

It is interesting, however, that Akhenaten still talks of 'propitiating the Aten' in Amarna hymns—a hint perhaps of the immense control needed to gaze into the dawn of

Above 172 Sculptor's trial piece with portrait heads of Akhenaten (Egyptian Museum, Cairo)

Facing page 173 Fecundity figure bearing offerings (Relief in the temple of Ramesses II at Abydos)

creation each day and to see, in this vast emanation of fiery solar energy, beneficent fructifying warmth streaming forth to earth. The devotion and reverence engendered by such an experience can be sensed in the beautiful lyricism of Akhenaten's hymns.

LIGHT, LIFE, SUSTENANCE: AN OVERFLOWING WORLD

So far we have dwelt on the solar light and life of the Creator, but there is a third, equally important, aspect which constantly recurs in Amarna religion—sustenance. Light, life and sustenance: these are the three strands continually running through the Amarna hymns.

Frequently, in traditional religion, food and sustenance are said to be the gifts of the annual Nile inundation, personified by the strange figure of Hapy, who is shown with a protruding belly and pendulous breasts, bearing food aloft in his hands. Everything in

his iconography points to the fecund life which comes forth with the returning waters each year (pl 173). But Akhenaten reshaped this relationship of food with the Nile into a strong avowal that the waters depend utterly on light. Now it is Aten who creates Hapy. Light controls the rhythm of the inundation waters

You made Hapy in the Dwat,
  You bring him as you desire,
To preserve the people,
  Even as you made them for yourself.[8]

Light is the true source of sustenance, the vital force needed for growth in plants and animals.

Such proclamations of light as the source of fecund life on earth help to explain Akhenaten's puzzling physiognomy in reliefs and sculpture, which has led some to conclude that he was either suffering from pathological illness or obsessed with candid portrayals of his actual physique—explanations which, however, entirely ignore the religious intent that lies behind so much of Amarna art.

In the first place, the king's emphasized breasts and protruding belly bring to mind the bodily characteristics

of the inundation god, Hapy. When this similarity is set alongside the hymns in which Akhenaten is praised by his subjects as an incarnation of Hapy then the link becomes even more plausible. Again and again, the bounty of the king is stressed by his followers, who hail him as, 'This thousandfold Hapy overflowing every day'.[9] And again, 'Hapy overflowing every day who preserves Egypt'.[10]

Or again, an official in Akhetaten describes his relationship with Akhenaten in the following way:

I propitiate him who lives by truth,
The Lord of Diadems, Akhenaten,
Great in his lifetime.
O Hapy, by whose command
One is powerful
The food and nourishment of Egypt,
The vital ruler who forms me,
Makes me, fosters me . . .
My Ka day by day.[11]

As the food-giving power, Akhenaten creates overflowing abundance in the city. Moreover, those stelae showing Akhenaten and Nefertiti together with their daughters, should also be understood as symbolizing the abundance of life embodied by the couple and not just as 'naturalistic' glimpses into palace life (pls 165, 179).[12]

The idea of the king as the guarantor of Egypt's fertility—as responsible for guiding, preserving and ensuring the fruitfulness of earth for his people—is by no means a new theme in royal eulogies. What is so startling in Amarna religion is the way this is so unequivocally linked with light. And nothing else but light.

Thus, to the sky belong light and life, emanating forth from a heavily incised convex orb of the sun, which is almost three-dimensional in appearance. From this globe arms extend downwards in rays of light, some holding out *Ankh*-signs of life towards the fecund figures of the king and queen, surrounding them with solar energy and radiance. And the living power which Akhenaten receives from the sun, he, in turn, feeds to his people, maintaining life on earth. It is said of him that he 'endows his house of everlastingness with millions and hundreds of thousands of things, who exalts Aten and magnifies his name'.[13]

Together the Aten and the king, the celestial manifestation of the divine Father and the terrestrial incarnation of the Son, share in the co-rulership of heaven and earth, symbolized by the fact that the Aten's names are inscribed in two cartouches exactly like the king's, and dated monuments are ascribed jointly to them. Together they embody light, life and sustenance in the kingdom.

Moreover, Akhenaten must have been well aware of how these embracing arms of the Aten might strike an initiated Egyptian. For there was a long-standing tradition of deities enfolding their offspring in a vitalizing embrace. For example, when Atum spat out Shu and Tefenet on the primeval hill, he poured life into them by taking them in his arms so that his *Ka* was in them. Or it is said of Osiris that he placed his arms around Horus

in order to become the *Ka* of his son. Henri Frankfort well articulated the significance of the embrace in Egyptian religion when he wrote that it is 'no mere sign of affection, but a true fusion, a communion between two living spirits, *unio mystica*'.[14]

Yet, and this is important, Akhenaten is not embraced by the supportive upward-reaching *Ka*-arms of the deity, but rather by arms which stretch downwards from the celestial orb above, arms which extend towards Akhenaten and Nefertiti on earth, perpetually transfiguring them in an embrace of light.

It is a startling translation, a new expression of the embrace between

Creator and offspring, which lays bare the meaning of Amarna rulership. Through this embrace the royal couple are quite literally and visually shown to be 'transfigured ones' in Akhetaten, in 'the Lightland of the Sun', their bodies infused with the divine power of celestial light and life, leaving not the slightest shadow of doubt that they are indeed transformed children of light, nourished and surrounded by light.

And, in turn, the king together with Nefertiti embodies all the bounty of Egypt for his people on earth. He is their *Ka*. For just as the Aten in the sky extends life-giving arms to Akhenaten and Nefertiti, so their fecund forms

161

Above 174 Akhenaten and Nefertiti as cult incarnations of the Heliopolitan cosmic deities, Shu and Tefenet. They are accompanied by three daughters shaking loop sistra (Relief in the tomb of Apy, el-Amarna)

Facing page 175 Akhenaten and Nefertiti, accompanied by three princesses, mediate the divine radiance of the Aten for their subjects. The royal couple, illumined by solar rays, lean from the palace balcony to reward Ay with gold necklaces. As the Aten gives life to the king and queen, so they transmit blessings to their people, enabling the great current of solar life to flow between heaven and earth. Ay, who was one of Akhenaten's most trusted officials—and who subsequently became the king of Egypt after the death of Tutankhamun—is accompanied by his wife, the royal nurse Teye (Relief in the tomb of Ay at el-Amarna)

are shown standing in the Palace Window of Appearances, reaching out gifts to their loyal officials, who hold arms upraised in a *ka*-like gesture (pl 175). The couple sustain the unending flow of solar life in Egypt, and together with the Aten they represent a triadic focus for the cult at el-Amarna. Officials, some of whom Akhenaten had promoted from quite humble origins, built small shrines in the gardens of their luxurious villas. There were altars in these shrines on which were placed stelae showing the royal family worshipping the Aten and similar stelae were kept on altars in houses (pls 165,179).

Nevertheless, Akhenaten frequently emphasizes that he, and he alone, is the sole mediator of this divine life for

Egypt and that Nefertiti is subordinate to him in the social hierarchy of Egypt. As he himself declares at the close of the *Great Hymn to the Aten*:

There is no one who knows you
Except your son Akhenaten,
You teach him your ways and your might.[15]

No longer are the cult deities worshipped in the darkest regions of temples, no longer are they known through inner devotion of the heart, or propitiated through magical practices. Simply the Sole God of Egypt is mediated through Akhenaten, and Akhenaten alone. He, and he alone, understands the source of divine light and life. Scholars have quite rightly compared this intense focus on the Pharaoh with the high degree of centralization in Old Kingdom Egypt, a time when kings built pyramids around which their subjects clustered, dependent entirely on the monarch for their well-being. And though there had undoubtedly been an intense shift of religious focus since Old Kingdom times, nevertheless, here too, at el-Amarna, all is centred on the king, presiding in a city where everything is tinged, shot through with the sun.

THE TRIPLE CREATOR: NAMING SOVEREIGNTY

By now it must have become obvious that to describe Akhenaten and Nefertiti as hedonistic sun-worshippers falls very wide of the mark. As twin worshippers of the Aten at the dawn of creation, the royal couple are, in fact, identified with the first born pair of Atum, incarnations of Shu and Tefenet. This can be seen in plate 174 which shows the couple worshipping before an open-air altar, alight with blazing offerings, as the rays of the sun stream down from the celestial orb above surrounding them with light. The king holds cartouches containing the divine names of the Aten into the sun-rays, and flanking the cartouches on each side is a small figure crowned with the characteristic feathers of Shu.

Small though this detail may be, the figures serve to emphasize Akhenaten's connection with the air god. Behind him stands Nefertiti, robed in a long flowing gown, who holds aloft similar cartouches. These have a single female figure squatting beside the divine solar names, her hands raised in praise. She is the correlative of the Shu figures and can be none other than Tefenet here.

But if further proof be required of Akhenaten's aspirations, it is only necessary to look at the names of the sun god, royally enclosed in two cartouches on monuments, which explicitly set out the nature of the deity worshipped in the Lightland-of-the-Sun. Like all Egyptian names, this name had to express the power, qualities and attributes of its owner, had to unfold the divine being and essence.

But how to name a deity about whom it is said that he 'creates with his arms, whom the sculptors do not know'?[16] What could encapsulate such a 'formless' being, one who is unknowable, and of whom it is said that he shines 'in their faces, but no one knows your passage'?[17] A radiant being, who is completely distant, completely other, yet at the same time is also completely near—an ultimate, intimate reality. Such were the dilemmas Akhenaten faced in naming the deity worshipped at Akhetaten. And obviously he reflected deeply about this, so much so that a new version of the sun god's name was substituted in the cartouches later in his reign, indicative of the king's constant search for understanding throughout his lifetime.

For there was nothing static in the City of the Sun, but rather a continual quest for ways of encapsulating the Beauty and Unity flowing through creation, of comprehending the underlying wholeness of existence. Sometimes Amarna hymns refer to the androgynous nature of the creator, who is both Mother and Father in the world, tenderly 'nursing' and 'feeding' the embryo in the maternal womb, soothing and stilling the crying child

163

with all the nurturing care and concern of a mother. This androgyny is highlighted in the following lines from the *Shorter Hymn to the Aten*:

People, herds and flocks,
All trees that grow on earth,
They live when you dawn for them,
You are Mother and Father
For those whom you have made.[18]

However, this 'Mother' aspect of deity is not emphasized in the official cult, or at least not in the divine names. These focus rather on the trinitarian nature of the solar Creator, whose name, in its earlier version, appears in the double cartouche as:

Re-Harakhti-who-rejoices-in-the-Lightland-in-his-*Name*-and-in-the-*Sunlight*-(Shu)-which-is-in-the-*Aten*.

The unity of the solar creator, named here as Re-Harakhti (Re-Horus-of-the-Horizon), is revealed through the light

Below 176 First Dynasty comb from Abydos showing three aspects of Horus. The name of King Wadj is enclosed within a representation of the palace facade (serekh) surmounted by a Horus hawk (Egyptian Museum, Cairo)

raying from the solar orb containing the mystic name. He is the Sole God with three aspects defined as:

(1) *Name* Re-Horus-of-the-Horizon, who rejoices in the eastern horizon

(2) *Sunlight* Emanation in the sunlight. *Shu* the word for sunlight in Egyptian is also, of course, the name of the air god, Shu, and a deeply significant connection. In Amarna art this emanating aspect is symbolized by arms holding 'life'-signs raying down through the air from the solar globe, so emphasizing the 'life' aspect of the deity.

(3) *Image* Visible manifestation as the celestial orb of the sun named Aten, which is the focus of the cult at el-Amarna.

Plate 177 shows Akhenaten supporting the divine names of the trinitarian solar Creator. Like the names of the Egyptian king these are inscribed in two knotted loops (or cartouches) called *shenou*, symbolizing 'everything which the sun encircles'. Akhenaten's pose here closely resembles that of Shu bearing aloft the sky, and the comparison is hardly likely to be accidental.

It is possible that Akhenaten reached back to the very earliest period of Egyptian history for inspiration when formulating this divine name. For example three aspects of the hawk god, Horus, are portrayed on a First Dynasty ivory comb found at Abydos (c 3000 BC). At the bottom of the comb, a hawk perches on the palace facade (the *serekh*), which contains the name of Wadj, one of the First Dynasty kings (pl 176). He is the ruler inhabiting the palace on earth. Above is another compelling image of Horus, this time as a gigantic bird hovering in the air with outstretched wings, which curve towards *was* sceptres of dominion at each side, symbolizing rulership and great might. At the top of the comb is yet another image of the hawk, this time sailing in a boat across the sky like the New Kingdom zenithal sun god. Right at the very beginning of

Egyptian dynastic history, then, there is a triple hawk god identified with the Egyptian king, whose rule encompasses the three realms of earth, air and sky.

However, the impulse for Akhenaten's trinitarianism is much more likely to have originated in Hatshepsut's intensely creative reign. Her threefold understanding of Amun-Re created a religious form suited to the age of piety and personal devotion of the heart practised by New Kingdom Egyptians (chapter ten). Hatshepsut's adherence to Amun-Re must have been anathema to Akhenaten—reliefs at Deir el-Bahri and elsewhere at Thebes were deliberately damaged during his reign.

Nevertheless her threefold innovations still reverberate in Amarna religion, albeit reformulated in ways appropriate to the worship of the celestial Aten.

As we have already seen the threefold Amun-Re appears as an Image King, a Life Deity and Primordial God (chapter ten). Akhenaten must have been well-acquainted with this tradition, to the extent that this triplicity reappears, drastically re-worked, in his own solar threefold formulation some 150 years later.

Now, however, the 'Image' aspect no longer applies to an earthly god who rules Egypt and appears with all the regalia of the Theban cult image, but rather to the great orb of the sun which is the focus of cult worship at el-Amarna. Now too the 'Life' aspect of Amun-Re becomes a radiant 'eye of light' beaming through the air in sun-rays, which are represented in reliefs holding 'life'signs.

The primordial aspect no longer relates to the Osirian realm, but rather to the 'Name' of the deity rising in the eastern lightland. To name means to call into existence, to know the essence of a deity or a person, and in Akhenaten's formulation the solar divinity, the great cosmic spirit, is named as the celestial Re-Horus-of-the-Horizon, who rejoices in the eastern horizon, the primordial realm from whence creation is brought into existence anew each day.

Yet even though such links with Hatshepsut's reign can be traced for the earlier name, eventually Akhenaten broke away from any semblance of connection with existing Egyptian tradition. Sometime betwen years nine and twelve of his reign a new—and most carefully thought-out—name begins to appear on monuments. Gone is any reference to the 'Air' manifestation of the Creator—either as sunlight or as the air god, Shu. Gone too is mention of the hawk-headed Horus of the Horizon, the magnificent dawn bird.

Akhenaten seems to have climbed still further up the ladder to the sky, moving closer to the supernal solar triad, as he drops sunlight—the radiant element—from the divine names, replacing it with the solar Father. Now the threefold aspects are composed of (1) *Name* (2) *Father* (3) *Image* (visible orb of the sun), and read as follows:

Re-the-horizon-ruler-who-rejoices-in-the-Lightland-in his-*Name*-and-in-*Father*-Re-who-is-come-as-the-*Aten*.[19]

The trinitarian Father is now known solely through his name and the great heated incandescent orb of the sun. And with this abandonment of the earlier name went also the last remaining hope of retaining any link with the rest of the Egyptian pantheon. As long as sunlight *(Shu)* streaming through the air to earth was an aspect of divinity, so too there remained the possibility of a connection with the air

177 An alabaster votive plaque showing Akhenaten supporting the divine names of the Aten in their earlier form. The king's pose resembles that of the air god Shu, bearing aloft the sky (Egyptian Museum, Berlin)

god, Shu, and, as importantly, his female counterpart, Tefenet—the cosmic pair with whom Akhenaten and Nefertiti were identified. Moreover, there also remained a link, however tenuous, with the rest of the Heliopolitan Ennead who were descended from this first-born pair: the sky goddess, Nut, the earth god, Geb, and their children, Osiris, Isis, Seth and Nephthys.

It meant, however, that Akhenaten was one step removed from the source of creation, still within a world of differentiated sexual duality. And in this new name, Akhenaten had taken to their ultimate conclusion the tendencies which had been present throughout his reign. He had finally resolved the tension between a kingship which implied a plurality of deities and one based exclusively on relationship with the divine solar Father.

All vestiges of the pantheon had gone. He had succeeded in articulating his vision of the supernal realm, the glorious unity of existence emanating from the trinitarian Father God. Yet, as he kicked away the last remaining rung of the ladder connecting sky and earth, so a great gulf opened, which as long as he was alive could be bridged. But what would happen after him?

It is not surprising to find the later phase of Akhenaten's reign marked by a fanatical outburst of iconoclastic activity. No longer could he tolerate the plural word for deities, which he ordered to be erased from inscriptions.

Now began too the persecution of Amun's cult at Thebes, the god who had bound solar light and life to phallic earth fertility, to the cycle of perpetual regeneration. His name was brutally hacked out from monuments at Thebes, even chiselled out from the tip of Hatshepsut's obelisk at Karnak some twenty metres high

(pl 122). Moreover, the words for 'truth' and 'mother', which incorporated the hieroglyphs of the goddess Maat and the vulture of Mut, now had to be spelt phonetically.

Akhenaten was intent on destroying the slightest image or trace which implied the presence of other deities besides the Sole God. In his quest for the unity of life, for the trinitarian Father, he had turned away from all cult forms other than the heated orb of the celestial sun.

For the first time in Egypt's history the nature of the solar Father had been expressed according to a threefold doctrine which excluded all other deities and provided the sole basis for the king's ritual practice. Yet although Akhenaten is sometimes associated with the rise of monotheism, his vision of divine radiance, his view of creation as an eternal process, and his use of a supreme triad to express divine reality, seem to be distantly echoed far more in Platonism and Neoplatonism. And despite the fact that his successors were unable to follow him along this path, he himself appears as a recognizable link in the long chain of mystics and spiritual seekers dedicated to the celestial realm of light and life.[20]

Which brings us finally to one other notable 'disappearance' in the City of the Sun that cannot go unmentioned here—namely the disappearance of the lovely Queen Nefertiti from official monuments sometime around year 13 of Akhenaten's reign. Had she died by this time? Or is her 'disappearance' yet another reflection of these disturbing events in the later phase of her husband's reign?

One intriguing theory suggests that Nefertiti had not vanished but simply adopted the trappings of masculine kingship, co-ruling with Akhenaten in his later years and eventually assuming the name of Smenkhkare as the ruler of Egypt when Akhenaten

178 An unfinished stela from Amarna probably depicting Akhenaten and Nefertiti. The queen wears the distinctive Red and White Crowns of Upper and Lower Egypt, which are traditionally worn by male rulers or by the Theban goddess Mut. The queen is here specifically associated with symbols of the united land, perhaps to emphasize her status as terrestrial ruler of Egypt (Stela of Pase, State Museum, Berlin)

died. Not all scholars agree with this daring interpretation of the evidence, however, sometimes preferring to associate Smenkhkare (whose name appears briefly in inscriptions at both el-Amarna and Thebes) with an ephemeral male successor ruling after Akhenaten.[21]

It is impossible to go into all the reasons for or against this hypothesis here. But should further archaeological proof be found in support of Nefertiti's identification with Smenkhkare, we do not have far to look for religious reasons why this 'masculinizing' of the queen may have been necessary.

As long as Akhenaten related to the air manifestation of the Creator—either as radiant emanatory sunlight or as the air god, Shu—so too the possibility of identifying the royal couple with the cosmic twins Shu and Tefenet remained viable.

As the male and female offspring of the Creator, they embody the ruling Majesty and Beauty in the land, with Nefertiti, herself, being an apparition of theophanic feminine radiance. Indeed she is described as 'The Great Queen, his beloved, rich in beauty, who propitiates the Aten with a sweet voice . . . who is at the side of the Sole One of Re for eternity'.[22]

But once Akhenaten had taken the drastic step towards ultimate sonship with Re—and replaced the emanatory radiance of divinity with the Father aspect in the divine name—so a feminine counterpart alongside him in the cult might well have seemed

179 An altar stela from a house shrine at el-Amarna with a scene of the royal family in the palace similar to plate 165. Here the warmth of human feeling is expressed as Akhenaten tenderly kisses his daughter Meretaten beneath the life-giving rays of the solar globe. Nefertiti holds Ankhesenpaaten in one arm and Meketaten sits on her lap excitedly drawing the queen's attention towards Akhenaten (Egyptian Museum, Berlin)

Facing page 180 Detail from plate 179 showing Ankhesenpaaten—the future wife of Tutankhamun—playing with a snake ornament attached to Nefertiti's crown

superfluous, a troublesome reminder of sexual differentiation within creation, and all that implied in the pantheon. Regardless of whether or not this was indeed Nefertiti's fate, the prevailing trends during Akhenaten's later years—above all the new name of Re and the king's intolerance towards the multiplicity of deities— would almost certainly have prohibited identifying the queen with Tefenet. On what basis then would she have been included in the cult?

For the first time the unthinkable became possible in Egypt, as the Sun King, step by step, succeeded in removing any theological justification for the feminine in religious practice. Once the link with Shu and Tefenet had been abandoned, there was simply no traditional archetypal role with which the queen, as solar priestess, could be identified in a ritual function. Judging by by the tenderness evident in many scenes from el-Amarna, Akhenaten was anything but a misogynist, yet it cannot be denied that the religious vision of his later years had become—perhaps unintentionally— essentially patriarchal.

Epilogue
The Return to Memphis

THE DEATH OF Akhenaten after a seventeen year reign is passed over in silence by his successors. Nothing remains to inform us about the eventual fate of 'the criminal of Akhetaten', as the Egyptians subsequently named him. No burials were found in the main burial chamber of the royal tomb, which lies in a remote desert area in the hills behind the great plain of el-Amarna but judging from the shattered remains of Akhenaten's granite sarcophagus lying in pieces on the floor of the tomb, the king's enemies had been at work here as elsewhere.

Fortunately the sarcophagus, which must have been made around the time when the new name of the Aten was being introduced, has been restored and is now in the Cairo Museum. It features a figure of Nefertiti at each exterior corner, her arms outstretched in protection for the king along each side.[1] Radical and consequential as ever, Akhenaten had changed yet another religious custom in Egypt with these four figures of the queen guarding the corners of a royal sarcophagus.

The exact nature of the succession is not at all clear but within a short space of time the throne of Egypt passed to a young boy. Later known as Tutankhamun, at the beginning of his reign he was still called Tutankhaten—which may be translated as *'Perfect is the Life of Aten'* or as *'Living Image of Aten'*. The decision to abandon the city of Akhetaten must have been taken early in his youthful reign though this could hardly have been on the orders of Tutankhamun himself, since he would have been scarcely a teenager at the time.

The identity of his parents has never been reliably established and is still a source of some controversy amongst scholars. He may have been a son of Akhenaten but there are various other plausible possibilities.[2] No one, however, questions his marriage to Ankhesenpaaten, *'She Lives for the Aten'*, one of the six daughters born to Akhenaten and Nefertiti (pl 179), a marriage which closely linked the new king with the Amarna family, and was probably a reason why Tutankhamun was excluded from 19th Dynasty king lists.

Responsibility for moving the troubled court presided over by this youthful pair must have fallen to Ay, who had been 'Commander of all the King's horses' during Akhenaten's reign, and a loyal supporter of the heretical king (pl 175). It was Ay, in fact, who was to rule Egypt for about four years after Tutankhamun's early death, evidence enough that the officials active in Akhenaten's reign were still controlling Egypt at the end of the 18th Dynasty.

Hints of the general confusion at the time of the exodus from Middle Egypt may be gleaned from the northern part of Akhetaten which was in the process of being developed when the decision to abandon the capital must have been taken. Here new houses were left in various stages of construction. Elsewhere, people seem to have bricked up the doorways of their houses, leaving behind caretakers, perhaps in the hope that one day it would be possible to return to the City of the Sun.

Nor did all move with Tutankhamun's entourage, some of the city's poorer members taking the opportunity to inhabit better quarters in the city; and it was probably not until the reign of Ramesses II that the solar temples themselves were dismantled, many blocks being carried away for the construction of a new temple built by Ramesses at Hermopolis, the ancient city of Thoth on the west bank of the Nile opposite el-Amarna.

Tutankhaten and Ankhesenpaaten soon dropped the Aten from their names in favour of the Theban god, Amun-Re, and became known as Tutankhamun—*'The Living Image of Amun'*—and Ankhesenamun—*'She Lives for Amun'*. Yet it was not to Thebes, the city of regeneration ruled by Amun-Re-Bull-of-his-Mother, that they returned.

Disheartened and confused by the events of Akhenaten's reign, the royal court made its way northwards to the ancient capital of Memphis at the apex of the Delta—*'The Balance of the Two Lands'* as the Egyptians sometimes called it. From here Tutankhamun issued a proclamation, which was inscribed on a stela discovered in the temple at Karnak. In it the young king vows to restore the old ways and end the chaos which had afflicted the god-forsaken land of Egypt, a country where

'The temples of the gods and goddesses from Elephantine to the marshes of the Delta had fallen into ruin, their shrines had fallen into desolation and had become mounds overgrown with weeds . . . The land was in confusion for the gods had turned away from this land . . . and their hearts were weak in their bodies'.[3]

The rift in Egyptian consciousness caused by Akhenaten's reign, so evident in this extract from Tutankhamun's proclamation, left the country with a deep need to return to its cultural roots at Memphis. Here in this revered city the god Ptah and the Sun Eye, Hathor-Sekhmet, reigned supreme; and the teachings of this ancient centre assumed ever greater importance with the arrival of the 19th Dynasty kings.

The Memphite 'wisdom of the heart' flourished again with renewed vigour in Ramessid Egypt, and the sequel to the present book not only traces Hathor's return after Akhenaten's reign but also uncovers her central place in the spiritual tradition of Memphis, which flowed, like the great current of the Nile, through the whole of Egypt.

Facing page 181 The Second Coffin of Tutankhamun which portrays the king with the emblems and attributes of Osiris (Egyptian Museum, Cairo)

Right 182 Detail of the scene on the back of Tutankhamun's throne showing Queen Ankhesenamun anointing the king. The scene is still strongly influenced by Amarna art, especially the intimate pose of the royal couple and the raying arms and hands of the Aten; moreover, the cartouches—which contain the later form of the Aten name—have been left untouched (Egyptian Museum, Cairo)

Short Bibliography

Assmann, J *Liturgische Lieder an den Sonnengott: Untersuchungen zur altägyptischen Hymnik 1.* Berlin 1969.

— *Der König als Sonnenpriester: Ein kosmographischer Begleittext zur kultischen Sonnenhymnik in thebanischen Tempeln und Gräbern.* Glückstadt, Hamburg and New York 1970.

— *Ägyptische Hymnen und Gebete.* Zürich and Munich 1975.

— *Re und Amun: Die Krise des polytheistischen Weltbilds im Ägypten der 18.–20. Dynastie.* Freiburg and Göttingen 1983.

— *Ägypten: Theologie und Frömmigkeit einer frühen Hochkultur.* Stuttgart Berlin Cologne Mainz 1984.

— 'State and Religion in the New Kingdom', in JP Allen *et al, Religion and Philosophy in Ancient Egypt.* New Haven, Connecticut 1989.

— *Maât, L'Egypte pharaonique et l'idée de justice sociale.* Paris 1989

Borghouts, J F *Ancient Egyptian Magical Texts.* Leiden 1978.

Calverley, A M, Broome, M F and Gardiner, A H (ed), *The Temple of King Sethos I at Abydos.* 4 vols. London and Chicago 1933-1958.

Derchain, P *Hathor Quadrifrons: Recherches sur la syntaxe d'un mythe égyptien.* Istanbul 1972.

Dorman, P F *The Monuments of Senenmut: Problems in Historical Methodology.* New York 1988.

Frankfort, H *Kingship and the Gods: A Study of Ancient Near Eastern Religion as the Integration of Society and Nature.* Paperback Edn. Chicago and London 1978.

Gardiner, A H *The Library of A Chester Beatty: Description of a Hieratic Papyrus with a Mythological Story, Love Songs, and Other Miscellaneous Texts.* London 1931.

— *Hieratic Papyri in the British Museum, Third Series, Chester Beatty Gift.* 2 vols. London 1935.

Germond, P *Sekhmet et la protection du monde.* Basle and Geneva 1981.

Griffiths, J Gwyn (ed) *Plutarch's de Iside et Osiride.* [Cardiff] 1970.

Kitchen, K A *Ramesside Inscriptions, Historical and Biographical.* c. 6 vols. Oxford 1968—

Knudtzon, J A *Die el-Amarna-Tafeln.* 3 vols. Leipzig 1907–1915.

Lexikon der Ägyptologie, 6 vols. Wiesbaden 1975–1986.

Lichtheim, M *Ancient Egyptian Literature: A Book of Readings.* 3 vols. Paperback Edn. Berkeley, Los Angeles and London 1975–1980.

Naville, E *The Temple of Deir el Bahari.* 6 vols. London 1895–1908.

Redford, D B *Akhenaten: The Heretic Pharaoh.* Princeton 1984.

Sandman, M *Texts from the Time of Akhenaten.* Brussels 1938.

Sethe, K *Amun und die acht Urgötter von Hermopolis.* Berlin 1929.

Tomb of Kheruef: Theban Tomb 192, The. Chicago 1980.

Troy, L *Patterns of Queenship in Ancient Egyptian Myth and History.* Uppsala 1986.

te Velde, H *Seth, God of Confusion: A Study of His Role in Egyptian Mythology and Religion.* Leiden 1977.

English translations of the *Pyramid Texts* and *Coffin Texts* may be found in

— R O Faulkner, *The Ancient Egyptian Pyramid Texts.* Paperback Edn. Warminster (No date).

— R O Faulkner, *The Ancient Egyptian Coffin Texts.* 3 vols. Warminster 1973–1978.

For English translations of the *Book of the Dead* see

— EA Wallis Budge, *The Book of the Dead: The Chapters of Coming Forth by Day.* London 1898 (with several reprints);

— TG Allen, *The Egyptian Book of the Dead: Documents in the Oriental Institute Museum at the University of Chicago.* Chicago 1960; TG Allen. *The Book of the Dead or Going Forth by Day.* Chicago 1974;

— RO Faulkner, *The Ancient Egyptian Book of the Dead.* London 1985.

There are also translations by P Barguet, *Le livre des morts des anciens égyptiens.* Paris 1967; E Hornung, *Das Totenbuch der Ägypter.* Zürich and Munich 1979.

Abbreviations

AcOr Acta Orientalia ediderunt societates orientales batava danica norvegica svecica. Leiden and Copenhagen.

ASAE Annales du Service des Antiquités de l'Égypte. Cairo.

BIE Bulletin de l'Institut d'Égypte. Cairo.

BIFAO Bulletin de l'Institut français d'Archéologie orientale. Cairo.

BiOr Bibliotheca Orientalis. Leiden.

BSEG Bulletin de la Société d'Égyptologie. Geneva.

BSFE Bulletin de la Société française d'Égyptologie. Paris.

CT A de Buck, *The Egyptian Coffin Texts.* 7 vols. Chicago 1935-1961.

GM Göttinger Miszellen. Beiträge zur ägyptologischen Diskussion. Göttingen.

JARCE Journal of the American Research Center in Egypt. Princeton.

JEA The Journal of Egyptian Archaeology. London.

JNES Journal of Near Eastern Studies. Chicago.

MDAIK Mitteilungen des Deutschen Archäologischen Instituts, Abteilung Kairo. Wiesbaden.

PT K Sethe, *Die altägyptischen Pyramidentexte.* 4 vols. Leipzig 1908-1922.

RdE Revue d'Égyptologie publiée par la Société française d'Égyptologie. Paris.

SAK Studien zur altägyptischen Kultur. Hamburg.

Urk K Sethe and W Helck, *Urkunden der 18. Dynastie.* Leipzig and Berlin 1906-1958.

Wb A Erman and H Grapow, *Wörterbuch der ägyptischen Sprache.* 7 vols, Belegstellen 1-5. Berlin 1926-1963.

ZÄS Zeitschrift für ägyptische Sprache und Altertumskunde. Berlin and Leipzig.

1 For a specific study of Egyptian queens see L Troy, *Patterns of Queenship in Ancient Egyptian Myth and History*. Uppsala 1986. There is also a discussion of queens in G Robins, *Women in Ancient Egypt*. London 1993, 21-55.

2 Extract from *Urk*.4.27,14-28,12.

3 For the role of the God's Wife see G Robins, 'The God's Wife of Amun in the 18th Dynasty in Egypt' in A Cameron and A Kuhrt (eds), *Images of Women in Antiquity*. London and Canberra 1983, 65-78.

4 It is extremely difficult to know from the surviving evidence who was responsible for erasing Hatshepsut's figure on monuments, and recarving her cartouches so that they contained the names either of Thutmose I or Thutmose II. It cannot always be assumed that everything was the work of her immediate successors. It has to be remembered that during Akhenaten's reign considerable havoc was wreaked on Theban temple reliefs, and undoubtedly Hatshepsut would have been a target. Moreover, there was considerable restoration work and recarving of monuments during the reigns of Haremhab, Seti I and Ramesses II, and Hatshepsut was not included in 19th Dynasty king lists.

5 Extracts from *Urk*.4.255-9.

6 After studying the evidence P Dorman in *Monuments of Senenmut*, 46-65 concludes that any attempt by Thutmose III to dissociate himself from Hatshepsut could only have begun late in his reign, and not before year 42. Dorman suggests this may have been concurrent with the conversion of the Karnak axis into a roofed processional way, which included changes to the court between the fourth and fifth pylons built by Thutmose I.

7 See below chapter 10 nn.4, 5.

8 For the different conceptions of the king's role which emerged during the New Kingdom see Assmann, 'State and Religion in the New Kingdom', 55-88.

Notes to Chapter 1 (pages 6–16)

1 Lines from one of the hymns to the uraeus published by A Erman, *Hymnen an das Diadem der Pharaonen*. Berlin 1911. For these lines *ibid*. 28. Translation of the hymns also in A Barucq and F Daumas, *Hymnes et prieres de l'Egypte ancienne*. Paris 1980, 55-71.

2 *PT* §1108c. The Second Dynasty seal is illustrated in P Kaplony, *Die Inschriften der ägyptischen Frühzeit* 3. Wiesbaden 1963, pl 125 (No 748). For a survey of the cobra goddess in the Old Kingdom see Sally B Johnson, *The Cobra Goddess of Ancient Egypt: Predynastic, Early Dynastic and Old Kingdom Periods*. London and New York 1990. She cites the earliest known example of the cobra on the king's brow on a First Dynasty ivory label showing King Den smiting enemies, ibid 52-53 (Catalog 10).

3 The original meaning of Hathor's name is uncertain. It is written *Hwt-Hrw* in Egyptian and scholars have often assumed that the writing reveals motherhood to be her principal function, as *Hwt* means 'house' or 'temple' and is used as a symbol of the mother. In a late text, for example, Hathor's name is connected with Horus in her womb: 'Whilst he is in the body of this goddess a house of Horus is prepared within her, wherefore her name is Hathor', H Junker, *Die Onurislegende*. Vienna 1917, 117. On the other hand E A Wallis Budge in *The Gods of the Egyptians or Studies in Egyptian Mythology* 1. London 1904, 428-429 suggested that Hathor's name means 'the House above', a region of the celestial sky where Horus, the great celestial hawk, has his dwelling. Indeed, late texts also make play on the *hr* element in Hathor's name, linking it with the verb *hrj* meaning 'far away', Junker, *op.cit*. 111-12. Both interpretations of the name were obviously meaningful for the Egyptians.

4 For example, in a section discussing 'intoxication' and 'ecstasy' Assmann, *Theologie und Frömmigkeit*, 185, cites the cult of Hathor at Dendara as a significant exception in Egypt. He emphasizes that intoxication and ecstasy (qualities particularly associated with Hathor) were not prominent in the total picture of ancient Egyptian religion.

5 For this episode in the *Book of the Dead* see H Kees, *ZÄS* 65 (1930), 65-83. Also T G Allen, *The Book of the Dead or Going Forth by Day*. Chicago 1974, 184. According to an inscription on the back of a 30th Dynasty granite shrine originally from Saft el-Hinna in the eastern Delta, a similar fate also befell the earth god, Geb. He entered the shrine of the uraeus to try to take possession of the snake, but the cobra spat out her poison towards him as he stretched out his hand, killing his companions and scorching Geb with her fearsome heat. Text translated in F Ll Griffith, *The Antiquities of Tell el Yahûdîyeh*. London 1890, 72-3 with pl 25.

6 *Papyrus Bremner-Rhind* 25, 2-4. Quoted in Germond, *Sekhmet*, 122.

7 From the 18th Dynasty tomb of May (Theban Tomb No. 130). V Scheil, *Tombeaux thébains de Mâi, des graveurs, Rat'eserkasenb, Pâri, Djanni, Apoui, Montou-m-hat, Aba*. Paris 1894, 549.

8 Borghouts, *Magical Texts*, 1 (No 1).

9 The phallic objects, together with other types of votive offerings discovered in Hathor's shrines are discussed by G Pinch, *Votive Offerings to Hathor*. Oxford 1993.

10 *CT* 6, 63l-64b.

11 See B Rothenberg, *Timna: Valley of the Biblical Copper Mines*. London 1972, 125-207; B Rothenberg, *The Egyptian Mining Temple at Timna* 1, London, 1988.

12 *PT* §534a-b. S Schott, *Altägyptische Liebeslieder*. Zürich 1950, 73 (1).

13 Translation and bibliography in Lichtheim, *Literature* 2, 197-9. See also E Hornung, *Der ägyptische Mythos von der Himmelskuh. Eine ätiologie des Unvollkommenen*. Göttingen 1982.

14 From a magical spell aimed at warding off danger on the last day of the year, Borghouts, *Magical Texts*, 12 (No 13).

15 G Maspero, *The Dawn of Civilization: Egypt and Chaldea*. London 1894, 23.

16 H Junker, *Der Auszug der Hathor-Tefnut aus Nubien*. Berlin 1911. See also K Sethe, *Zur altägyptischen Sage vom Sonnenauge, das in der Fremde war*. Leipzig and Berlin 1912.

17 The warning was inserted by a New Kingdom scribe copying the classical maxims of the Old Kingdom sage Ptahhotep, see Z Zába, *Les maximes de Ptahhotep*. Prague 1956, 285-6. Quoted also by P Derchain, *SAK* 2 (1975), 74.

18 Quoted from Germond, *Sekhmet*, 21 and 73.

19 J Yoyotte, *BSFE* 87-8 (1980), 49-50, 64. The statues were subsequently removed by later Pharaohs for placement in their own temples.

20 M Alliot, *Le culte d'Horus à Edfou au temps des Ptolémées*. Cairo 1954, 491.

21 From a magical spell for warding off the breath of the plague of the year, Borghouts, *Magical Texts*, 14 (No 14). Immediately before naming Hathor as 'mistress of the stream', the magician invokes the child of raging Sekhmet: 'O son of Sekhmet, power of powers, son of a murderer, the raging one, O son of Hathor, mistress of the stream . . .'

22 See the vivid description in G Maspero, *op.cit*. 22.

23 *Papyrus Chester Beatty 1*: Verso. Published by A H Gardiner, *The Library of A Chester Beatty*, 27-38 and pls 16-17, 22-6, and 29-30. There are various translations of the poems, see M Lichtheim, *Literature* 2, 181-6 (with bibliography). Also J L Foster, *Love Songs of the New Kingdom*. New York 1974, 44-61.

24 Word-play based on the number of each stanza is very important throughout the cycle of the poems. So, for example, here in the seventh stanza, with its theme of releasing the lovesick youth from his suffering, there is an obvious link between the number seven (*zfh*) of the stanza and the word for 'to remove evil', to 'release' or 'loosen' (*sfh*).

25 See Germond, *Sekhmet*, 75-81 for the seven stanzas at the end of the litany associated with Sekhmet's seven arrows. As well as these seven arrows, there were also the seven Hathors who were closely linked with individual fate, as in the story of *The Doomed Prince* when they appear at the prince's birth to predict that he will die either through a crocodile, a snake or a dog, Lichtheim, *Literature*, 2, 200. They are also invoked in magical spells, Borghouts, *Magical Texts* (Nos 1, 24, 74, 108).

Notes to Chapter 2 (pages 18–22)

1 Borghouts, *Magical Texts*, 54. These three phases or transformations of the sun god have been particularly studied by Assmann, *Liturgische Lieder*, 43-44, 335-339; *Re und Amun*, 54-95.

2 *Papyrus Louvre 3292*. Translation in G Nagel, *BIFAO* 29 (1929), 47; Assmann, *Liturgische Lieder*, 336.

3 See n.1. In the sun-hymns the uraeus is often associated with Re's power over enemies in the midday phase.

4 *Papyrus Louvre 3292*. G Nagel, *BIFAO* 29 (1929), 40; Assmann, *Ägyptische Hymnen*, 152 (No 45).

5 Lines from Chapter 15B III of the *Book of the Dead*, Assmann, *Liturgische Lieder*, 37 (ll.10-14).

6 H Frankfort, *Ancient Egyptian Religion: An Interpretation*. Paperback Edn. New York, Hagerstown, San Francisco, London 1961, 133. See also Assmann, 'State and Religion in the New Kingdom', 63-6 for a discussion of the solar journey. Assmann describes the journey as a process in time requiring 'the constant overcoming of a constant counterforce or gravitation towards stand-still and disintegration'.

Notes to Chapter 3 (pages 23–37)

1 EA 3. Knudtzon, *Die el-Amarna-Tafeln* 1, 71 (ll.18-20). Quoted in Redford, *Akhenaten*, 52. For a translation of the Amarna letters see also W L Moran, *Correspondance diplomatique du pharaon*. (Translation by D Collon and H Cazelles). Paris 1987. For this letter see *ibid*. 66-7.

2 *Tomb of Kheruef*, pl 24.

3 Plato, *Laws*, 656-7. For ancient Egyptian dances in general see E Brunner-Traut, *Der Tanz im alten Ägypten nach bildlichen und inschriftlichen Zeugnissen*. Glückstadt, Hamburg and New York, 1938; H Wild, 'Les danses sacrées de l'Égypte ancienne' in *Les danses sacrées*. Paris 1963, 33-117

4 Translation from E F Wente, *Tomb of Kheruef*, Text, 47-8.

5 *Ibid*.47.

6 For the uterus associated with the transformative aspects of the oven and fire (either as the place where seeds are roasted or as the furnace for smelting metals) see M Eliade, *The Forge and the Crucible*. Paperback Edn. Chicago and London 1978, 38, 56-61; E Neumann, *The Great Mother: An Analysis of the Archetype*. Paperback Edn. Princeton 1974, 284-6.

7 *Tomb of Kheruef*, pls 35-6.

8 Translation and bibliography in Lichtheim, *Literature* 1, 94-6; Assmann, *Ägyptische Hymnen*, 421-3 (No 201).

9 A Mariette, *Dendérah: description générale du grand temple de cette ville* 1. Paris 1870, pl 31. The hymn accompanies a scene of the king offering a jar of wine to the enthroned goddess. It is translated in Lichtheim, *Literature* 3, 107 (Hymn 1). Dances for Hathor were particularly characterized by springing or acrobatic movements, accompanied by the sound of finger-clicking, clappers or sistra. F Daumas in *ZÄS* 95 (1968), 15 noted a text at Dendara which describes the movements performed by Hathorian musicians in night-time dances for the goddess: 'Singers, vital and beautiful, are intoxicated by speedily moving their legs out before them'. Daumas suggested this was a kind of *zikr* designed to bring on an altered state of consciousness during the ritual.

10 *CT* 4, 181c ff. Morenz compared Ihy's birth from the cosmic egg with the birth of the Orphic Eros and suggested a connection between Egyptian and Orphic traditions, S Morenz and J Schubert, *Der Gott auf der Blume: Eine ägyptische Kosmogonie und ihre weltweite Bildwirkung*. Ascona 1954, 59.

11 (Spell 368). *CT* 5, 30a-c.

12 (Spell 495). *CT* 6, 76i-j.

13 *CT* 4, 183c-h.

14 *CT* 4, 161b-e. The Egyptians referred to death as 'taking possession of' or 'capturing' a person during the journey into the afterlife, see J Zandee, *Death as an Enemy according to Ancient Egyptian Conceptions*. Leiden 1960, 85-6. To use these same words, therefore, in connection with Ihy highlights his opposition to death.

15 It is thought that Ihy's name is probably a diminutive of the word *jḥ* 'cattle', *Lexikon der Ägyptologie* 3 (1980), col 125.

16 R E Witt, *Isis in the Graeco-Roman World*. London 1971, 288 n29 cites a Christian tradition that the Golden Calf was made in the likeness of Apis, the sacred bull of Memphis.

17 *Urk*.4.1725,5.

18 See W Westendorf, 'Ursprung und Wesen der Maat, der altägyptischen Göttin des Rechts, der Gerechtigkeit und der Weltordnung' in *Festgabe für Dr. Walter Will zum 70.Geburtstag am 12. November 1966*. Cologne, Berlin, Bonn and Munich 1966, 201-25.

19 *Urk*.4.384,15-385,3.

20 E Otto, *Die biographischen Inschriften der ägyptischen Spätzeit: ihre geistesgeschichtliche und literarische Bedeutung*. Leiden 1954, 143.

Notes to Chapter 4 (pages 38–51)

1 Lines from the Tura hymn to Amun-Re, A el-Mohsen Bakir, *ASAE* 42 (1943), 87, pl 4 (l7). Another hymn praises Re-Harakhti as 'the adorned youth, possessor of attraction', *Urk*.4.2096,12.

2 *Urk*.4.19, 3-6. In a scene on Hatshepsut's red quartzite shrine at Karnak, Hathor acclaims Hatshepsut as being 'like the one in the horizon', P Lacau and H Chevrier, *Une chapelle d'Hatshepsout à Karnak* 1. Cairo 1977, 248.

3 Translation of the text and bibliography in R Hari, *Horemheb et la reine Moutnedjemet ou la fin d'une dynastie*. Geneva 1964, 208-14 and pl 37, fig.60. See also A H Gardiner, *JEA* 39 (1953), 13-31.

4 See L Keimer, *BIE* 37(1) 1956, 215-57.

5 See M Gimbutas, *The Language of the Goddess: Unearthing the Hidden Symbols of Western Civilization*. San Francisco 1989, 134-7 for the association of the snake and cattle in different cultures. Gimbutas notes the widespread belief in snakes as household guardians, protecting the family and domestic animals, especially cows.

6 W Helck, *Die Ritualszenen auf der Umfassungsmauer Ramses' II in Karnak*. Wiesbaden 1968, pl 34.

7 *Urk*.4.286,14-16. The shrine has never been published in its entirety, but its inscriptions have been translated by H W Fairman and B Grdseloff, *JEA* 33 (1947), 12-33. For a description of the shrine's decoration see S Bickel and J-L Chappaz, *BSEG* 12 (1988), 9-24.

8 *Urk*.4.287,5-9. According to Bickel and Chappaz, *op.cit.* 20, the cartouches in this scene date from the reign of Seti I, who restored the shrine after the Amarna period. So the scene itself may date from his reign. But that it is in the spirit of Hatshepsut's reign may be gleaned from a relief in Hathor's shrine at Deir el-Bahri showing the leonine-headed goddess, Weret-Hekau, beneficently acclaiming Hatshepsut's power as she holds out her *menit*-necklace towards the sceptre held by Amun, Naville, *Deir el Bahari* 4, pl 101. By contrast, the dread aspect of Weret-Hekau comes to the fore at Karnak when she proclaims about Hatshepsut: 'I cause that dread of her is in the hearts of the *Rekhyt*-people', Lacau and Chevrier, *op.cit.* vol 1 238; vol 2 pl 11 (Block 261).

9 Article by E Fennel in *The Times* (27 October 1986).

10 Sinuhe B 65-6. The story is translated in Lichtheim, *Literature* 1, 222-35.

11 Sinuhe B 44-5. Similar phrases are used about Ramesses II on the *Hittite Marriage Stela:* 'The great chiefs of every land . . . retreat in fear,

terror of his person is in their hearts, Kitchen, *Ramesside Inscriptions* 2, 241, 3-10. Likewise Thutmose III says he compelled all lands to come 'bowing before my *Bas*, terror of me is in the hearts of the Nine Bows', *Urk*.4.161, 14-15.

12 A H Gardiner, *JEA* 4 (1917), 35-6 and pl 9

(ll 7-9); W Schenkel, *Memphis. Herakleopolis. Theben: Die epigraphischen Zeugnisse der 7.-11. Dynastie Ägyptens.* Wiesbaden 1965,283-4 (No 477).

13 O Keel, *Das Böcklein in der Milch seiner Mutter und Verwandtes. Im Lichte eines altorientalischen Bildmotivs.* Göttingen 1980, 82, 142-4.

Notes to Chapter 5   (pages 52-64)

1 A B Edwards, *A Thousand Miles up the Nile.* Paperback Edn. London 1984, 286-8.

2 A Erman, *Die ägyptische Religion.* Berlin 1905, 3. Describing the complexities of Egyptian religion, Erman wrote: ' Every epoch accordingly increased the disarray of the general conceptions . . . and enlarged the mass of religious details which so delighted the Egyptian theologians, and is a horror for us'.

3 *Saturae* 13, 93.

4 Griffiths (ed), *Plutarch's de Iside et Osiride*, 219. Lucan, (*Pharsalia* 8, 832) wrote that the sistrum arouses grief.

5 É Chassinat and F Daumas, *Le temple de Dendara* 7. Cairo 1972, 91 (with pl 622). Quoted in F Daumas, *RdE* 22 (1970), 68.

6 É Chassinat, *Le temple d'Edfou* 4. Cairo 1929, 342 (8-9).

7 In Chapter 2 of my doctoral thesis *Cult Objects of Hathor: An Iconographic Study* (Oxford University 1984. Unpublished), I have suggested that the names *sḫm* (sekhem) and *zššt* are not the names of two distinct types of sistrum (ie the naos and loop sistrum), but rather reflect two different classifications of the object. On the one hand, the sistrum is a sound-producing instrument (*zššt*) and, on the other, it is an object held in the hand as an instrument of power (*sḫm*) like a sceptre, especially the *sekhem*-sceptre.

8 PT §682e-f. Likewise, the uraeus is said to be 'flaming of face against enemies', P Derchain, *Le papyrus Salt 825 (B.M. 10051), rituel pour la conservation de la vie en Égypte.* Brussels 1965, 142 XIII 3. The solar king's power to deprive people of life and breath is vividly encapsulated in a text on the Middle Kingdom stela of Sehetepibre: 'the nose is blocked when he falls into a rage, they breathe his air when he is content', see Lichtheim, *Literature* 1, 128.

9 PT §1568. This fear of being severed from the source of life, namely from the beneficent face of the sun god is expressed in a hymn to the Pharaoh which begins '(Turn) your face to me,

O rising sun', Assmann, *Ägyptische Hymnen*, 497 (No 240).

10 *Papyrus Chester Beatty 1*: Recto. Published by Gardiner, *The Library of A. Chester Beatty*, 8-26 and pls 1-16. Translation in Lichtheim, *Literature* 2, 214-23.

11 From a hymn at Philae, F Daumas, *ZÄS* 95 (1968) 12 §20 (l 5),13.

12 *Urk*.4.613,16-17.

13 *Reliefs and Inscriptions at Karnak* 1. Chicago 1936, pl 59B. There are several versions of Waset's hymn at Karnak, see W Helck, *MDAIK* 23 (1968), 119-27; *The Temple of Khonsu* 2. Chicago 1981, pl 179; *ibid*. (Text), 54 5. This theme of the serpent goddess as Lady of the Two Lands, manifesting in her local cult forms, is also important in Graeco-Roman litanies for Hathor-Sekhmet.

14 F Daumas, *ZÄS* 95 (1968),12 §20(ll 3-4), 13.

15 Translation in Lichtheim, *Literature* 1, 216-17.

16 Hymn on a stela now in the Louvre (C 100). See W Max Müller, *Die Liebespoesie der alten Ägypter.* Leipzig 1899, pl 16; Schott, *Altägyptische Liebeslieder.* Zürich 1950, 100 (No 39).

17 The episode is described by Clement of Alexandria in *Protrepticus* 2, 20-1. The similarities with the Egyptian episode have been noted by several writers, see, for example, J Przyluski, *La grande déesse: Introduction à l'étude comparative des religions.* Paris 1950, 156-7; F le Corsu, *Isis: Mythe et Mystè*res. Paris 1977, 60. F Ll.Griffith, in *Stories of the High Priests of Memphis: The Sethon of Herodotus and the Demotic Tales of Khamuas.* Oxford 1900, 33 n.3, remarked on the similarity between Baubo's name in the Eleusinian Mysteries and the name of Ta-Bubu, a priestess from Bubastis, who appears as a temptress in the demotic story of *Setne Khamwas and Naneferkaptah.* The fact that this beautiful priestess also comes from Bubastis is interesting, because Herodotus (Book 2, 59,60) described rites there in which women display their genitals.

18 There is a similar episode in a Japanese Shinto myth involving the sun goddess Amaterasu. Filled with despair because of her brother's misdeeds, she locks herself away in a rocky cavern. Her withdrawal plunges the world into gloom, causing great consternation among the rest of the pantheon. Then the young goddess Ama no Uzume adorns herself with plants and begins to dance on a tub at the cave's entrance. As she drums with her feet, she is carried away with excitement, and proceeds to take off her clothes before the assembled 800 deities, who all roar with laughter at her antics. Puzzled by this loud noise, Amaterasu peeps out to discover why they are laughing, a little ray of light issues from the cave, just sufficient for the assembly then to persuade their goddess of light to return and banish darkness from the world. I Lévy in *Mélanges Franz Cumont* 2. Brussels 1936, 817-45 compared this myth both with Baubo in the Eleusinian Mysteries and with Hathor's undressing before Re in Egypt.

19 Cf also the beginning of the story of *Setne Khamwas and Naneferkaptah* where princess Ahwere relates how her father, the Egyptian Pharaoh, wanted her to marry the son of an army general rather than her brother whom she loved. Her humorous reply to her father, when she mischievously mimics his wish, completely dissolves his fixity of purpose: 'I laughed and Pharaoh laughed' she says. See F Ll. Griffith, *op.cit.* 85-87; Lichtheim, *Literature* 3, 127-8.

20 A van Gennep, *The Rites of Passage.* Paperback Edn. London 1960, 111-12. His analysis was based on the study of A Moret, *Du caractère religieux de la royauté pharaonique.* Paris 1902, 75-113.

21 Van Gennep, *op.cit.* 112.

22 M Eliade, *Yoga: Immortality and Freedom.* Paperback Edn. Princeton 1973, 220-5.

23 A H Gardiner, *JEA* 36 (1950), 7.

Notes to Chapter 6   (pages 65–8)

1 F Petrie, *Seventy Years in Archaeology.* London (No date), 106.'

2 *Papyrus Harris 500*, Recto 4, 7-4,9. Text in W Max Müller, *Die Liebespoesie der alten Ägypter.*

Leipzig 1899, 22. Translation in Lichtheim, *Literature* 2, 190.

3 From stanza 6 of the cycle of seven poems in *Papyrus Chester Beatty 1* (see chapter 1 n.23).

'Brother' and 'sister' are frequently used in the love poetry, not as a kinship term, but in the sense of 'lover' or 'beloved' in order to express the close relationship between the youth and girl.

1   *PT* §446c. The early origins of Amun are problematic and not all scholars agree that Amun was originally one of the primordial deities of Hermopolis, as suggested by Sethe, *Amun*, 79-87. Others have preferred to link him either with Min right from the beginning, or with a local god worshipped between Koptos and Hermopolis in Upper Egypt, see E Otto, *Lexikon der Ägyptologie* 1 (1975), cols.237-8 for a summary of the various suggestions. The first known mention of Amun at Thebes is on an 11th Dynasty stela, see W M F Petrie, *Qurneh*. London 1909, pl 10.

2   *Urk*.4.364,2-3.

3   From a hymn in the temple of Hibis, Assmann, *Ägyptische Hymnen*, 292 (l.109); Sethe, *Amun*, 97.

4   From a late text at Medinet Habu, Sethe, *Amun*, 102 (§217). The theme of Amun as an indwelling deity within all things dates back to the New Kingdom, see *Lexikon der Ägyptologie* 1 (1975), col.245.

5   For the divine bodies of the gods (especially Re's body) made of gold see F Daumas, *Revue de l'histoire des religions* 149 (Paris 1956), 6-7. Why Amun-Re's body should be painted blue in reliefs has never been satisfactorily explained, though there is the suggestion that it characterizes him as a sky deity, *Lexikon der Ägyptologie* 1 (1975), 239.

6   For religious developments in the First Intermediate Period and the Middle Kingdom and their influence on New Kingdom piety see Assmann, *Theologie und Frömmigkeit*, 194-232; Assmann 'State and Religion in the New Kingdom', 68-71.

7   Cf *The Instructions for Merikare*, a text which probably dates from the Middle Kingdom, where it is stated that the office of kingship has been instituted by the sun god for the benefit of humanity, and to guard against injustices: 'Well-tended are the people, the cattle of god. he made sky and earth for their sake . . . he made for them rulers in the egg, leaders in order to strengthen the backs of the weak', *Merikare* (from lls.130-6). Translation in Lichtheim, *Literature* 1, 106. Discussed by Assmann, *Theologie und Frömmigkeit*, 201-4. In another text, again probably composed during the Middle Kingdom, the king's role in the solar cult is described. It states that Re has placed the king on earth 'for ever and ever, in order to judge humanity and propitiate the deities, and set truth in place of wickedness', Assmann, *Sonnenpriester*, 22; *Theologie und Frömmigkeit*, 11.

8   Lines from a hymn to Amun-Re inscribed on a votive stela of Nebre from Deir el-Medina, Lichtheim, *Literature* 2, 105-7. The crisis of the Amarna Revolution resulted in a surge of hymns expressing personal piety and devotion to the deities during the Ramessid period, but such expressions also occur before Akhenaten's reign, see G Posener, *RdE* 27 (1975), 195-210.

9   In the Old Kingdom and Middle Kingdom *Wisdom Literature*, the deity responsible for creatively ordering the world is simply referred to as 'the god'. He is also a hidden god, known in the human heart, as in *The Instructions for Merikare* where it is said: 'the god who knows characters is hidden' (l.124), Lichtheim, *Literature* 1, 105. In other texts it is obvious that the sun god is meant. But what is clear is that many of these earlier ethical traits were incorporated into the New Kingdom cult of Amun-Re.

10 Assmann suggests that this move towards a religion based on personal piety and a theology of divine will ultimately contributed to the waning of Pharaonic rule. He argues that the Egyptian social structure was unable to change sufficiently to accommodate the new religious developments. The emphasis on the god of the individual and personal religious experience led to a decline in the old concept of Maat, which had hitherto maintained social cohesion. As the collective identity embodied by the Pharaoh weakened, so the clergy became the dominant force in Egyptian society, see Assmann, 'State and Religion in the New Kingdom', 80-2. Also Assmann, *Maât*, 135-41.

11 *Urk*.4.611,15-612,6. Translation in Lichtheim, *Literature* 2, 35-9.

12 *Papyrus Harris 1*. See H D Schaedel, *Die Listen der grossen Papyrus Harris: Ihre wirtschaftliche und politische Ausdeutung*. Glückstadt, Hamburg and New York 1936, 51. According to the papyrus 86,486 people were employed in the service of Amun throughout Egypt, 12,364 at Heliopolis and 3,079 at Memphis.

13 *Urk*.8.144(210); Sethe, *Amun*, 30 §47.

14 The identification with Hathor is suggested, for example, by S Allam, *Beiträge zum Hathorkult (bis zum Ende des Mittleren Reiches)*. Berlin 1963, 11; Frankfort, *Kingship*, 172-3, 385 n.64; Troy, *Patterns of Queenship*, 54. Another image from Hierakonpolis of a cow head with stars on the tips of the horns, on the forehead and ears occurs on a vase now in the Ashmolean Museum, Allam, *op.cit.* pl 1.

15 Cf the motifs in the shrines of Level VII which include vultures, stylized bulls, a pregnant female, and a female with long streaming hair, J Mellaart, *Çatal Hüyük: A Neolithic Town in Anatolia*. London 1967, 105-17; 166-8.

16 *PT* §2203-4. Similarly, *PT* §728-9, §809, §2002-3.

17 From the New Kingdom *Crossword Hymn to Mut*, H M Stewart, *JEA* 57 (1971), 96 (l.48, horizontal text) with pl 26.

18 *Ibid*. 103 (l.64, vertical text) with pl 26.

19 *Ibid*. 91 (ll.10,11, horizontal text) with pl 25. See also U Verhoeven and P Derchain, *Le voyage de la déesse libyque: Ein Text aus dem 'Mutritual' des Pap.Berlin 3053*. Brussels 1985, for a text praising the arrival of the propitiated goddess Mut in the Delta region after her sojourn in the desert. She is a beneficent solar goddess who subsequently journeys through the towns of Lower Egypt and Thebes, hailed by her loyal subjects. The text has obvious parallels with the arrival of the raging Sun Eye from Nubia in Graeco-Roman temple inscriptions. The authors date the composition of the text about Mut to the New Kingdom.

20 Lines from *Urk*.4.21

21 In a late hymn to the Heliopolitan Hathor with the four faces at El Kab, Nekhbet is hailed as the southern face of Hathor, see P Derchain, *El Kab I: les monuments religieux à l'entrée de l'Ouady Hellal*. Brussels 1971, 55 with 12*-13*. The hymn is also quoted by Derchain in *Hathor Quadrifrons*, 4. See also a scene in the New Kingdom shrine of Setau at El Kab in which Nekhbet is shown with Re-Harakhti. According to Derchain she manifests here as the solar goddess who returns from the distance, Derchain, *op.cit.* 71-3, with pl 33.

22 M Eliade, *Yoga: Immortality and Freedom*. Paperback Edn. Princeton 1973, 239.

23 *CT* 4, 65j, 66c, f-g. Quoted in te Velde, *Seth*, 43.

24 P Derchain, 'Mythes et dieux lunaires en Égypte' in *La lune: mythes et rites*. Paris 1962, 41.

25 *Urk*.8.74 (89b). In the same text it is said that Khons is 'conceived on the day of the new moon, born on the second day of the month, and becomes old after the 15th day', see Derchain, *op.cit.* 43.

26 *WB*.3.300,14.

27 *CT* 4, 65k-l, 66a (Spell 310). Similarly Spell 311.

28 From Chapter 83 of the *Book of the Dead*. See J Zandee, *BiOr* 10 (1953), 110.

29 See above n 25.

30 *CT* 4, 67o-s.

31 *CT* 4, 66m, 66o-p. The *Pyramid Texts* also invoke this demoniacal side of Khons on behalf of the king: 'It is Khons who kills the lords, cutting their throats for the king, taking away their entrails for him', *PT* §402a-b. Discussed by J Zandee, *BiOr* 10 (1953), 111.

32 *CT* 4, 67i.

33 The ritual for propitiating Sekhmet was preserved in the liturgical library of Edfu and is shown on temple walls. It consisted of slaughtering four geese and four oryx which were offered together with jugs of beer (or wine) to the bloodthirsty goddess, see Germond, *Sekhmet*, 253.

34 For Khons as a healer and exorcist see the late text on the *Bentresh Stela* from Karnak now in the Louvre (C 284). This tells how the holy cult image of Khons was taken to the country of Bakhtan to heal Ramesses II's sister-in-law who was plagued by a demon. Translation in Lichtheim, *Literature* 3, 90-94.

1 H Gauthier, *Les fêtes du dieu Min*. Cairo 1931, 139-40.

2 *Ibid.* 138-40. Many of the epithets cited by Gauthier date from the Graeco-Roman period.

3 L Keimer, *ZÄS* 59 (1924), 143.

4 S Hassan, *Hymnes religieux du Moyen Empire*. Cairo 1928, 159.

5 Much of the evidence for the connection of Isis with 'Bull-of-his-Mother' dates from the New Kingdom and later, but her mother-son relationship with Min or Min-Horus dates back at least to the Middle Kingdom, see M Münster, *Untersuchungen zur Göttin Isis vom Alten Reich bis zum Ende des Neuen Reiches*. Berlin 1968, 129-37.

6 Gauthier, *op.cit.* 137.

7 Frankfort, *Kingship*, 188.

8 The importance of the ancestral statues in the Min festival, and their link with the dynastic succession through the mystery of Bull-of-his-Mother was emphasized by H Jacobsohn, *Die dogmatische Stellung des Königs in der Theologie der alten Ägypter*. Glückstadt, Hamburg and New York 1939, 29-40; Frankfort, *Kingship*, 188-9.

9 *Papyrus d'Orbiney* (British Museum 10183). Translation and bibliography in Lichtheim, *Literature* 2, 203-11.

10 See M J Vermaseren, *Cybele and Attis: The Myth and the Cult*. London 1977, 16-24, for early forms of Cybele's cult. Vermaseren associates Cybele with the goddess Kubaba, who was worshipped at Carchemish and also as far south as Ugarit in the second millennium BC. She is said to have been the goddess who was later worshipped by the Phrygians in Anatolia. For the association of Cybele and Attis see *ibid.* 88-95. The eunuch priests of Cybele were obviously a familiar sight in Alexandria from the 3rd century BC onwards, see P M Fraser, *Ptolemaic Alexandria* 1. Oxford 1972, 278. For possible Syrian origins for some parts of the story see E Brunner-Traut, *Lexikon der Ägyptologie* 4 (1982), col. 700.

11 There is an interesting comparison with the strange bull sacrifice carried out on the island of Atlantis, mentioned by Plato, *Critias* §119. There too the bulls wandered freely, and the main feature of the sacrifice was contact of the victim's blood with a pillar or post on which the laws of the land were carved. The sacrificial bull was led to the column where it was slain; and then some of its blood was dropped into a bowl of wine which the king drank, swearing he would act according to the laws inscribed on the column. Perhaps in Egypt as well, there was some kind of ritual slaughter involving a pillar and ritual blood, which underlies this episode of the story.

12 *Papyrus Dublin 4*. Translation in Assmann, *Ägyptische Hymnen*, 467-8 (No224,l.8).

13 Lines from a sun-hymn inscribed on the dorsal pillar of Khaemhet's statue in the Brooklyn Museum. Translation in Assmann, *ibid.* 162 (No 55B).

14 Calverley, *Temple of King Sethos* 2, pl 36. The text is above the procession of standards preceding the king.

1 Borghouts, *Magical Texts*, 32 (No 46).

2 *Papyrus Chester Beatty 3*, Recto 11,1ff; Gardiner, *Hieratic Papyri in the British Museum* 1 (Text), 20. Quoted in te Velde, *Seth*, 56.

3 For the five different versions of this text (which is often referred to as the story of Anat and Seth) see now J van Dijk, ''Anat, Seth and the Seed of Prē'' in H L J Vanstiphout *et al* (eds), *Scripta Signa Vocis. Studies presented to J.H.Hospers*. Groningen 1986, 31-51.

4 Griffiths (ed), *Plutarch's de Iside et Osiride*, 146-7 (ch 19).

5 *Papyrus Chester Beatty 3*, Recto 10,11; Gardiner, *Hieratic Papyri in the British Museum* 1 (Text), 19.

6 Te Velde, *Seth*, 56.

7 *Papyrus Chester Beatty 1*, Recto. Published by Gardiner, *Library of A.Chester Beatty*, pls 1-16. Translation and bibliography in Lichtheim, *Literature* 2, 214-23.

8 Te Velde, *Seth*, 51-2.

9 Episode recounted in a magical spell for warding off poison, Borghouts, *Magical Texts*, 51-5 (No 84).

10 From Ani 4,6-7 and Ani 7,7-8. Translation in Lichtheim, *Literature* 2, 137, 140.

11 *Papyrus Jumilhac* 3,1ff; J Vandier, *Le papyrus Jumilhac*. Paris (No date), 114.

12 I have been unable to trace the present whereabouts of this terracotta, but it was first published by J Millingen, *Annali dell'Instituto archeologico* 15 (fasc 1) 1843, 72-97 with pl E. See also F Winter, *Die Typen der figürlichen Terrakotten* 2. Berlin and Stuttgart 1903, 197 (No 6), where its museum number is listed as Berlin, Antiquarium 4875. It is cited as 'der bekannte italienische Terrakotto' under the heading 'Baubo' in K Ziegler and W Sontheimer (eds), *Der kleine Pauly: Lexikon der Antike* 1. Stuttgart 1964, 845. F Neumann, however, associates the figure with Isis in *The Great Mother: An Analysis of the Archetype*. Paperback Edn. Princeton 1974, 139-40, though he interprets the pose as symbolizing fertility.

13 Lichtheim, *Literature* 3, 178; te Velde, *Seth*, 56.

14 For a discussion of this practice see the chapter on Egyptian divination by J Ray in M Loewe and C Blacker (eds.), *Divination and Oracles*. London 1981, 186-7. Also W R Halliday, *Greek Divination: A Study of its Methods and Principles*. London 1913, 159-62.

15 Griffiths (ed), *Plutarch's de Iside et Osiride*, 139-41 (Ch 14).

16 J Ray, *op.cit.* 184, 186-7, suggests that the practices arose from Mesopotamian influence. However, it is quite possible that the evidence for divination has simply not been preserved from earlier periods, a point made by J Baines in discussing oracles and other forms of divination, *JEA* 73 (1987), 88-94. He cites New Kingdom documents from Deir el-Medina relating to 'the seer' or 'wise woman'. There are also star-gazers and people who predict events from observations of winds mentioned on the *Israel Stela*, see H Brunner, 'Zeichendeutung aus Sternen und Winden in Ägypten' in W Röllig (ed), *Das Hörende Herz: Kleine Schriften zur Religions-und Geistesgeschichte Ägyptens*. Göttingen 1988, 224-9. Brunner thinks these people were not part of the official court circle.

17 E Otto, *Das ägyptische Mundöffnungsritual* 2. Wiesbaden 1960, 53-9 (Scenes 9-10).

18 Griffiths (ed), *Plutarch's de Iside et Osiride*, 146-7 (Ch 19).

19 Borghouts, *Magical Texts*, 88 (No 129).

20 *Herodotus* 2 (Chapter 63). See also A B Lloyd, *Herodotus, Book II: Commentary 1-98*. Leiden 1976, 285-7.

21 Translation from H Kees, 'Aegypten' in A Bertholet (ed), *Religionsgeschichtliches Lesebuch* 10. Tübingen 1928, 35 (No 55). The episode happened on day 26 of the first month of the Inundation season, which the calendar states is definitely a bad day on which nothing should be undertaken.

22 J C Goyon, *Confirmation du pouvoir royal au nouvel an [Brooklyn Museum 47.218.50]*, Cairo 1972 (Text), 54-5.

23 É Chassinat and M de Rochemonteix, *Le temple d'Edfou* 2. Cairo 1918, 44; te Velde, *Seth*, 44.

24 *PT* §594a.

25 Te Velde, referring to Sir Alan Gardiner's idea that the missing 1/64 was supplied magically by Thoth, suggests that each fraction does not remain on its own but is united with its invisible counterpart in a higher synthesis: 1/64 unites with its counterpart and becomes 1/32, and so on until the final result is not 63/64 but a totality in which nothing is lacking, *Seth*, 48.

26 See P Derchain, 'Mythes et dieux lunaires en Égypte' in *La lune: mythes et rites*. Paris 1962, 25; te Velde, *Seth*, 43.

27 Te Velde, *ibid.* 32.

Notes to Chapter 10 (pages 116-29)

1 For the two tombs of Senenmut at Deir el-Bahri see P F Dorman, *The Tombs of Senenmut: Architecture and Decoration of Tombs 71 and 353.* New York 1991.

2 The nature of the relationship between Hatshepsut and Senenmut (who seems to have been unmarried) has been the subject of some speculation over the years. That it was close and highly personalized cannot be doubted, as suggested by statues of Senenmut tenderly nursing Hatshepsut's daughter, Neferure. Also the central band between the astronomical images on the ceiling in Senenmut's tomb contains the royal names of Hatshepsut followed by Senenmut's name. To link the Pharaoh with one of her subjects in an inscription placed among the celestial stars would have been deeply meaningful to the Egyptians, a sign that their lives were cosmically interwoven in the stellar circuit,

see Dorman, *ibid.* 139 (with pl 85) for the inscription.

3 Assmann, 'State and Religion in the New Kingdom', 69. For Hatshepsut's importance in the new religious developments, *ibid.* 71-2.

4 Assmann, *Re und Amun*, 145,153

5 *Ibid.* 145-54.

6 Z Wysocki, *MDAIK 42* (1986), 228; see also a further article in *MDAIK 48* (1992), 233-54.

7 The quotes here are from *Urk.* 4.361-9.

8 The birth scenes are described in detail in H Brunner, *Die Geburt des Gottkönigs: Studien zur Überlieferung eines altägyptischen Mythos.* Wiesbaden 1964.

9 *Urk.*4.219,13-220,6.

10 *Urk.*4.339,16-340,2.

11 Like so much else surrounding Hatshepsut, her tomb (Tomb 20) is not without controversy. It is the earliest datable royal tomb in the Valley of the Kings, though J Romer in *JEA* 60 (1974), 119-33; *Valley of the Kings.* London 1981, 194-5, thinks that it originally belonged to Thutmose I and was then taken over and extended by Hatshepsut for her own burial alongside her father. E F Wente, *JNES* 41 (1982), 164 n.26 agrees with Romer for other reasons. Other scholars, however, think that Tomb 38 may have been Thutmose I's original tomb, and that Hatshepsut had her father reburied in her own tomb during her reign. It has even been proposed that Thutmose I's tomb lay somewhere between Dra-Abu-el-Naga and the Valley of the Kings and is still to be discovered, L Gabolde, *SAK* 14 (1987), 78-81. Similarly, no tomb has been safely established as belonging to Thutmose II, though Tomb 42 in the Valley of the Kings has been suggested. So it is quite possible that Hatshepsut was the first to build in the Valley of the Kings.

Notes to Chapter 11 (pages 130–8)

1 This extract from Plato, *The Symposium*, translated by Walter Hamilton, Penguin Classics 1951, pp 93-95, is reproduced by permission of Penguin Books Ltd.

2 Redford, *Akhenaten*, 235.

3 S Freud, *Der Mann Moses und die monotheistische Religion.* Amsterdam 1939, 35-54.

4 For a discussion of 'the new solar religion' see Assmann, *Re und Amun*, 96-143; *Theologie und Frömmigkeit*, 235-243.

5 (British Museum 826). Translation in Lichtheim, *Literature* 2, 86-9.

6 From a hymn on a 19th Dynasty stela belonging to Didia (British Museum 706). Kitchen, *Ramesside Inscriptions* 1, 330 (l.12).

7 Hymn translated by Assmann, *MDAIK* 27 (1971), 4-5 (ll. 4-5).

8 Cf. the hymn on the stela of Suti and Hor cited in n.5. Also the Cairo hymn to Amun-Re on a papyrus dating to the reign of Amenhotep II, Assmann, *Ägyptische Hymnen*, 199-207 (No 87).

9 The question of whether there may have been a coregency between Akhenaten and his father Amenhotep III is much disputed, with some scholars even suggesting a period of nine or twelve years. Others prefer a shorter period. No double-dated documents have been found, which would prove their joint rule conclusively, so that most of the present evidence remains circumstantial. For a survey of the evidence see W J Murnane, *Ancient Egyptian Coregencies.* Chicago 1977, 123-69. Murnane believes that most of the evidence relating to the coregency theory is unsatisfactory and that, at most, the coregency would have ended by the time Amenhotep IV changed his name to Akhenaten, *ibid.*231-3.

10 E Edel, *Zu den Inschriften auf den Jahreszeiten-reliefs der'Weltkammer' aus dem Sonnenheiligtum des Niuserre.* Göttingen 1961, 239-43; Assmann, *Theologie und Frömmigkeit*, 71.

11 *CT* 2, 161a.

12 *Kingship*, 153, 380-1 (nn. 26-27). An alternative etymology was suggested by H Kees, who linked the word *bn* with *wbn* to 'rise' or 'shine'. For convincing reasons against the *wbn* etymology as primary see J Baines, *Orientalia* 39 (1970), 391-2.

Notes to Chapter 12 (pages 139–54)

1 The suggestion is put forward independently by both J D Ray, *GM* 86 (1985), 86-7; L Bell, *JNES* 44 (1985), 293.

2 EA No 26. Knudtzon, *Die el-Amarna-Tafeln* 1, 226-7 (ll. 49-51). Quoted in Redford, *Akhenaten*, 166-7.

3 The relationships within the royal family at el-Amarna are a highly controversial topic. It is known that Teye, the wife of Ay, who was one of the leading figures at Akhenaten's court, was Nefertiti's nurse, but the suggestion that Ay was Nefertiti's father is unproven. Nefertiti's sister is named as Mutnodjme on the monuments at el-Amarna. She is perhaps to be identified with Queen Mutnodjme, the wife of King Haremhab.

4 See R Winfield Smith and D B Redford, *The Akhenaten Temple Project 1: Initial Discoveries.* Warminster 1976; D B Redford, *The Akhenaten Temple Project 2: Rwd-mnw, Foreigners and Inscriptions.* Toronto 1988. The Franco-Egyptian Centre at Karnak are also studying evidence from the ninth pylon at Karnak which has yielded no less than 12,000 blocks.

5 C Traunecker, *BSFE* 107 (1986), 23-7.

6 Akhenaten's titulary on the boundary stelae at el-Amarna, Sandman, *Texts,* 120. Translation in Lichtheim, *Literature* 2, 49.

7 The royal wadi seems to have been an important point of orientation at el-Amarna. R A Wells in *SAK* 14 (1987), 313-33 suggests that the smaller Aten temple is oriented towards there; and also that sunrise in the vicinity of the wadi during February and October was significant for the temple. On the basis of this hypothesis Wells has used astronomical data to calculate possible dates for the founding of Akhetaten. His dates have been challenged by R Krauss in *GM* 109 (1989), 33-36, who nevertheless accepts the general proposition advanced by Wells. G Martin suggests that the smaller Aten temple might have been intended as a funerary temple for Akhenaten, G T Martin, *The Royal Tomb at El-'Amarna ii: The Reliefs, Inscriptions and Architecture.* London 1989, 30 n.4

8 A R Schulman, *JARCE* 3 (1964), 58-9, with n.63. In his article, Schulman emphasized the army's influence during Akhenaten's reign.

9 Translation from A K Grayson, *Assyrian Royal Inscriptions* 1. Wiesbaden 1972, 49. Quoted in Redford, *Akhenaten*, 235.

10 EA No 1. Knudtzon, *Die el-Amarna-Tafeln* 1, 64-5 (ll. 75-6), 66-7 (ll.85-7).

11 Sandman. *Texts*, 94 (ll. 16-20)-95 (ll. 1-2). Translation of the great hymn to the Aten in Lichtheim, *Literature* 2, 96-100.

12 Sandman, *Texts*, 175, 11ff. Inscription on a stela of Bak and his wife now in Berlin, see W Kaiser, *Katalog Ägyptisches Museum*. Berlin 1967, No 766. The artistic canon used by Amarna artists for portraying the human figure has been studied by G Robins in a series

of articles, *GM* 64 (1983), 67-72; *GM* 84 (1985), 51-64; *GM* 88 (1985), 47-54.

13 The mourning scenes are shown in two chambers of the tomb. The dead princess is clearly Meketaten in Room *gamma*, see G T Martin, *The Royal Tomb at El-'Amarna, ii: The Reliefs, Inscriptions and Architecture*. London 1989, 42-8. More problematic is the dead mother's identity in the relief in Room *alpha*, as the accompanying texts have been destroyed. Martin, *ibid*. 37-41, suggests that

this may be a portrayal of Tutankhamun's birth, with the mother perhaps Kiya, Akhenaten's secondary wife. It seems more plausible though that the scenes relate either to Meketaten's death again or to another princess. Significantly, the scene of the rising sun in Room *alpha* (pl 168) was reworked to obliterate two figures of princesses, perhaps, as Martin suggests, because they had died whilst work was in progress in the tomb, *ibid*. 31 with n.11.

Notes to Chapter 13 (pages 155–68)

1 G Bachelard, *The Poetics of Reverie: Childhood, Language and the Cosmos*. Paperback Edn. Boston 1971, 186.

2 Sandman, *Texts,* 95 (ll. 9-12).

3 *Ibid.* 95 (ll. 17-20).

4 Lines from the *Short Hymn to the Aten*. Sandman, *ibid.* 11 (ll. 6-16). Translation and bibliography in Lichtheim, *Literature* 2, 90-2.

5 Sandman, *Texts,* 15 (ll. 7-10).

6 *Ibid.* 13 (ll. 9-13).

7 *Ibid.* 93 (ll. 12-15, 17-18), 94 (l. 1-3).

8 *Ibid.* 95 (ll. 2-3).

9 *Ibid.* 92 (l. 4).

10 *Ibid.* 91 (l. 13).

11 *Ibid.* 16 (ll. 8-10). Inscription from the Amarna tomb of Meryre. The link between Akhenaten's physiognomy in reliefs and the inundation has been suggested by some scholars, for example, Germond, *Sekhmet*, 240 with n.3. J Baines in *Fecundity Figures: Egyptian Personification and the Iconology of a Genre*. Warminster 1985, 320-1, points out certain features of fecundity figures which may be connected with the Karnak colossi of Akhenaten (Amenhotep IV), but, on the whole, he expresses doubt about linking fecundity figures with Akhenaten's iconography (see *ibid.* 118).

12 It is worth comparing the Amarna family scenes of Akhenaten and Nefertiti with much later developments in the iconography of Hapy during the Roman period. He became associated with a female companion, Euthenia, who personified abundant life. She is sometimes shown holding a cup whilst surrounded by children, or offering a crown to her partner, see L Kákosy, *JEA* 68 (1982), 290-8.

13 Sandman, *op.cit.* 121 (ll. 6-11).

14 Frankfort, *Kingship*, 134.

15 Sandman, *op.cit.* 95 (ll. 16-17). Nefertiti's dependence on Akhenaten is stated in the text on the boundary stelae at el-Amarna. She is said to be 'under the authority of Pharaoh', with her children in turn being 'placed under her guidance', Sandman, *op.cit.* 126 (ll. 1-8). See also Lichtheim, *Literature* 2, 50. The inscription on a reconstructed shabti belonging to the queeen (the only one of its kind so far known) describes her as being 'favoured by Akhenaten'. For a reconstruction of the shabti see C E Loeben, *MDAIK* 42 (1986), 99-107. The names of the Aten on the shabti are in the earlier form, so the object must have been made before the last known occurrence of Nefertiti on Amarna monuments.

16 *Urk.*4.1971,12 13.

17 Assmann, *MDAIK* 27 (1971), 9 (No 2) = Sandman, *op.cit.* 93 (ll. 16-17).

18 Sandman, *op.cit.* 12 (ll. 3-12).

19 The translation of the name is problematic but I have followed the one proposed by G Fecht, *ZÄS* 85 (1960), 109-117; R Anthes, *ZÄS* 90 (1963), 6. See also B Gunn, *JEA* 9 (1923), 175-176. Gunn drew attention to the importance of the sun god's 'father' aspect in official titulary at el-Amarna.

20 Although Akhenaten expressed his religious beliefs according to trinitarian notions, he is sometimes linked with the development of the monotheistic Hebrew religion. E Hornung states that, although it is difficult to establish conclusively Akhenaten's influence on the Old Testament, he, nevertheless, emerges as 'the first monotheist' in history, see 'Die Anfänge von Monotheismus und Trinität in

Ägypten' in K Rahner (ed.), *Der eine Gott und der dreieine Gott: Das Gottesverständnis bei Christen, Juden und Muslimen*. Munich and Zürich 1983, 63-4. On the other hand, J Assmann compares the early religion of Israel with the New Kingdom movement of personal piety, and argues that this movement, whilst contributing to the decline of Pharaonic rule, ultimately found a viable social expression in Israel: Assmann, 'State and Religion in the New Kingdom', 80-2.

21 One of the main reasons for identifying Smenkhkare with a female ruler is that the throne name occurs in a feminine form. The identification of Smenkhkare with Nefertiti was suggested by J R Harris in a series of articles, *GM* 4 (1973), 15-17; *AcOr* 35 (1973), 5-13; *AcOr* 36 (1974), 11-21. See also J Samson, *Amarna. City of Akhenaten and Nefertiti: Nefertiti as Pharaoh*. Warminster 1978, 133-9. This is opposed by R Krauss, *Das Ende der Amarnazeit: Beiträge zur Geschichte und Chronologie des Neuen Reiches*. Hildesheim 1978, 43-53. He thinks that Akhenaten's eldest daughter, Meretaten, succeeded him before marrying King Smenkhkare. Yet another theory is proposed by W Helck in *MDAIK* 40 (1984), 159-67, who argues that the most important female in the later years of Akhenaten's reign after Nefertiti's disappearance was Kiya, one of Akhenaten's secondary wives, whose name appears on blocks from el-Amarna. Helck suggests that she was subsequently ousted by a faction loyal to Meretaten and Ankhesenpaaten, the daughters of Nefertiti.

22 From a hymn in the tomb of Ay, Sandman, *op.cit.* 92 (ll. 15-17).

Notes to Epilogue (pages 169–71)

1 See G T Martin, *The Royal Tomb at El-'Amarna i: The Objects*. London 1974, 13-16. The official discovery of the royal tomb was made by Alessandro Barsanti in 1891. Because of the various items of funerary equipment found in the tomb, it is thought that Akhenaten had a

normal royal burial, see G T Martin, *The Royal Tomb at El-'Amarna ii: The Reliefs, Inscriptions, and Architecture*. London 1989, 4 n.2.

2 It has been suggested that Tutankhamun may have been Akhenaten's son, born to another of the king's wives—perhaps Kiya who appears

on some monuments at el-Amarna. Other suggestions are that he was a son of one of Queen Teye's daughters, or a descendant of Thutmose IV from some collateral branch of the family.

3 *Urk.*4.2027,3ff.

SOURCES OF THE ILLUSTRATIONS

Frontispiece: Cobra collar—photo courtesy of the Griffith Institute, Ashmolean Museum, Oxford

1 Ahmose-Nefertari—photo courtesy of the Kestner Museum, Hannover

2 Stela of Ahmose and Tetisheri—photo Kurt Lambelet

3 Ahmose-Nefertari—see plate 1

4 Hathor and Amun-Re crown Hatshepsut—photo AMR

5 Statue of Hatshepsut—photo Kurt Lambelet

6 Cobra jewel—photo F J Gladstone

7 Statue of Amenhotep III—photo Thomas B Hartwell

8 Name of Hathor—photo AMR

9 Hathor and Re-Harakhti—photo AMR

10 The Serpent Eye—after J Vandier, *Tombes de Deir el-Médineh: La tombe de Néfer-Abou.* Cairo 1935, pl 21

11 Statue of Hathor—photo Thomas B Hartwell

12 Statue of Sekhmet—photo AMR

13 Relief of Hapy—photo AMR

14 Shu enticing the raging lionness back to Egypt—after G Roeder, *Der Tempel von Dakke* 2. Cairo 1930, pl 115

15 Lute-playing monkey—photo AMR

16 Dancing Bes—photo AMR

17 Musicians in Ramose's tomb—photo AMR

18 River procession—after É Chassinat, *Le temple d'Edfou* 10(2). Cairo 1960, pl 126

19 View of the Dendara temple—photo AMR

20 Damaged face of Hathor—photo AMR

21 Relief of female guest—photo AMR

22 Hathor face—photo AMR

23 Vignette of Khepri—photo AMR

24 Vignette of Ankhesenenmut and Re in the solar boat—photo AMR

25 Vignette of the young sun child—after A Piankoff and N Rambova, *Mythological Papyri, Texts.* New York 1957, 22, fig 3. Copyright 1957 by Böllingen. Reproduced by permission of Princeton University Press

26 Scene above the entrance to Ramesses X's tomb—after J F Champollion, *Monuments de l'Égypte et de la Nubie* 3. Paris 1845, pl 271

27 Neferabet propitiating the uraeus—after J Vandier, *Tombes de Deir el-Médineh: La tombe de Néfer-Abou.* Cairo 1935, pl 17

28 Sed Festival dancer—photo AMR

29 Statue of Amenhotep III—photo Thomas B Hartwell

30 Libation scene—photo AMR

31 Dancers in Amenhotep III's third Sed Festival—photo AMR

32 Sed Festival dancers—photo AMR

33 Hathor, Amenhotep III and Teye—photo AMR

34 Sed Festival dancers—photo AMR

35 Sed Festival scene—after *Tomb of Kheruef,* pl 24. Courtesy of the Oriental Institute of the University of Chicago

36 Sed Festival musicians—photo AMR

37 Relief of Hathor—photo AMR

38 Scene of dawn dancers—after N deG Davies and AH Gardiner, *The Tomb of Antefoker, Vizier of Sesostris I, and of his Wife, Senet (no.60).* London 1920, pl 23

39 Ihy statue—photo courtesy of the Griffith Institute, Ashmolean Museum, Oxford

40 Scene of cattle crossing water—after H Wild, *Le tombeau de Ti* 2. Cairo 1953, pl 114

41 Head of Queen Teye—courtesy of the Ägyptisches Museum, Berlin (Foto Margarete Büsing)

42 Vignettes from the papyrus of Ani—after EA Wallis Budge, *The Book of the Dead: An English Translation of the Chapters, Hymns, etc., of the Theban Recension, with Introduction, Notes, etc* 1. (Second Edition). London 1953, 365

43 Relief of Maat—photo courtesy of the Soprintendenza Alle Antichità, Florence

44 Seti I offers Maat—photo Kurt Lambelet

45 Rebus of Amenhotep III's name—after H Brunner, *Die südlichen Räume des Tempels von Luxor.* Berlin and Mainz 1977, pl 13

46 Statue of Senenmut holding the serpent Renenutet—photo courtesy of the Brooklyn Museum, Charles Edwin Wilbour Fund

47 Sennedjem at the horizon gates—photo Uni-Dia slide (No 37005)

48 Statue of King Haremhab and Queen Mutnodjme—photo courtesy of the Museo Egizio, Turin

49 Gold pendant of Weret-Hekau—photo F J Gladstone

50 Egyptian crowns—graphics F J Gladstone

51 View of Hatshepsut's temple—photo AMR

52 Sistrum-shaped temple column—photo AMR

53 Gold pectoral—after O Keel, *Das Böcklein in der Milch seiner Mutter und Verwandtes. Im Lichte eines altorientalischen Bildmotivs.* Göttingen 1980, 78, fig 39

54 Interior of the Hathor shrine at Deir el-Bahri—photo AMR

55 Relief of Hathor suckling Hatshepsut—after Naville, *Deir el Bahari* 4, pl 104

56 The Speos Artemidos—photo AMR

57 Scarab and *menit*-necklace—photo Uni-Dia slide (No 39548)

58 Relief of Hathor and Seti I in the Louvre—photo Musées Nationaux, Paris

59 Detail of Hatshepsut relief—photo AMR

60 Statue of a Ramessid queen—photo AMR

61 The Hathor cow in her rock shrine—photo Egypt Exploration Society, London

62 Statue of the Hathor cow—photo courtesy of the Egyptian Museum, Cairo (Mustapha Maksoud)

63 Isis shaking her sistrum before Amun-Re—photo AMR

64 Colossus of Ramesses II—photo AMR

65 Detail of plate 63—photo AMR

66 (a) Two naos sistra—after L Klebs, *ZÄS* 67 (1931), 60

66 (b) A loop sistrum—after L Klebs, *ZÄS* 67 (1931), 62

66 (c) A gold naos sistrum—photo F J Gladstone

67 Musicians at Thebes—after G Foucart, *Tombes thébaines, nécropole de Dirâ' Abû'n-Nága: 3 le tombeau d'Amonmos,* 4. Cairo 1935, pl 31

68 Triad of Hathor, King Menkaure and nome goddess—photo AMR

69 Loop sistrum from Tutankhamun's tomb—photo courtesy of the Griffith Institute, Ashmolean Museum, Oxford

70 Unfinished statue of Akhenaten and daughter—photo AMR

71 Coronation sequence—after A H Gardiner, *JEA* 36 (1950), pl 2 (opp. p 5)

72 Hathor shaking her sistrum before Amun-Re—photo AMR

73 Statue of the cobra goddess—photo F J Gladstone

74 Frontal view of pl 73—photo Kurt Lambelet

75 *Menit*-counterpoise—photo AMR

76 Nebamun hunting in the marshes—photo AMR

77 Vignette of an ithyphallic god—photo AMR

78 Entrance to Luxor Temple—photo AMR

79 Statue of Senwosret III—photo Kurt Lambelet

80 Statuette of Amun-Re—photo AMR

81 The Theban triad—after L Lamy, *Egyptian Mysteries: New Light on Ancient Knowledge.* London 1981, 11

82 Wadjet and Nekhbet motifs—photo AMR

83 Relief of Nekhbet—photo AMR

84 Queen Nefertari—photo AMR

85 Statue of Khons—photo AMR

86 View through Karnak temple—photo AMR

87 Relief of Isis, Ramesses II and Min-Amun—photo AMR

88 Predynastic vase—photo courtesy of the Staatliche Museen zu Berlin, Ägyptisches Museum

89 Min Festival scenes—after *Medinet Habu 4: Festival Scenes of Ramses III.* Chicago 1940, pl 196 A-B. Courtesy of the Oriental Institute of the University of Chicago

90 Ramesses III seated in his palanquin—photo AMR

91–95 Min Festival scenes—after *Medinet Habu 4: Festival Scenes Of Ramses III.* Chicago 1940, pl 196 A-B. Courtesy of the Oriental Institute of the University of Chicago

96–97 Royal hairdressing scenes—photos courtesy of The Brooklyn Museum, Charles Edwin Wilbour Fund

98 Laundry scene—courtesy of the School of Archaeology and Oriental Studies, University of Liverpool

99 Female arms receiving the sun—after A Piankoff and N Rambova, *Mythological Papyri, Texts.* New York 1957, 41 fig 25. Copyright 1957 by Böllingen. Reproduced by permission of Princeton University Press

SOURCES OF THE ILLUSTRATIONS

INDEX